THE SOCIAL AND ECONOMIC
HISTORY OF JAPAN

THE
SOCIAL AND ECONOMIC
HISTORY OF JAPAN

By

EIJIRO HONJO

Member of Japan Academy

Emeritus Professor at Kyoto University

NEW YORK

RUSSELL & RUSSELL · INC

1965

FIRST PUBLISHED IN 1935
REISSUED, 1965, BY RUSSELL & RUSSELL, INC.
BY ARRANGEMENT WITH EIJIRO HONJO
L. C. CATALOG CARD NO: 65-18809
PRINTED IN THE UNITED STATES OF AMERICA

PREFACE

THE present work is a collection, methodically arranged, of my articles published in the 'Kyoto University Economic Review', the memoirs of the Department of Economics in the Imperial University of Kyoto, and it is hoped that it will give the reader a general idea of the social and economic development of Japan. Especially in regard to the social and economic state in the Tokugawa period and the changes that came over social and economic conditions in the period of transition from the Tokugawa Shogunate to the Meiji Restoration the reader will be able to gain a fairly good knowledge.

The study of the social and economic history of Japan has made remarkable progress in this country in recent years, and the results of many valuable researches have been made public either in book form or in magazine articles. But as these books and articles are mostly written in Japanese, very few of them have been made known to the Western scientific World. The author will be satisfied if the present volume will do something to meet the want hitherto felt in this regard.

Here all matters are dealt with summarily, because the author has mainly aimed at the exposition of the course of events in broad outlines, and also because he deliberately refrained from too detailed a description and discussion of facts in the belief that it would be rather tiresome to those who come in Contact with the social and economic history of Japan for the first time. My works in Japanese deal more minutely with the course of events, and any reader who may desire fuller information is referred to them.

This volume is published as a memoir of the Nihon Keizaishi Kenkyūsho (the Institute for Research in Economic History of Japan), which was established in Kyoto in 1933. The circumstances connected with the establishment of this Institute and the work being carried on by it at present are summarised in the supplement.

EIJIRO HONJO

Kyoto

May 1935

AUTHOR'S NOTE

The author takes great pleasure in the publication of this book made possible through the kind cooperation of Russell & Russell. When first published in Japan, it was printed in a limited number of copies and was permitted to go out of print.

I look forward to the wider dissemination of this book among those readers of all nationalities interested in Japanese economic history.

This is an introductory work on the economic history of Japan. The author will be gratified if this work is helpful to those who are interested in this particular department of research and, also, if it proves to be a handy guide to those scholars willing to delve deeper into the subject.

January, 1965   EIJIRO HONJO

NOTE

1. As regards the dates herein contained, the years are those of Christian era, but the months and days are in accordance with the Lunar calendar, which was in vogue in Japan prior to the Meiji Restoration. Therefore the dates in this book do not exactly accord with those by the Western calendar.

2. The titles of books written in Japanese and the nouns of Japanese origin seldom or not at all used in English are given in Italics. The Japanese ideographs for these are printed in the appendix, some of which are given in explanatory English.

3. In the Japanese expression the singular and plural are the same in form. Such being the case, Japanese nouns printed in Italics in this volume, e.g. *daimyō*, *han*, etc., are used in the same form whether in the singular or in the plural.

4. The author is greatly indebted to Mr. Leonald Goroku Masui, *M.A.*, *B.A.*, and Mr. Hisashi Terao, of 'The Japan Chronicle' for the translation of the original articles from Japanese into English with which this volume is compiled; to the late Professor Eadward Clarke of the Department of Literature in the Imperial University of Kyōto for its revision; to Mr. Shinsuke Takagi, Assistant of the Department of Economics in the same University and Mr. Keitarō Amano, Assistant Librarian of the same Department, for reading the proof and preparing the appendices and indices.

CONTENTS

PART I

PART II

DETAILED CONTENTS

PART I

SUPPLEMENT

THE DEVELOPMENT OF THE STUDY OF ECONOMIC HISTORY IN JAPAN

APPENDICES

INDICES

PART I

CHAPTER I
THE SOCIAL ORGANISATION AND THE SOCIAL PROBLEMS

SECTION I
CHANGES IN POLITICAL AND SOCIAL ORGANISATIONS

1. SOCIETY BASED ON THE *SHIZOKU* SYSTEM (CLAN SYSTEM)

The constitution of the *shizoku*. The political and social organisations in Japan of remote ages were based on the *shizoku* system. The *shizoku* means a community embracing a number of households of the same ancestry or those which believed themselves to be of the same ancestry. The households constituting it include not only those of direct descent but those of collateral lines. Each *shizoku* community had its head who ruled all component households, while each household was led by its master. To each of these *shizoku* or *uji* belonged a body called *be*

or *tomo* and also another body called *yakko*.
Although an *uji* was a community of those of
the same ancestry, such was not necessarily the
case with the *be*. As they belonged to some *uji*,
they came by degrees to assume the name of
that *uji*, and finally regarded themselves as of the
same ancestry as their chief, their claim being
recognised by outsiders also. The *uji* was thus
a community founded on the belief of its component units that they belonged to the same
ancestry. The *uji* also worshipped their guardian
god, which it called *ujigami*, and their reverence
for their *ujigami* served to strengthen the ties of
community binding them together. Such being
the case, it may well be said that the *uji* was a
community consisting of those who were not only
of the same ancestry but of the same religious
faith.

The *kabane.* In connection with the *uji*
system, it is necessary to make some explanation of
the *kabane*. Some *kabane* were derived from the
names by which persons were called or honorific
titles that they enjoyed, and some were granted
by the Imperial Court, while others were derived
from the names of their hereditary offices. Thus,
there was at first no clear distinction among the
members of a community in regard to standing.
As time went by, however, they came to symbolise
the status or position peculiar to different families,
and this distinction was officially recognised by
the Imperial Court. A system relating to this

was subsequently inaugurated under which the *kabane* was conferred on influential persons. In this way, the *kabane* came to indicate the status and standing of families.

The *shizoku* system and the organisation of the State. In the ancient days when the *shizoku* system operated in perfect form, the administration of the State was conducted along the lines of this system. To begin with, in those times the *uji* were inseparably associated with Government offices. All offices, big and small, were hereditarily held by the *uji-no-kami* (patriarchs or heads of the *uji*). For instance, the *ōomi* who were in charge of the State administration were appointed from among the heads of *uji* of the Imperial lineage, while the *ōmuraji* were assigned to the heads of *uji* of the *kami* (deity) lineage. The *kuni-no-miyatsuko* and *tomo-no-miyatsuko* offices, the occupants of which participated in local and sectional administrative business, were also held by the heads of certain *uji*. Thus, there existed a close relationship between the administrative organs and the *uji*.

Regarding the rule of the country, although the territory over which the Emperor held sway gradually widened in extent, not all the people in Japan were under the direct rule of the Emperor in those days. Then the territory held directly by the Imperial *uji*, that is, by the Emperor and the members of the Imperial Family, and its inhabitants only were under the direct rule of the Emperor. Over all other regions the Emperor had no direct sovereignty or control; they were ruled by him only indirectly through the heads of the *uji* concerned. In other words, the Emperor, as the head of the Imperial *uji*, directly ruled the territory and its inhabitants belonging to the Imperial *uji*, on the one hand, and, on the other hand, in his capacity as sovereign of the country he controlled the heads of all other *uji*, who had under their direct rule their respective regions and people. The *shizoku* system was nothing more or less than an administrative system.

Thus, it will be seen that in remote times in this country, social order was established along consanguineous lines, and the State was organised on the basis of this order. Such being the case, people of high social standing, or in other words, those of noble pedigree who possessed great wealth and many people under their direct rule, occupied high administrative posts. For instance, *ōomi* and *ōmuraji* were higher than *omi* and *muraji* in both official and social standing, while *omi* and *muraji* were of higher standing, politically and socially, than *kuni-no-miyatsuko* and *tomo-no-miyatsuko*. Higher still than *ōomi* and *ōmuraji* was the Emperor. Those who constituted the nobility in those days had *uji* and *kabane*. So also did the hereditary heads of the various *be* and the chiefs of local tribes. A class of people called the *be*, who engaged in various kinds of industry and other activities as followers of these high-class people, assumed the name of the *uji* to which they belonged, though they did not possess any *kabane*. They were semi-free people, whose social position was much lower than that of the nobility. Further below in rank were the *yakko* who had neither *uji* nor *kabane*, but possessed *na* (personal name) only. These were slaves, pure and simple. The people belonging to the *be* and the *yakko* classes lived by labour as the governed classes. In the society of those days, all services or occupations were, generally speaking, hereditary.

In short, there was no distinction yet between the social system and the State organisation. Both were based on a combination of *shizoku*. The *shizoku* system not only furnished the nucleus of the social organisation of ancient times but formed the basis of matters, administrative, military and religious.

2. SOCIETY BASED ON THE *GUNKEN* SYSTEM
(PREFECTURAL SYSTEM)

The collapse of the *shizoku* system. With the changes of the times, the *shizoku* system, which constituted the nucleus of the political and social organisations of this country in ancient days, came to engender many evils, until it underwent a complete change in the Taika Reform.

In politics, various powerful *uji* began to act with increasing arrogance, and rivalry for power and reciprocal hostility set in. This led to the ruin of these *uji* one after another, until the sovereign power of the State reverted to the Emperor. In the meantime, the population went on increasing year after year, with the result that it became impossible for people belonging to the same *uji* to live in one and the same district to the exclusion of all others, and a commingling of those belonging to different *uji* became unavoidable. As the proverb " Near-by strangers are better than relatives afar " has it, consanguineous relations came to be held of less importance than the territorial ties that bound inhabitants of the same region. This gradually paved the way for the creation of regional bodies in place of communities bound by consanguineous ties. Furthermore, the importation of Chinese and Korean civilisations and systems in rapid succession rendered it impossible for the increasing desires of the noble classes to be satisfied by the economic system so far ruling. If considered from this point of view only, it was inevitable that reform of some kind should be effected. Confucianism and Buddhism, which were introduced into this country, were incompatible with the ideas underlying the *shizoku* system and the faith of ancestor-worship, and they awakened in the people individualistic ideas, which ran counter to the community ideas, which had been prevalent before.

Owing to various stimulations and changes,

coming both from within and from without, the *shizoku* system had been gradually decaying. Advantage was taken of the fall of the Soga family from its high estate to establish the direct rule of the Emperor over the entire territory and people of the country, and for the creation of an authoritative State in which rule was detached from the *shizoku* system. In other words, a society based on the *gunken* system came into being. This embodies the Taika Reform.

The organisation of the State after the Taika Reform. In the Taika Reform (in 646), four great policies were proclaimed, namely, the establishment of the *gunken* system, the alteration of administrative districts, the reform of the land system and the collection of various taxes. These certainly embodied a revolutionary change of the political and social organisations.

In the days when the *shizoku* system operated, the Emperor's rule of the territory and people was only indirect, except over such territory and people which belonged to the Imperial *uji*, but in the Taika Reform, the private ownership of land and people was prohibited, and they were put under the direct control of the State. Moreover, the custom of hereditary occupation of Government offices by the heads of the *uji* was done away with, and a new system was introduced under which men of talent, even if they belonged to the lower grades of *uji*, were given high Government offices in which they could participate in the administration of State affairs. In consequence, the heads of *uji* very often held Government offices subordinate to those occupied by some of their followers. In this way, the consideration of pedigree was left out of all account in the choice of occupants of high Government offices, and the State administration was made absolutely independent of the *shizoku* system. The administrative organisation, which was formerly based on the *shizoku* system, was so changed that the Central Government was divided into eight Departments embracing many offices, and *kokushi* and *gunshi* officials were appointed to administer local affairs. This is what was called the *gunken* system. With the introduction of this system, the social and political importance of the *uji* entirely disappeared.

In consequence of the Taika Reform, the *be* class of people, public and private, was abolished, and most of these people were converted into *ryōmin* or common law-abiding people, while a section continued their servile existence. That class of people possessing *uji* and *kabane*, formed the nobility. As Buddhism prospered, the Buddhist priests came to constitute a special class, wielding an influence in no wise inferior to that of the nobility. The *ryōmin* were free citizens who chiefly engaged in the cultivation of *handen* (fields granted by the Government). In those days, there were many slaves, who, forming the working classes, played an important part in

supplying industrial labour, in putting waste land
under cultivation and in many other directions.

3. SOCIETY BASED ON THE *SHŌEN* SYSTEM
(MANOR SYSTEM)

The rise of aristocracy. In the Taika Reform,
the *shizoku* government gave way to the *gunken*
system, and Government offices were thrown open
to talent. But in the Central Government, the
uji of influence tried hard to exclude one another
until the Fujiwara family monopolised political
power. This brought aristocracy into being, and it
appeared as though things had reverted to *shizoku*
politics. In the provinces, with the development
of the *shōen* system, the old system of private
ownership of land and people returned, and the
principle of the public ownership of land was
undermined. The Heian period may, in these
circumstances, rightly be called the age of *shizoku*
politics or of aristocracy in fact, if not in name.

The Taika Reform was not necessarily
prompted by the general progress of civilisation
among the people. In those days, the people as
a rule derived no benefit from the splendid civilisation that then existed. It prevailed in limited
circles only ; it was enjoyed by the nobility and
other upper-class people exclusively. The capital
was built on a magnificent scale, and the noble-
men who lived there peacefully developed luxurious habits and indulged in the pleasures of

poetical composition and musical performances. The masses, on the other hand, had nothing to do with the civilisation of those days, being condemned to a life of penury. Owing to the exceedingly inadequate means of communication then available between the capital and the provinces, it was extremely difficult for the Central Government to deliver its orders to the provinces and get them obeyed. The civilisation in the central parts of the country did not extend to the provinces. On the whole, the civilisation of Japan in the Heian period was the civilisation of Kyōto, the then capital, and nothing more than that.

In short, although a brilliant civilisation existed among a section of the upper-class people in the Heian period, as in the preceding Nara period, there was a lack of communication and and contact between the upper and lower classes and between the capital and the provinces. To make matters worse, land had fallen more and more into private possession and the *shōen* system finally came into existence. This system brought various new social phenomena and problems, and a peculiar social order eventually developed out of it.

The organisation of the State based on the *shōen.* In the Taihō-ryō, the memorable Ordinance issued in the Taihō era (701–703), the principle was laid down that land should be public property and not be owned by private individuals.

This system soon crumbled away, however. Many private fields were put under cultivation in the shape of the so-called *shōen*.

In those days, land formed the sole property. Since the basic principle of public ownership of land failed to operate and the cultivation of private fields was officially recognised, fields of various kinds, the private ownership of which was forbidden under the system then ruling, gradually fell into quasi-private possession. The Imperial Court, shrines and temples, peers in Kyōto and local men of influence strove to add to their landed property, and powerful persons often abused their position and influence to possess themselves of the fields of others. The land controlled by *kokushi* (provincial authorities) in their official capacity was a public possession, and the people living thereon had the duty of paying taxes and other imposts, but the land annexed in the manner stated above was what was called the *shōen* of the shrines, temples and powerful families concerned, and these *shōen* enjoyed a sort of extraterritoriality in that they were practically exempt from all imposts. Such being the case, some landowners in the provinces voluntarily contributed their land to local magnates with a view both to evading public exactions under their protection and to adding to their local influence. As the land belonging to temples also enjoyed similar exemptions, there were cases where people either contributed their farms and estates to temples or built temples on their own authority so as to secure such exemptions for their own benefit on the pretext that the land belonged to these temples. In this way, local magnates gained more and more influence, and the lands of small farmers were gradually annexed by them, with the result that the whole country threatened to become *shōen*-ised.

As afore-said, the *shōen* was exempt from the duty of paying taxes to the Central Government. The inhabitants on the *shōen* vowed allegiance to the lord of the district and tilled the land, paying taxes to the lord. Thus, the land and its people were turned into the private possessions of their lord, instead of being the public land and public citizens as in the former period. The result was that the authority exercised by the Central Government over the provinces was considerably weakened. The *shōen* was virtually independent of the rule of the Central Government, and there was no connection or unity whatever between these *shōen* districts. Although in the organisation of the State of those days, there existed a Central Government, it existed only in name. The situation actually prevailing then was the rival and mixed existence of limited areas of public land belonging to the State, and extensive *shōen* land belonging to the Imperial Family, peers, local magnates and temples.

I have already mentioned the practice of

annexing land freely resorted to in those days,
and this led to the creation, on the one hand, of
those who, as owners of extensive tracts of land,
wielded great influence, and, on the other hand,
of many discontented people, who were either
unable to own any piece of land or, deprived of
their land, obliged to clear out of their native
districts. Brigandage became rampant in many
provinces in consequence, but the Central Government was powerless to suppress it. In the meantime, local magnates gradually increased their
military power. In order to protect themselves
against invaders, they kept many retainers and
followers. In this manner, the way was steadily
paved for the acquisition of political influence by
military leaders.

4. SOCIETY BASED ON THE DECENTRALISED HŌKEN SYSTEM (FEUDAL SYSTEM)

The meaning of *hōken* (feudalism). The term
hōken is used in contrast to the term *gunken*.
In the *gunken* system, the country had for its
head the Ruler who superintended State administration in fact as well as in name. Under this
system, the whole country was divided into many
administrative districts called *gun* or *ken*, to each
of which Government officials were appointed to
transact administrative business. These officials
did not own, as their feuds and subjects, the
districts and people which they were ordered to

rule. Nor were their offices hereditary or permanent with them. They were occasionally transferred to other posts in different districts. On the contrary, in the *hōken* system, the sovereign existed only in name, and the feudal lords, who nominally vowed allegiance to the sovereign, possessed lands of their own, which, with a few exceptions, were ruled by their descendants generation after generation. The inhabitants in these feuds belonged to their respective lords as their subjects, and pursued each his own vocation under their rule. The relationship of master and servant existing between the lord and the inhabitants of his fief, and the feudal character of territory were the two essential factors of the feudal system.

The feudal system was born of a desire for a secured existence which has become general after an unsettled and insecure social life which had previously prevailed. In turbulent times, it is only natural that national power should become decentralised, and it is certainly no easy task to bring this disrupted society back into unity so as to form a perfect centralised State. This is especially so when creation of an unrest and unsettled society was the result of the effeteness of the Central Government, which caused the local magnates to administer local affairs by their own initiative and energy. In other words, the creation of an unsettled society was due to the gradual diminution of State power, with the corresponding extension of private power. The only way to bring a stable society into existence in such circumstances was, therefore, to develop the system of private protection so that society might be bound by ties such as exist between master and servant. This is the reason why the feudal system sprang up after the turbulent times. At the beginning, the feudal system partook largely of the nature of divided authority, but later it gradually assumed the character of centralisation of power. Small feuds were by degrees annexed by bigger ones, and the bigger ones gained more influence in consequence until they conceived the idea of undertaking the task of maintaining the stability of the State as a whole.

In short, territorial and personal connections formed the essential factors of the feudal system, and one prominent feature of the society based on the feudal system was the existence of the relationship of master and servant between the governing and the governed classes. With the changes of the times, however, the feudal system took on different aspects, as has already been explained. There is a wide difference between the feudal system that ruled in the Kamakura period and after, and that ruling in the Tokugawa period. The one was characterised by decentralisation of power, while the other was contrariwise marked by centralisation of power. For this reason, the feudal system of the middle ages of this country is called the decentralised feudal system.

When we say that the political and social organisations of Japan in and after the Kamakura period became feudal, we do not simply mean that the *samurai* class became feudal. We also mean that society as a whole became feudal. For instance, the relationship of master and servant similar to that which existed in the *samurai* class subsisted between masters and their employees in commercial circles. The same spirit of devotion as was displayed by *samurai* towards their lords was shown by servants to their masters among the common people. Servants stood to their employers in the relationship of lord and retainer. In those days, vocational classes sprang up, and those belonging to these classes gradually gained in social influence. Those of the same trade combined to monopolise certain lines of business among themselves, allowing no incursion by outsiders into their settled spheres of activity. The relationship of master and servant was firmly established and class distinctions were recognised, with the result that all people found their proper positions. It was one characterisitic of the feudal society that privileges were held in respect. Such was in the natural order of things as stability of society was the aim of the feudal system.

The ruling spirit of insubordination. The social conditions underwent marked changes during the period between the Namboku period (Southern and Northern Dynasties) and the Muromachi period. The word "insubordination" truthfully illustrates the state of things prevailing in those times. The will to supplant those of higher but effete classes manifested itself in all walks of life. It was, in a word, an age of rule by deputation. Not only in politics but in all circles, usurpation of power was the order of the day. The head temples were despoiled of their power by branch temples, and master priests were evicted from their places of authority by their disciples. Particularly noteworthy were the attempts made by the low-class people to supplant the upper-class people and the poor to control the rich.

The constant and long-drawn-out disturbances in those days deprived all classes, high and low, of their security of living, and all were reduced to financial straits, morality falling to a very low level. While there were some people who amassed enormous wealth, there were a large number of people who were reduced to penury. The low-class people, who were condemned to an insecure existence under the pressure constantly brought to bear upon them by this disparity between the rich and the poor, gradually nursed a spirit of insubordination against the high class people, and this discontent found violent expression in a sort of social movement called *tsuchi-ikki* (riots). These riots reflect the prevalent spirit of insubordination in those days.

5. SOCIETY BASED ON THE CENTRALISED
HOKEN SYSTEM (FEUDAL SYSTEM)

The establishment of the centralised feudal system. When he was appointed Shogun in the eighth year of Keichō (1603) and assumed the supreme military power, Tokugawa-Ieyasu held sway over the various feudal lords by virtue of his office as Shogun, on the one hand, and was the lord of his own feud, on the other. His feud, or *tenryō* as it was called, covered one fourth of the area of the whole country, if put together. It was distributed in 47 out of the 68 provinces, into which the country was divided. All the places of political importance and all big cities constituting commercical and industrial centres were under his direct control, and he appointed *bugyō* and *daikan* officials to govern these places. All other districts except those belonging to the Imperial Family, shrines and temples belonged to the *daimyō* (feudal lords), and the administration of affairs in these fiefs was, on the whole, left to the self-rule of their lords. Among these fiefs were those belonging to the three branch Tokugawa families in Kii, Owari and Mito provinces, and the fiefs belonging to *fudai-daimyō* (feudal lords in hereditary vassalage to the Tokugawas) and those belonging to *tozama-daimyō* (feudal lords not in hereditary vassalage) were, so to speak, interwoven with one another. In the Jōkyō-Genroku era (1684–1703), the *daimyō* with a fief yielding more than 10,000 *koku* of rice totalled 240, of which 45 produced over 100,000 *koku* of rice. Whereas the fief of Lord Maeda, of Kaga province, who was the most important *daimyō*, did not produce more than 1,020,000 *koku*, the Tokugawa Shogunate held a fief, the quantity of rice produced in which was variably put at from 4,000,000 to 8,000,000 *koku*. In any case, it is clear that the Tokugawas possessed an influence far superior to that of the *daimyō*. It is, of course, undeniable that the wide extent of the *tenryō* (the Shogunate fief) put the Tokugawas in the predominant position, but at the same time the fact must not be lost sight of that the influence of the Tokugawas was further enhanced by the wise policies pursued by able and perspicuous Shoguns, who successively held the exalted position in the early days of the Tokugawa Shogunate. By inaugurating the *sankin-kōtai* system (alternative sojourns of *daimyō* in Edo, as Tōkyō was then called, in the Shogun's service), distributing the fiefs adroitly, arranging inter-marriages between *daimyō*, etc. and imposing levies on rich *daimyō* in connection with engineering works in Edo, the Tokugawa Shogunate held the *daimyō* well in hand. While on the other hand, it followed the exclusionist policy towards outside countries so as to avert disturbing influences and stimulants from abroad against the maintenance of order at home. These measures combined to enhance the power and influence of the Tokugawa Shogunate to the diminution of the influence of the *daimyō*. Thanks also to the some measures, the centralised feudal system was perfected and tranquillity was maintained at home during the régime of the Tokugawa Shogunate for more than 250 years.

The centralised feudal system obtained in the Tokugawa Shogunate, and historians regard this period as one in which the feudal State was consummated. It, therefore, follows that the establishment of the class system and the rigorous maintenance of the relationship of master and servant, which are the characteristics of a feudal society, were eminently manifest in the period. These characteristics were evident in many circles. For instance, in politics the popular slogan was to adhere to the old rules and discard the new ways, and official inspectors called *ōmetsuke* and *metsuke* were appointed to see that the Shogunate order were faithfully obeyed. Everything went by the established etiquette and rules, and there was no freedom of speech or of the press such as it then was. Although the way was opened for the secret submission of views to the authorities, free debate of political matters by masterless *samurai* was frowned upon. The system of *kabunakama* (guild system) operated in all kinds of pursuits, and nobody outside the group was allowed to engage in the same trade. An apprentice was promoted to the status of an artisan after a cer-

tain period of apprenticeship, and it was not until
he had formally introduced himself to those in
the group and obtained their formal sanction that
he was allowed to become one of the trade. From
the study of Chinese classics, Japanese poetry and
the military arts of archery, fencing and horse-
manship down to the light accomplishments of
the tea ceremony, flower arrangements, etc., the
established formality was rigidly adhered to.
Once one became a pupil under a master of a
certain school, no matter whether it was in regard
to learning or light accomplishments, one was
forbidden to turn one's back on the learning or
the accomplishments of that particular school
under penalty of being stigmatised as a heretic.
These are characteristic of a feudal society, and
it is no wonder that a society with such characteristics should have been marked by inactivity
and conservatism.

Exclusionism. In the Tokugawa period, the
centralised feudal system was established at home,
while towards the outside world an exclusionist
policy was pursued. This brought about an age
of tranquillity extending over 250 years. To close
the country was not, however, the original intention of the Tokugawa Shogunate. Tokugawa-
Ieyasu, the first Shogun, laid down the fundamental policy of peaceful intercourse with other
countries, and endeavoured to gain profit by promoting trade. The policies adopted by Spain and
Portugal towards our country at the time were

unfortunately too much wedded to what is called mercantilism. Those countries were obsessed not only by the desire to acquire gold and silver but by designs of territorial acquisition. They sent to these shores missionaries together with merchants, so that they might control the spiritual world of this country through the religious propaganda of these missionaries, while deriving material interests from the trade with this country, which they strove to develop through the efforts of their merchants. As these political ambitions were gradually revealed, there arose differences and difficulties of varying kinds, which impeded the intercourse between these countries and Japan, eventually resulting in the adoption of the exclusionist policy by the Tokugawa Shogunate.

The exclusionist policy, contrary to the policy adopted in the early days of the Tokugawa Shogunate, revoked the throwing open of the country to foreigners. I will now explain how this policy was operated on several sides. Let me first consider how it affected the propagandism of Christianity. At first, the Tokugawa Shogunate connived at Christian evangelical work, but after the eighteenth year of Keichō (1613), it was absolutely vetoed. As regards the travel abroad of Japanese citizens, it was at first encouraged, but later a general embargo was put on it, only the ships officially sanctioned were allowed to go abroad. After the thirteenth year of Kan'ei (1636), even this exceptional arrangement was done away with, and not only were people forbidden to go abroad but those who were abroad then were not allowed to come home. So far as the advent of foreigners to these shores is concerned, the Portugese were deported, contrary to the open door policy originally laid down, and the request of British subjects for permission to resume trade relations was rejected, Dutch and Chinese citizens only being allowed to engage in trade with the Japanese at Nagasaki. The intercourse with the Dutch was more restricted than that with the Chinese, however, for they were allowed to take up their residence in the limited area of Dejima only. Lastly, as to the foreign trade. At first, the whole country was thrown open to foreign intercourse, but later the trade ports were reduced in number, and restrictions were put on methods of commercial transactions, the period of anchorage and sojourn. Nay, even the amount of trade was restricted. Thus it will be seen that at the beginning the Tokugawa Shogunate adopted the open door policy towards all countries, then closed the country to Portugal, and finally the country was closed to all countries except China and Holland. In short, the exclusionist policy was adopted by degrees. Moreover, as the trade relations with Holland and China remained unmolested, the exclusionist policy was by no means absolute.

SECTION II

SOCIAL PROBLEMS IN VARIOUS AGES

1. SOCIAL PROBLEMS IN THE *SHIZOKU* RÉGIME

The social problems in these days referred to land. Annexations of land gave rise to various questions.

Annexations of land. The agricultural age began in remote times in Japan, a fact which accounts for the importance which has always attached to land. As already explained, in the system ruling in remote days, the direct rule of the Emperor over the land and the people was limited to those belonging to the members of the Imperial Family. All other *uji* were led by their respective heads. They belonged to the Emperor only indirectly. Consequently, there existed two kinds of land — one owned by those of the Imperial lineage and the other owned by men of influence. As the land in the Imperial possession increased in extent year by year, so did the land owned by men of influence go on expanding. "Some annexed tens of thousands of acres of land, while others owned not the size of a pin's head," as an old writing has it. The tendency to annex land was manifest even in very ancient times. Some ambitious *uji* even attempted to annex estates belonging to the Imperial Family.

The question of *uji* and *kabane*.   As already mentioned, pedigree was held in high esteem in these times.   People of dignified *uji* and *kabane* occupied high positions, socially, and politically, and these possessed themselves of extensive areas of land by utilising their positions.   In point of wealth also, they occupied a superior position.   In such circumstances, there developed a natural desire among the people generally for high *uji* and *kabane*, and some people went the length of forging pedigrees so as to secure a high social position and amass wealth.   This was the cause of the confusion of *uji* and *kabane*, which it was attempted to adjust by the so-called *kugadachi* method.   Thus, a disparity between the rich and the poor was marked in remote times already, and this bred problems of various kinds.

2. SOCIAL PROBLEMS IN THE *GUNKEN* RÉGIME

The Taika Reform brought the form of government based on the *shizoku* system to ruin.   It also prohibited the private ownership of land and people, and the *handen* system was introduced, but the operation of this system was attended with supreme difficulties.   The growth of population, the increase of human desires and the elevation of the standards of living caused a shortage of arable fields, and this led to the reclaiming from the wilderness and cultivation of private fields.   The system of private ownership gradually

supplanted the old system, and then the annexation of lands recurred. Besides the nobility and
the common people, there sprang up many slaves
from various causes. These slaves engaged in
the cultivation of fields, the construction of
temples and many works of labour by order of
their masters.

The grant and recovery of *handen* fields.
The grant and recovery of *handen* fields took
place in regard to certain stipulated land. The
fields to be supplied as *handen* were public property and no private ownership was recognised
regarding them, only usufruct being recognised as
a matter of principle. Each household was supplied
with a stipulated tract of land, and no single individual formed the subject of the right. When a
child attained the age of six, a boy was given 2
tan (one *tan* being .245 acre) and a girl two-thirds
of the area, that is, one *tan* 120 *bu*. The land
granted to each person was called *kubunden*.

This rule of granting and recovering *handen*
fields was enforced comparatively widely at first
in the country, but later it ceased to be enforced
rigidly, partly because it involved troublesome
procedure and partly because it was easily turned
to account by crafty and fraudulent persons.
Even in the Gokinai district, where, it being in
close proximity to the capital, the authority of
the Imperial Court ought to have been forcibly
felt, the *handen* system failed to operate during
a few score years. If this was the case in the

Gokinai district, the state of things ruling in the outlying districts may well be imagined. Besides *kubunden*, there were various kinds of fields, which proved a serious impediment to the operation of the *handen* system. Moreover, with the increase of population, there occurred a shortage of fields, and this necessitated the encouragement of cultivation of waste lands. In the seventh year of Yōrō (723), an instruction was issued to all provinces ordering the cultivation of private fields. Under the new order, those who newly made ponds and put waste land under cultivation were allowed to own their new fields in three generations, while those who put waste land under cultivation by utilising the ponds and irrigation facilities already existing were allowed to own their new fields during their lifetime. In later year (743), this law was so revised as to turn such fields into the permanent property of their cultivators, as there was fear of such fields being looted and allowed to go to waste as the period for their restitution to the Government approached. After this, there developed a tendency for people to get private fields in preference to cultivated fields, which partook of the nature of *handen*, and the rich people vied with one another in putting waste land under cultivation. The result was that the private lands owned by influential families grew more extensive in area than public lands. In this way, the *handen* system gradually gave place to the so-called *shōen* system. The motive underlying the creation of the *handen* system was to rectify unfairness in the distribution of wealth by establishing the State ownership of all land, but this object was completely defeated, and through the introduction of the system of clearing land, the distribution of wealth became unfair again.

There also operated the *chin-so* system in this period. By *chin* was meant the rent collected in advance at the time of sowing seeds in spring, while *so* meant the payment of the rent at the time of harvesting crops in autumn. It was somewhat similar to the farm tenancy system introduced in later ages. Under this system, which recognised the transfer of the usufruct of land, the rich proceeded to annex lands, while the poor losing their lands were turned into tenant farmers. Thus, it will be seen that this system also contributed to the accentuation of the disparity between the rich and the poor.

The disparity between the rich and the poor. Annexation of lands caused a wider gulf between the rich and the poor, as already mentioned, and the great disparity that existed between them can be gathered from other facts also.

The Taihō-ryō (Ordinance of the Taihō era) divided all households in the country into nine classes according to the amount of wealth they possessed. It is clear from the census registers of the day that slaves were mostly kept by households belonging to the higher orders. In other words, the majority of slaves were concentrated among a small number of the rich. This fact may be cited as one illustration of the great disparity then existing between the rich and the poor.

A register record compiled in the province of Echizen in the second year of Tempyō (730) and that compiled in the province of Tajima in the second year of Tempyō-Shōhō (750) give the following number of the households of the different classes:—

class	1st	2nd	3rd	4th	5th	6th	7th	8th	9th	others
Echizen	1	4	7	4	5	8	11	13	45	920
Tajima	–	–	–	–	2	2	3	11	69	327

From the above, it will be seen that there were very few households belonging to the upper classes, while those belonging to the lower classes were very numerous. This is another example testifying to the great disparity between the rich and the poor.

Needless to say, land was the only source of economic power in this period, and there operated the *kubunden* and the "private fields" systems, on the one hand, and the farm tenancy system was in force, on the other, the labour of slaves being utilised under the latter system. These facts formed the principal causes of the social problems of the day.

3. SOCIAL PROBLEMS IN THE *SHŌEN* RÉGIME

In this period, the more important social problems were furnished by the question of land-ownership and by the vagrants who, deprived of their land and property, and unable to bear heavy burdens of taxation, forsook the places of their birth.

The land question. As already explained, the *kubunden* system was not enforced strictly, and the increase of population necessitated the cultivation of waste lands, which resulted in the increase of private fields, this rendering the operation of the *kubunden* system all the more difficult. After the law was enacted in the fifteenth year of Tempyō (743) under which private fields became the permanent property of their cultivators, there was a remarkable increase of private fields. As this caused many and far-reaching evils, prohibitory or restrictive orders were frequently issued, but all these efforts had little effect in checking the general tendency. The *shōen* fields went on increasing and public fields witnessed as remarkable a decrease. In the reign of the Emperor Gosanjō (1069–1073), an office was created with the object of adjusting matters relating to *shōen*. The idea was to create no new *shōen* fields and abolish those *shōen* fields, which were either of dubious origin or obstructive of the administration of State affairs. Earnest efforts were made to enforce this new rule, but the desired results were not reaped, as the authorities were powerless to apply the new rule to the possessions of the former *Kanbaku* Fujiwara-Yorimichi, and moreover, as there were many fields which were created by Imperial order in the reign of the above-mentioned Emperor. In the reign of the Emperor Shirakawa, who succeeded the Emperor Gosanjō on the Throne, not only was this office abolished but there was a positive increase in the number of *shōen* fields belonging to temples, in consequence of the Emperor's adherence to Buddhism. In the reign of the Emperor Toba, the above office was again created, but as official investigations were not strictly conducted, no effectual check could be put on the increasing tendency of the *shōen*. As already explained, *shōen* fields enjoyed a sort of extraterritoriality, and there was consequently an increasing number of people who sought to evade public exactions under the protection of local magnates by contributing their land to them. This practice accentuated the tendency to annex land, to make the gulf between the rich and the poor wider.

The *rōnin* (vagrants) question. In the closing days of the Heian period, the acreage of public fields and lands greatly decreased and the whole country threatened to be turned into *shōen*. As *shōen* fields were exempt from taxation, the local Government officials resorted to extortions in resulting from order to make up for the dwin-

dling revenue this diminution of public fields and
lands, and the poor people who could not bear
heavy burdens were obliged to leave their native
places for other districts.   These poor people
turned into what are called *rōnin* (vagrants) in
the *Ōchō* period.

Another cause of forced vagrancy was *suiko*.
Suiko means the system under which the rice
plants on official and private fields were rented
to farmers in spring and the tenants paid the
rent together with interest thereon after the harvest in autumn. This system was inaugurated
from the worthy motive of relieving farmers in
distress, but later it came about that the State
expenditure was defrayed from the profit made
out of the operation of this system, and even the
rich were made to rent such rice plants and pay
the stipulated dues. The interest on private *suiko*
was, as a rule, 100 per cent. per annum, and
that on public *suiko* 50 per cent. Although the
quantities of rice plants to be rented out for *suiko*
purposes were officially fixed according to the
size and other circumstances of the provinces,
the local Government officials rented out rice
plants in excess of the stipulated quantities so as
to pocket the balance. Men of influence and
those under their protection refused to obey the
orders of the local Government officials. They
declined to rent the rice plants allotted to them.
Again, some of those, who were obliged to rent,
strove to escape the obligation by offering a bribe

to the officials. In such circumstances, heavier burdens devolved on honest people who did not shirk the duty, and when the time for paying their dues came round, they could not meet their obligations. When they were in financial straits, farmers rented high-interest rice plants, thoughtless of the future, only to find themselves unable to pay their dues when they were called upon to pay them in due time. In such cases, they had their houses, already hypothecated, confiscated. They also had to part with their fields and lower themselves to the position of labourers, until at last were obliged to flee from their dear homes to become vagrants in strange provinces. Many of these unfortunate people settled down on *shōen* land, which was immune from taxation, and either were employed in the work of putting waste lands under cultivation or they engaged in diverse menial works. In a sense, the *shōen* furnished a refuge for the people who had deserted their native places because of their inability to put up with extortions.

4. SOCIAL PROBLEMS IN THE DECENTRALISED *HOKEN* RÉGIME

In this period, the whole country was divided among local men of power and influence. Many influential men asserted their authority everywhere, and the spirit of class antagonism pervaded the entire commünty. The war cry of rioters had the ring of a new class strife. Of the riot (*tsuchi-ikki*) I will treat in the next section. In this section I will deal with the land question and *tokusei*.

The land question. Landownership at this time was of a very complex nature. One tract of land had, besides its *de facto* lord, one or two or more *de jure* lords, who were called *honsho* or *ryōke*. The owner of the land, who put it under cultivation, finding it impossible to stand the persecution of the local Government officials, chose to make a man of influence its nominal lord, and in some cases selected one or more nominal lords in a man or men of higher rank and influence. This led to joint ownership of one tract of land, and to the division of the profit accruing from the land among its different lords. Such being the case, the actual income to each from a wide tract of land was comparatively small. As, moreover, the crops sometimes failed, the feudal Government did much to encourage thrift among the people. An anecdote of Saimyōji-Nyūdō (Hōjō-Tokiyori), an ex-Regent, sitting talking at night with no better relish than *miso* (bean-paste) to feast upon, and another of Matsu-shita-Zenni, Tokiyori's mother, making a patch on a paper screen, illustrate the enthusiasm with which the campaign of thrift was carried on by the feudal Government.

Since the fief territory was the main source of revenue for the feudal Government, restrictions were put on the sale, mortgage transfer, etc. of the land. Even when a son succeeded to his father's fief, he was called upon to obtain the sanction of the feudal Government. With regard to the land which was newly bestowed on persons in recognition of their merits, its sale was prohibited, lest it should fall into the hands of those *samurai* who were not amenable to the control of the feudal Government, or of farmers and merchants, as it would impair the financial power of the Government. The custom of assigning the post of Shogun to Imperial Princes or *kuge*-nobles opened the way for the spread of *kuge* tastes to Kamakura and other Kantō districts, and luxurious habits came to prevail. The difficulty of living arising in consequence compelled *gokenin* (low-grade vassals of the feudal Government) to dispose of their land or mortgage it by some means or another. As preventive measures, the feudal Government laid down the rule that transactions in such land between *gokenin* should be effected at the original price and that the land which passed into hands of non-*gokenin* could be recovered without compensation. The poverty of the *gokenin* was, however, so great that these devices could not prevent their land from passing into other hands. As the last resort, the feudal Government adopted the *tokusei* system so as to invalidate the sale, lease and giving in pledge of land.

Tokusei. By *tokusei* is meant the practice of repudiating all rights and obligations concerning contracts of sale, lease and mortgage signed within a certain stipulated period. It was in accord with the spirit of *tokusei* that the mortgage and sale of the land owned by *gokenin* was invalidated in the fourth year of Bun'ei (1267). The *Tokusei* Order, which is most popularly cited, is the one issued on March 6th of the fifth year of Einin (1297). It consists of many clauses, the more important of which provide for the strict prohibition of the mortgage or sale of the landed property of *gokenin,* and for its restoration without compensation, to the original owners of any such lands which were sold or mortgaged by *gokenin* to other *gokenin* in the past, except that which was sold or mortgaged twenty years before by legal means. With regard to the land which had passed into the hands of non-*gokenin* or *bonge* the above-mentioned prescription was not recognised. With regard to loans of money, it was stipulated that no lawsuit about such matters should be accepted. This rule applied to the people generally as well as to *gokenin.* An exception was, however, made in favour of those who pawned their things in order to borrow money from pawnbrokers (*dosō*). This *Tokusei* Order, which was strikingly partial toward debtors, caused great uneasiness in economic circles, and it had the effect of depriving the *gokenin* of all means of raising money. In such circumstances, the Order was revoked after a year's operation. The extent of the shock that the Order caused to the economic world may be gathered from the fact thats in the transactions effected, even after the cancellation of the Order, in regard to the sale or mortgage of land, deeds were prepared, in which was inserted that the seller or pawner undertook that he would never assert his claim to the land, even if another *Tokusei* Order were issued.

The *Tokusei* Order in the Kamakura period was intended for the repudiation of debts for the benefit of a *samurai* class called *gokenin*, but in the following Muromachi period, the low-class common people agitated for the issue of a *Tokusei* Order in their desire to get their repudiated. With a view to compelling the feudal Government to accept their demand, they caused riots. The objects of the attack and spoliation of these rioters were always *sakaya*, *dosō* and similar rich parvenus. Since the days of the Hōjō régime, the *sakaya* and *dosō* played the part of monetary organs as money-lenders, and they belonged to the propertied class. The *tokusei* riots in the Muromachi period to say nothing of the *Tokusei* Order issued in the Kamakura period are traceable to the growing disparity between the rich and the poor.

5. SOCIAL PROBLEMS IN THE CENTRALISED
HOKEN RÉGIME

The development of currency economy and

the rise of the *chōnin* class in the Tokugawa
period widened the gulf between the rich and the
poor. It was the established policy of the Tokugawa Shogunate to maintain the class system and
eliminate all causes inimical to this system. In
the actual social life, however, there was a general
impoverishment of the farmers and *samurai*, on
the one hand, and the enrichment of the commercial and industrial people generally, on the
other. This phenomenon caused many farmers
to give up the plough to become merchants or
artisans. The custom also came into vogue for
samurai to adopt the sons of rich merchants
with an eye to the wealth of the parents of their
adopted sons. The Tokugawa Shogunate adopted
various policies in order to check the tendency
toward the increasing of the disparity between
the rich and the poor or to dispose of this problem successfully. The more important among
these policies were the prohibition of the sale of
land, the issue of the *Kien* Order, the imposition
of *goyōkin*, and the regulation of the price of rice.
With regard to the popular agitations such as
peasants' riots and rice-riots, I propose to deal
with them in the next section.

The prohibition of the sale of land. In the
Tokugawa period, the sale of land was vetoed.
The prohibitory law in this respect was enacted
in March of the twentieth year of Kan'ei (1643),
and it continued in force until the closing days
of the Tokugawa Shogunate. The Mito-Han was,

however, free from this prohibition. As a matter of fact, land was pledged and allowed to pass into other hands on various pretexts, and as the transfer of land went on, such practices were legally prohibited. This law was promulgated because of the fear that if the sale of land was legally recognised, many farmers might lose their property. It was feared that the possession of more and more lands by rich men and the loss of their lands by small farmers might bring about a state of things in which all the lands belonging to a village might fall into the hands of one or two rich men of the village or possibly even into those of other villages. In short, the law aimed at preventing the desertion of their villages by impoverished farmers and the increase of the disparity between the rich and the poor in consequence of the annexations of land. The same motive underlay the restrictions on the partition of lands. The Shogunate feared that if the partition of lands on the part of small farmers among their children was allowed without restriction, there would be created numerous poor farmers, who could not make both ends meet, and so it prohibited the partition of lands, unless the farmer possessed an estate of more than one *chō* (2.45 acres) in acreage, which would yield more than 10 *koku* (50 bushels) of rice. It does not appear that this prohibitory law was strictly enforced, however.

The *Kien* Order. In the first year of Kansei

(1624), Lord Matsudaira-Sadanobu issued a famous order. In view of the fact that the accumulated debts contracted by *hatamoto* and *gokenin* (low-grade direct retainers of the Tokugawa Shogunate) from *fudasashi* (money-lenders) reduced many *samurai* families to distress, he issued an order under which all these debtors were excused from the duty of paying their debts, provided they were contracted before the fourth year of Temmei (1784). As regards the debts contracted after the fifth year of Temmei, the debtors were ordered to repay at the rate of 3 *ryō* a year for each 100 *hyō* (bales) of rice which they got as stipend from the Shogunate, irrespective of the amount of their debts, the interest to be paid being fixed at one *bu* per month for each 50 *ryō* borrowed. This order was the same as the *Tokusei* Order in the Kamakura period in nature, except for the difference that in this order provision was made for the instalment payments of some of the old debts. Fifty odd years later, the Tempo Reform was carried out. On December 14th of the fourteenth year of Tempo (1843), an order was suddenly issued, according to which *hatamoto* (debtors) were bidden to pay their debts to *fudasashi* (creditors) in twenty-year instalments, without interest, regardless of the date of repayment of the debts. The above-mentioned two orders were designed to relieve the *samurai* class of the dire financial straits to which they were then reduced, but it incidentally throws a sidelight on the remarkable difference in point of wealth existing between the *samurai*, who constituted the ruling class, and the *chōnin*, or the governed class, at the time.

Goyōkin. *Goyōkin* is a levy which was temporarily and optionally imposed chiefly on *chōnin* in order to make good the deficit in the State treasury. The reason for this imposition was that while the *samurai* were the descendants of those who had rendered services to the State on various battle fields, and they themselves were serving the State by proceeding to Edo by turns under the *sankin-kōtai* system, and farmers were producing foodstuffs by toiling on the farm all the year round, the *chōnin* sat idly and amassed big fortunes. That they were able to lead a peaceful life was all due to the favours conferred on them by the State. In order to repay these favours, it was argued, they ought to contribute a part of their wealth to the State coffer. The levy was a forced loan or a benevolence, to all intents and purposes. It was another attempt to to check the growing wealth of the rich. It may be regarded in the light of an economic question arising between classes or the question of disparity between the rich and the poor.

The *goyōkin* device was frequently resorted to after the Hōreki era (1751-1763), and the import was mainly levied on rich merchants in Edo, Ōsaka and other big cities. Some scholars of the day expressed approval of this system and urged the necessity of reducing the difference between the rich and the poor by checking the growth of wealth on the part of the rich. For instance, in his memorial to the Shogunate, Uesaki-Kuhachirō says: "If all means fail to find the wherewithal, I advise you to levy *goyōkin* upon rich merchants in Edo, Kyōto, Ōsaka and all other cities in order to raise the money neces- sary to meet the State expences, while at the same time trying to relieve the farmers. I notice that even in these days rich tradespeople and merchants are making good profits. For many years past, the agricultural interests, which are the main source of the country's strength, have been declining, and the commercial interests, which are of secondary importance, have been prosper- ing, with the result that things have reached a deadlock. In such circumstances, it is advisable that the surplus wealth of merchants should be collected to the end that the poverty of the farmers be lessened. Moreover, if you see that farmers take rank of merchants in all things, farmers will gradually come to hold their occupa- tion in due respect, and the number of those farmers who desert their native villages to lead town life now will decrease. While, on the other hand, merchants will come to envy the lot of farmers, whom they now hold in disdain. This will bring agriculture and commerce back into their proper position." Thus, he suggests that by imposing *goyōkin* on rich merchants, the deficit in the State revenue can be made good, on the one hand, and the class system can be maintained.

The regulation of the price of rice. In this period, *samurai* and farmers were suppliers of rice, while merchants and industrialists were consumers of the cereal. Their interests were in consequence in conflict. Fluctuations in the price of rice produced far-reaching effects on the financial position of the Shogunate and *daimyō*, and on the interests of all classes of society, so it was necessary not only for financial and economic reasons but for the harmonisation of the conflicting interests of different classes that the price of rice should be properly regulated. Although the *samurai* and farmers were desirous of the price being maintained at a high level, they did not like to excite discontent in commercial and industrial circles by disregarding their interests, for discontent might foment hostility among them against the *samurai* class and the destruction of the class system might result. So, they had to devise measures to prevent a violent rise in the price of rice. Thus, it will be seen that the regulation of the price of rice was undertaken not merely as an attempt to solve the question of the prices of commodities, but for the purpose of bringing the conflicting interests of all classes into harmony. Especially during and after the régime of Tokugawa-Yoshimune, the eighth Shogun, various policies were adopted for forcing up or reducing the price of rice. Nothing definite is known as to the actual results of these measures, but it is clear that the price of rice was influenced more by the condition of the rice harvest than by artificial policies.

SECTION III

VARIOUS PHASES OF SOCIAL MOVEMENTS

In the previous section, I have given a brief explanation of social problems in various periods. Below I will dwell upon some social movements recorded in the history of the times.

1. *TSUCHI-IKKI* IN THE MUROMACHI PERIOD

Tsuchi-ikki. *Tsuchi-ikki* means a riot caused by the populace. It is also called *tokusei-ikki*, because such riots were very often caused for the purpose of forcing the Government to issue a *Tokusei* Order. As already mentioned, the *Tokusei* Order in the Kamakura period was meant to repudiate the debts of *gokenin*, but the *tokusei* riots in the Muromachi period were started by the low-class people for the purpose of getting their own debts cancelled.

There sprang up a sort of monetary organ called *mujinsen* about the time the Hōjō family reigned supreme, and those who ran this business had storehouses for keeping goods pawned. These storehouses were called *dosō* (earth storehouse) becouse they were plastered with earth in order to avoid destruction by fire. Later, *sake* merchants ran the same business as a subsidiary business and consequently *sakaya* and *dosō* represented the business between them. They were pawnbrokers in later days. The feudal Government, which was in financial straits, levied heavy taxes on *dosō* and *sakaya*, and as well demanded heavy contributions from them whom it regarded as an abundant source of revenue. As for *sakaya* and *dosō*, they resorted to various devices to protect their interests against the unfavourable condition of affairs then prevailing. Some of them made popular shrines and temples the patron of their land or sought the protection of influential *kuge* peers and *samurai* leaders by acting as though they were their employees. Heavy taxation led to higher rates of interest on pledges, and, moreover, some of them resorted to profiteering at the expense of poor pawners, with the result that strong complaints and resentment prevailed among the populace against *sakaya* and *dosō*. What with the social system ruling, famines and epidemics, the financial circumstances of the masses were desperate, and riots were the ebullitions of the discontent which they could no longer keep down. The rioters broke into the storehouses of *sakaya* and *dosō* and looted them, destroyed the IOUs in their keeping, and pressed the Government for the issue of a *Tokusei* Order for the repudiation of their debts.

These riots were not confined to Kyōto and neighbourhood. They spread to the provinces. Indeed, they became a common evil in this period. The populace were not the only party concerned in these disturbances, but *kuge* and *samurai*, who were economically on the verge of bankruptcy, were evidently in secret collusion with the rabble. It is perhaps more correct to interpret them as acts of insubordination on the part of the poor against the rich.

Kuni-ikki. In some cases, riots assumed a different aspect. For instance, of the riots which broke out in the first year of Eikyō (1429) in Harima, Ise, Tamba, Settsu and Iga provinces, the one which occurred in Harima province had for its slogan "Down with the *samurai*," and the mob defeated the troops under Akamatsu-Mitsu-suke, the Shugo of the province, in the fight that ensued. In this case, the rioters aimed at the elimination of the *samurai* class; it was an attempt to undermine the social system then ruling. One which broke out in Yamashiro province was even more violent in nature.

This riot broke out in the seventeenth-eighteenth year of Bummei (1485–1486). At that time, the feud between Hatakeyama-Masanaga and Hatakeyama-Yoshinari was still going on. The two Hatakeyamas set up their respective new barriers in Yamashiro province, cut off the means of mutual communication, and occupied the land belonging to shrines and temples. As these steps put many hardships on the inhabitants of the province, the local inhabitants ranging from fifteen or sixteen to sixty years of age held a conference on December 11th of the seventeenth year of Bummei, and adopted resolutions urging the withdrawal of the contending troops, the restitution of the land belonging to shrines and temples, and the removal of the new barriers. They even organised troops and pressed the two Hatakeyamas for the acceptance of their demands. The *samurai* troops under the Hatakeyamas were sufficiently overawed by the menacing attitude of the improvised militia and withdrew, leaving the militia to undertake the guard duty within the province. On February 13th of the following year, a second mass meeting was called at the Byōdōin Temple at Uji. At this conference, laws were made and rates of taxation were fixed. Even the lands belonging to shrines and temples were taxed. All administrative affairs in the province were transacted by the representatives of the inhabitants. This form of rule seems to have lasted for quite a long time.

About this time, Kii province was also put under the rule of the populace. "It rid itself of the local magistrate and the farmers were the masters of the province," as an old written record describes the state of things then prevailing in the province. There were also religious riots started by believers in the Ikkō Sect or by ad-herents of the Nichiren Sect. The Ikkō riot in

Kaga province was a most notable example of the kind. In this case, the local magistrate was driven out of the province and the administration of the province was temporarily carried on by the mob.

In short, riots represented a big social movement of the non-propertied classes carried on intermittently for about a century. It is not correct to regard them simply as acts of violence committed by lawless people. If the low-class people had abided by their hard lot meekly and by force of habit, no trouble might have occurred, but as they lived in an age in which a rebellious spirit was manifest in all classes, and, moreover, as they were conscious of their ability to defy authority, such troubles were bound to occur. That their agitation took the form of an appeal to brute force may be taken as an illustration of the spirit of this age.

2. FARMERS' RIOTS IN THE TOKUGAWA PERIOD

The position of the farming population. In Japan, agriculture developed in very remote days, and it formed an important industry. In the Tokugawa period, special importance was attached to it. Notwithstanding this, however, the lot of the farmers was a very hard one. Their freedom of action was ruthlessly restricted, and they were treated as though they were merely instruments for producing taxes.[1]

The farmers constituted the large majority of
the people at the time, and yet their life was so
wretched. The pent-up discontent found violent
expression in the form of insubordination and
revolt against their feudal lords and Government
officials. Riots were the last and the only weapon
left in their hands for employment in an attempt
to escape their hardships and to protect themselves from the oppressive rule.

Farmers' riots. A farmers' riot was a revolt
against the feudal lord or officials on the part of
the farmers of a village or villages. The farmers
were always groaning under heavy burdens of.
taxation, and when in times of famine or poor
crops the authorities failed to take appropriate
measures for their relief, they rose in open revolt.
When the angry farmers of a village, led by their
ring-leaders, made a rush for the seat of the local
government in a body, the villagers *en route* who
shared their resentment and hardships joined the
mob. Thus, like a snowball, the rioters grew in
number as they went, until they sometimes reached
tens of thousands. They beat drums, blew horns
and rang bells as they proceeded, flying straw-
mat banners and carrying weapons in the shape
of bamboo spears, sickles, hoes, etc.

The farmers were forbidden to band together
and make a forcible appeal to the authorities. It

---

[1] cf. chap. VIII.

was called *totō* for farmers to concoct plots in a
body, and it was called *gōso* for them to band
together for making a forcible appeal to the
authorities, while for them to desert their villages
by common consent was called *chōsan*. Farmers'
riots generally passed through three stages, that
is, *totō*, *gōso* and rioting. In some cases, farmers
resorted to *chōsan*. For instance, in the first year
of Hōreki (1751), a few thousand farmers in
Katsuda district in the Tsuyama-Han, unable to
put up with the heavy taxation, deserted their
villages in a body, carrying their food, on the
pretext that they were going to Ise to pray to the
Grand Shrine there for the removal of maladministration. It is also on record that many farmers
in Iyo province crossed the border into Tosa
province and those in Tosa province fled into Iyo
province. The flight of many farmers in Awa province into Tosa province is also a historical fact.

Farmers' riots broke out often in the Tokugawa period. Particularly frequent were they in
the middle and latter days of the Tokugawa
Shogunate. In some cases, a few score riots
occurred in one district. Inasmuch as such a riot
was essentially directed against the feudal lord or
the local magistrates, one would think that it was
limited to the district concerned, but as maladministration by the provincial officials and the
financial straits of the farmers were matters which
were common to all provinces, the trouble was
highly contagious, and one riot led to many others

in other provinces.   Unlike movements based on doctrines, they were not carried on according to deeply-laid plans, nor were they capable of being sustained.   They were temporary agitations.   Like fireworks, they flared up, but only for a time.

Most riots succeeded.   The ring-leaders were, of course, either crucified, beheaded, banished or sentenced to heavy penalties, but the majority of their demands were accepted.   The *samurai* who were attacked by the mob fled into the castle. Instead of taking any warlike action, they sent out negotiators to arrange terms with the mob, and the negotiations ended, in many cases, in the acceptance of the demands of the agitating farmers.   At any rate, the farmers' riots in the Tokugawa period formed an important social movement as positive acts of hostility (negative acts of hostility in the case of *chōsan*) on the part of farmers against the authorities.

3. FARM TENANCY DISPUTES IN THE TOKUGAWA PERIOD

The farm tenancy system.   The farm tenancy system was in general operation in the Tokugawa period.   While there were people, on the one hand, who, owing to the difficulty of living or the undeveloped idea of land due to imperfect utilisation of land, took little care of their lands, there were people, on the other hand, who, by annexing lands, got possession of so extensive an area they had to engage others to cultivate it. As big landowners increased in number, the operation of the farm tenancy system became general. Thus, there sprang up two classes of farmers— big farmers who did not engage in farm work themselves, and tenant farmers who had no land of their own to cultivate. There were also a class who cultivated their own land, and farm labourers who could not even get land to tenant.

Farm tenancy was of two kinds—*myōden-kosaku* and *shichiji-kosaku*. It was called *myōden-kosaku* to tenant land belonging to landowners, and *shichiji-kosaku* it was called to tenant mortgaged land. The common form of farm tenancy was for landowners to lease their land to small farmers. Tenancy for a term of over twenty years was called *eikosaku* (perpetual or long-term tenancy). There were also two kinds of *shichiji-kosaku*, namely the tenancy of land in pledge by its owners (*jiki-kosaku*), and the tenancy of such land by persons other than its owners (*betsu-kosaku*).

I will describe afterwards the hard lot of the farmers generally,[2] and it is hardly necessary to say that the life of tenant farmers was simply wretched.

Farm tenancy disputes. It may appear at first sight that it was to mutual benefit that the countryfolk who had no other means of earning a livelihood should tenant land and that big land-

[2] cf. chap. VIII.

owners should put their extensive lands out to tenancy, but as a matter of fact the interests of both were not always in accord.   The former were gradually relegated to the position of the oppressed and the latter assumed the position of oppressors, and trouble very often arose between them.

Farm tenancy disputes were recorded as early as the Kyōho era (1716–1735). In the ' Minkan-Seiyō' occurs the following passage : " In a year of Kyōho, the rice crop was particularly poor, and towards the end of the next year tenant farmers in many villages abandoned their tenanted lands to their owners, as if by common consent, refusing to cultivate them.   This embarrassed the landowners considerably, and they did their utmost to placate their tenants by either consenting to reduce the rent or by giving them some money towards the cost of fertilisers.   Although in this way the trouble was settled, there was still left on the hands of landowners some lands which they could not any tenant farmers to cultivate. They, therefore, engaged farmers and bought horses to cultivate them themselves.   Their personal cultivation convinced them all the more that it was by no means paying to tenant farm land, for they found that involved cultivators in heavy expense in fertilisers, etc."

The research of the farm tenancy on Fukano at Kawachi province, newly reclaimed farm, shows that there was constant trouble between tenant farmers and their landowners or the manager of the farm. The tenant farmers agreed among themselves to keep under strict surveillance the doings of the managers who came into frequent collisions with them, because of the selfish and arrogant attitude adopted by them in the collection of the rent. It is also clear from documents dated January of the fifth year of Meiwa (1768) and the second year of Kansei (1790), that whenever trouble occurred a make-shift solution was reached by an exchange of memorandums between the disputants.

About the era of Kōka or Kaei (1844–1853), the tenant farmers comprising three or four hundred households at Honjo, Musashi province, made a point of preferring to their landowners a demand for a reduction in the rent every year, when the time for paying their rent came round, on the pretext of a poor harvest. In order to meet this situation, twelve landowners of the village organised a landowners' guild and passed resolutions, according to which tenant farmers were forbidden to be out on the day of collecting the rent, those who were absent on such a day, despite the advanced notice, were to be blacklisted and denied the tenancy of the fields of these landowners, tenant farmers were forbidden to pay in rent rice, barley, peas and beans, etc. of inferior quality. It was also resolved that the amount of reduction to be made on the rent should be fixed by the majority vote among the members of the landowners' guild, and that tenant farmers who complained of the rates of reduction should be blacklisted, denying them the tenancy of their fields. Since then, it is said that tenant farmers ceased to make unreasonable demands in regard to the reduction of the rent. This does not, however, show that disputes between landowners and tenant farmers were settled satisfactorily. It simply means that tenant farmers yielded to the oppressive rule of landowners.

From the above, it will be seen that disputes between landowners and tenant farmers existed as far back as the middle period of the Tokugawa Shogunate. The methods adopted by the disputants in carrying on their disputes and pressing their demands were practically the same as those used in similar disputes in the actual present.

4. *UCHIKOWASHI* (WRECKING) AGITATIONS IN THE TOKUGAWA PERIOD

Rice riots. *Uchikowashi* means, in effect, rice riots. Those poor people who were hard up on account of a violent rise in the price of rice caused a riot, which was joined by outlaws. These rioters raided pawnbrokers and *sake* merchants as well as rice shops, and demolished the buildings and looted rice and other articles, or bought them at absurdly low prices under intimidation. These riots were the outcome of the antagonism of the poor against the rich and the monopolists of interests. They were in most cases caused by tradespeople in big cities. While farmers' riots represented the revolt of farmers against the authorities, *uchikowashi* was the manifestation of the hostility of the poor against the rich.

As emergency measures for coping with *uchikowashi* agitations, the authorities tried to make each street of a city take steps for self-defence. They also prohibited all people from going out of doors when such trouble was going on, while doing all they could to bring the offenders to justice. At the same time, the Shogunate granted rice and money to poor people and undertook to sell rice at moderate prices. On the other hand, it afforded protection to retail rice dealers so that they could resume business, and urged rich men and public-spirited persons to give relief to the poor. Besides, it simultaneously pursued policies for the regulation of the price of rice, such as the rice transportation policy, the reduction of consumption, the restriction of *sake* production, and the sale of rice in storage.

Many cases of *uchikowashi* broke out in the different eras of Kyōho, Temmei, Tempo, and Keiō, but the most notorious of all was one which occurred in the Temmei era (1781–1788).

The *uchikowashi* riots of the Temmei era. What is popularly known as the Temmei *uchikowashi* took place in the seventh year of Temmei (1787). Owing to the unfavourable weather conditions experienced since the previous year, the rice crops failed in many provinces. In the seventh year of Temmei (1787), the business depression, coupled with a shortage of rice, forced the price of rice still higher up. The price of rice, which was quoted at 61 *momme* in February of the fifth year of Temmei (1785) rose to 101.5 *momme* in December of the following year and to 181 to 187 *momme* in July of the seventh year of Temmei. The poverty-stricken people, who had been on the verge of starvation since the autumn of the preceeding year owing to the high prices of commodities, raided the residence of Chaya-Kichiemon at Isemachi, Temma, Ōsaka, in large numbers on the night of May 11th, and proceeded to wreck the furniture. On the following day, they made raids on rice shops and forced them to sell rice at preposterously low prices. Their refusal to comply was the signal for taking out rice and other cereals by force, and wrecking the shops into the bargain. The shops attacked exceeded 200. Not only rice merchants but all other tradespeople were so terror-stricken that many of them closed their shops, with the result that serious incovenience was caused to the officials and the citizens generally. The general closing of rice shops proved a particularly hard blow to the poor people who, being in the habit of buying rice in small quantities, had no stock of rice. The Shogunate prohibited people from going out to see the trouble going on, to say nothing of vetoing their joining in the rioting. Guards were kept in each street, and arrests of the rioters were

strictly effected. Instructions were also issued to
the denizens of each street to see that the necessary relief was afforded to those in distress, and
the public was urged to give alms to the needy.
The retail rice dealers received official protection
and they were ordered to notify the authorities of
the persons who might attempt to use force
against them to make them sell rice at unreason-
ably low prices. It is said that some retail rice
merchants made palings of logs in their shops
and either handed rice to buyers or received
money from them through small gaps in the fence.

Ōsaka was not the only place where riots
were caused by poor people. Similar troubles
broke out in Kyōto, Fushimi, Kōriyama, Sakai,
Wakayama, Ishinomaki and many other places
in the Kinki, Tōkai, Chūgoku, Kyūshū and North-
East districts about the same time. The most
violent of all was the one that occurred in Edo.
The first victims of this *uchikowashi* in Edo were
rice shops near Ōgibashi bridge, Honjo, and at
Rokkenbori, Fukagawa, which were attacked by
a mob and wrecked on May 18th. The trouble
spread rapidly, and by the dawn of the 22nd of
the same month, disturbances occurred in many
places, and troops were finally called out to suppress the rising.

The above-mentioned *uchikowashi* riots were,
of course, different from political riots in nature,
but judging from the fact that rich people as well
as rice merchants were attacked by the mobs,

they may be viewed in the light of the violent
expression of hostility on the part of the poor
against the rich, though it is allowable that their
attacks on rich people were partly due to the
force of circumstances.

Section IV

Addendum

The collapse of the Shogunate régime.   As
already mentioned, the centralised feudal system
operated in the Tokugawa period, in which class
distinctions and the relationship of master and
servant were strictly maintained.   Things were,
however, undergoing a constant change.   The
merchant class seized the money power in our
country, and many feudal lords, who were reduced
to financial straits, had to look to them for the
supply of funds required for administrative purposes.   In such circumstances, they became conscious of their powerful influence with the *samurai*
class, while, on the other hand, the authorities
found it no longer possible to ignore the interests
of the commercial and industrial classes.   In the
latter days of the Shogunate, especially during and
about the Meiwa, An'ei and Temmei eras (1764–
1788), farmers and *chōnin* (merchants) caused riots
in many places—a demonstration of the spirit of
insubordination, which permeated many classes in
those days.   The fact that they frequently rose

in revolt against the *samurai* class, instead of submitting meekly to their oppressive rule, indicates at once the loss of influence on the part of the *samurai* class and the endeavours made by the common people to elevate their own position. In the meantime, the study of Japanese classical literature found increasing favour among the people, and there was at the same time a growth of loyalism. Moreover, the embargo on the importation of Western books slackened after the rule of Tokugawa-Yoshimune, with the result that the study of things Western came into vogue. There was a growing number of people who denounced the exclusionist and retrogressive policy and urged the necessity of adopting the open door and progressive policy. In this way, the new spirit was gradually fomented. The overtures made by foreign countries to this country in the closing days of the Tokugawa Shogunate asking for the opening of the country to foreign intercourse and trade furnished an opportunity for a political change, and this, coupled with many causes, political, economic and spiritual, finally brought about the Restoration.

The Meiji Restoration. The grand work achieved at the threshold of Meiji was at once the Restoration of the country to the Imperial sovereignty and the establishment of a new order. The Shogunate and all the feudal lords returned their fiefs to the Imperial House and the *han* were replaced by the prefectures. The whole land of Japan and her people reverted to the possession of the Emperor. This political unity brought about what is called the Restoration of the Imperial Government, and the Five Imperial Oaths laid down the new constitutional national policy, which means the establishment of a new order.

So far as the relations with the outside world are concerned, the Restoration means the opening of the country, after a long period of seclusion, to intercourse with advanced Western countries. Politically, however, Japan was saddled with extraterritoriality, which denied her the status of an independent country on an equality with other countries. In economic matters, she was deprived of tariff autonomy, restrictions in the shape of conventional tariff being put upon her. In order to claim the position of equality with other countries in political matters, it was necessary to enhance the national resources and promote economic development. This was the reason why the Government pursued a policy of direct interference during the first ten years of Meiji and did its utmost to lead the nation by launching many Government enterprises. The industrial development in the Meiji era is traceable to the intensive protection which the Government extended to various industries. With the development of industry, a capitalistic society was established, and the new organisations, political and social, were steadily developed until they reached the Western level. This political, economic and social progress was due largely to the fact that the merits of Western systems were adopted to make up for the shortcomings of Japanese systems. The Meiji civilisation was created by absorbing and assimilating Western civilisation, just as the Japanese civilisation in remote and middle ages owed much to the stimulation of imported civilisation.

The social organisation. The Restoration caused revolutionary changes not only in political matters but in social matters. The feudal system gave place to the system based on the centralisation of power. Class discrimination, which was at once stern and intricate, was abolished. The social system which ruled in the Tokugawa period was completely undermined as an antiquated régime.

The *samurai* class which possessed property in the shape of lands, returned their possessions to the Imperial Family on the abolition of the *han* in favour of the prefectures, and got hereditary pension bonds in return. They were forbidden to wear two swords, which was formerly their privilege, and they had to make their life and living conform to the new currency economics. They entered the business world, but they were proverbially poor hands at business, and as merchants they proved complete failures. Hereupon, the Government devised plans to give employment to them, and encouraged them to organise national banks, railway and other companies, so as to make them operate these businesses along Western lines. This was a success. As business men of progressive ideas, they finally came to constitute a new influence in the Japanese economic world, with the result that they played an important part in effecting a big reform in the social and economic organisations of this country. It is, indeed, a curious irony of fate that the *samurai* class, who formerly despised money, should have ended by constituting themselves as the forerunners of the present-day Japanese businese world.

The *chōnin* class, which gained much influence in the Tokugawa period, also lost the privileges and protection which they had enjoyed before, and they had to earn their own living in a world of free competition. The former *chōnin* were gifted with the idea of saving, it is true, but they lacked either initiative or spirit of enterprise or a taste for business. It is, therefore, no wonder that in a capitalistic society, which was ushered in after the Restoration, the nucleus was furnished by low-class *samurai* rather than by those belonging to the *chōnin* class. The new capitalist class was somehow brought into being, and a capitalistic society was established. On the other hand, there existed a multitude of labourers and proletarians, and these formed Labour against Capital. Sandwiched between Capital and Labour were the middle-class farmers, merchants, industrialists, and salaried men. The tripartite existence of the capitalists, the middle-class people

and the non-propertied class gave rise to a variety
of social problems.

**The social problem is a question of wealth and
poverty.** Even remote and medieval ages were
not from the question of wealth and poverty, but
in those days it did not take the form of strife
between the rich and the poor. It was a problem
of disparity in wealth between different social
classes. After the middle ages, however, there
were gradually created the rich and the poor
classes, though with a somewhat blurred line of
distinction at first, and a sort of social movement
arose between these classes. The *tsuchi-ikki*, to
which reference has already been made, was a
case in point. From the point of view of the
social classes, rioting was a conflict between the
people within the same social class, but it may
more properly be described as a conflict between
the rich and the poor classes. The same thing
may be said of *uchikowashi* and farm tenancy
disputes in the Tokugawa period. In the middle
ages, there sprang up what were called vocational
classes, and these classes witnessed a steady
development in the Tokugawa period. In consequence of the creation of the rich and the poor
classes and vocational classes, there gradually
occurred conflicts between the rich and the poor,
in addition to those within the same social class
or between different social classes. This was the
forerunner of the class strife subsequently developing between the economic classes which came

into being after the Meiji Restoration.

As already explained, even before the Meiji era, there were troubles which embodied conflicts between the rich and the poor classes rather than a question of wealth and poverty between social classes. On the whole, however, social classes retained their characteristic features in the pre-Meiji periods and the troubles were mainly between different social classes. Conflicts between the rich class and the poor class, though they occurred, were rather subordinate to those between the several social classes. After the Meiji Restoration, the social classes lost their significance, though they remained, and the economic classes that sprang up assumed much importance. Conflicts between the rich and the poor economic classes came to form important social problems in consequence. Thus, the so-called social problems or class strife of the pre-Restoration days and of the post-Restoration days are different in kind. Herein lies the significance of the Meiji Restoration, if it is studied from the point of view of the history of social movements.

CHAPTER II

THE ECONOMIC DEVELOPMENT

SECTION I

FACTS OF THE DEVELOPMENT

1. FROM SELF-SUFFICIENT ECONOMY TO LOCAL ECONOMY

In the ancient time when the *shizoku* system prevailed, the solidarity of society was based upon blood relationship. The principal means of production at that time were land and labour both of which belonged to each *uji* which ruled over the subject groups of *be* and *yakko*, the latter people being engaged in manual labour. The people of that time had already passed the period of hunting and fishery and had entered that of agriculture. Thus, it was clear that they lived in an era of land economy.

Each *uji* at that time was engaged in a particular occupation at the head of the people of the *be* who were occupied in manual labour. The people of the *be* were also engaged in agriculture and fishery in addition to the particular occupation of each *be*, and thus earned the necessaries of their daily life. Such must have been their ordinary mode of existence. One would, therefore, be jumping at a conclusion, should he venture to judge from the existence of different occupations that there was a systematic division of labour among the inhabitants in ancient times. Nor is it certain that each *uji* lived a communistic life by itself as a whole. As time passed, all the members of the same *uji* no longer lived in the same place ; they lived in different places. (An example of this may be found in the fact that the Imbe *uji* was different in the provinces of Kii, Awa, Sanuki and Tsukushi.) It is impossible to conceive that by the time the *uji* system was at the height of its development, an individual *uji* constituted an economic unit. On the contrary, the family was the economic unit, all the members of family being occupied in its work under the direction of its head. In some cases, bodies somewhat larger than the family — a group of families or of members of a *be* — were probably engaged in self-sufficient economy as an economic unit. In some exceptional cases, a small *uji* might have been an economic unit, but, generally speaking, it was the family that formed the foundation of economy. In short, the economic order of ancient times in Japan was one of land economy based upon gentilitial or clan relations. In principle, it was an economy of self-sufficiency, with the family as the economic unit and the association of the *be* as the centre of the labour system. The *uji* greatly contributed towards the development of agriculture and of other industrial arts by employing the members of a family, and, more particularly, the people of the *be*, in the development of land and other manual labour. However, there is another important factor that should not be lost sight of and that is the influence of foreign culture and Buddhism upon the progress of the economy of the time.

Intercourse between Japan and Korea was carried on from early times in the history of this country. Japan freely imported culture from Korea, especially after the Korean principalities became subjected to her. Many Koreans became naturalised in Japan. Some of them brought with them such industrial technologies as sericulture, weaving, ceramics, carpentry and leather manufacturing, while others imported gold, silver, jewels and textiles. Buddhism found its way into Japan during the reign of the Emperor Kimmei (540–572) and its spread greatly affected not only the religious faith of the people, but also the nation's economic and social life ; its effects upon architecture, sculpture and industrial arts were at once direct and profound. It is clear that the changes brought about by foreign relations and the introduction of Buddhism, coupled with the industrial policy of the period, contributed greatly towards the economic development of the country.

With the lapse of time, the population of the country increased and territorial relations came to play a more important rôle than blood relationship. After the Taika Reform abolished the government by *uji* and created a centralised government in its place, the *uji* ceased to have great importance. The provisions of the Taihō-ryō dealt with the *ko* or family but not with the *uji*. Thus, the political and legal unit had shifted from the *uji* to the *ko*. In the world of economy, the ownership of land shifted from the *uji* to the Emperor, as the result of the distribution of land under the *handen* system; the right of using land and deriving profits therefrom also shifted from the *uji* to the *ko* whose position as an economic unit became more clearly established than in former times. The necessity of supplementing the labour power of the members of families made the labour power of slaves increasingly important. In short, the *ko* or the big family system functioned as an economic unit. Both shrine and temple could be regarded as a family which lived a self-sufficient economic life and was engaged in land economy.

Foreign culture and Buddhism also exercised much influence on the economic development of this time. But no less important were the use of slave labour and the distribution of land under the *handen* system, both of which were the important features of the time. The majority of slaves were employed in productive work, men being engaged in agriculture and women in seri-culture and weaving. Some were employed in industrial and domestic work. The disintegration of the *handen* system set in when the scarcity of fields came to be felt with the rapid increase

in the population.   Encouragement of the development of new fields by private hands became inevitable and this resulted in the break-up of the
public ownership of land, in the development of
private fields and in the formation of the *shōen*.
The next period was marked by the phenome-
nal development of the *shōen* system.   In each
shōen there was a *shōke* or residence of its lord or
his representative, and was inhabited by persons
who tilled the soil and produced all necessaries of
daily life.   A *shōen* was also inhabited by persons
having no fixed domicile and who were employed
by the lord of the *shōen* or by other wealthy
landlords.   The *shōen*, in short, formed an individual economic area.   There is reason to believe
that a self-sufficient economy was carried on also
in a *shōen*.   The *shōke* was not necessarily located
at the geographical centre of a *shōen*.   However,
the life of a *shōen* must have been carried on
with the *shōke* as its centre.   This may be seen
in the fact that the governance of a *shōen* was
directed by the *shōke*, and that taxes in kind
were first conveyed to the *shōke* or to a warehouse usually situated nearby and then properly
distributed afterwards.   But at that time, it appears that money came to be coined and used
especially in cities; the appearance of these cities
being also a phenomenon of the times.   In and
around the capital and other important points, the
old self-sufficient economy faced changes.
Thus, although in principle the economic

order of the old centralised government was self-sufficiency, currency became increasingly used and the people lived a currency life to a certain degree. After political power passed into the hands of the *samurai* class in the Middle Ages, a rapid advance was made in this respect ; a handicraft industry was developed, cities expanded, commercial transactions were carried on more and more extensively, and commission merchants and exchange business also made their appearance. Although the coining of money was discontinued for some time, currencies of small denominations (chiefly Chinese coins), were used quite extensively. Trade was carried on with countries beyond the seas, and communication with oversea countries was carried on with increasing vigour. These economic phenomena indicate that the people of the time were not satisfied with the old time domestic economy or *shōen* economy and that they had expanded local economic area and developed currency economy to a certain extent. However, they continuously held land as the centre and agriculture as the foundation, of their economic life. In other words, while in ancient times agriculture was the only industry, in the middle ages besides agriculture there were also industry and commerce ; and the classes of artisans and tradesmen came into existence. True, the great majority of the people still were engaged in agriculture, and tradesmen and artisans followed their vocations under the protection of the Imperial Court, the aristocracy, shrines and temples. At any rate, one may say that commerce and industry had definitely come to be distinct vocations.

I have already dwelt on the close relations between ancient economy and Buddhism. Now, there were similar relations between shrines and temples on the one hand and economy on the other in the middle ages. There are many facts showing that the development of industry was made under the ægis of religious establishments. The development of lands, the introduction of special agricultural products (such as tea, for example), the development of architecture and sculpture, the holding of commercial fairs in front of some shrine or temple and on the days of their festivals, and the manufacture and sale of medicines and other products — these will be sufficient to show the close relations between the industrial development of the middle ages and shrines and temples. There is no doubt that the formation of *monzen-machi* (streets in front of temples and shrines) in all parts of the country was the natural result of the religious establishments, which were the only places of safety during the Middle Ages, a period marked by civil disturbances. As I have already pointed out, people carried on business under the protection of shrines and temples. Some entrusted their precious documents and treasures to these sacred places in order to protect them from the destruction and pillage of warfare. Shrines and temples also acted as financial organs and made loans; made co-operative credit facilities known by the names of *mujin* and *tanomoshi*; and utilised bills of exchange. Thus, the position of shrines and temples in the financial mechanism of the country was very important. In the communications of the time, the establishment of barriers known as *sekisho* during the middle ages also had close relations with shrines and temples.

2. FEUDAL ECONOMY OF EXCLUSION IN THE TOKUGAWA PERIOD

Each *han* in the Tokugawa period enjoyed comparative autonomy, carried on a self-sufficient economy within its walls, different *han* having different systems of currency as well as other systems of their own. But the period did not have a purely local economy as did the former times; its economy had gradually assumed a national character, due to the political unification of the entire realm. The continued maintenance of peace led to the development of the business world and the expansion of markets. It was not an uncommon event, even as early as the Jōkyō (1684-1688) and the Genroku (1688-1704) eras, that the sea products of the northern part of the country should be sold at Edo, the seat of the feudal Government, and the merchants of the northern *han* carried on business transactions in Kyōto, the ancient capital in the central

part of the country. The silk textile called
Nishijin-ori was in great demand by the *daimyō*
throughout the entire realm. The *sake* produced in the towns of Ikeda, Itami and Nada
was first conveyed to Bakan, the chief point for
the reception and distribution of freights for
Kyūshū and the northern districts and then
shipped to the territories along the coast of the
Japan Sea and in Kyūshū. The same national
beverage was also shipped to Edo to be used by
its inhabitants and not a few commission merchants there amassed a fortune. The oil made
from rape-seed, a plant very extensively raised in
the central part of Japan, was shipped to Edo
and other important points. Such products as
the bleached textile of Nara, cotton cloths of
Kawachi, candles of Aizu, bears' gall produced in
Kaga and Etchū, salted yellow-tail of Tango, sea-
weeds of Matsumae — these were all first sent to
the three great cities of Edo, Ōsaka and Kyōto,
and then distributed in different parts of the
country. It was the city of Ōsaka which was
the centre of commercial activities at that time.
The *daimyō* had their warehouses in Ōsaka to
which they sent their native products to be sold.
There was a regular freight service between Edo
and Ōsaka thereby facilitating the transportation
of the products of Ōsaka and nearby provinces
to the Kantō or Eastern Japan. The products
of all provinces were first assembled at Ōsaka
and then were distributed to all parts of the

country by various routes. Cognisance should be taken of the fact that the merchants of Ōmi and the drug peddlers of Toyama travelled throughout the entire country. Industrial arts such as lacquer and drapery were transplanted in the Kantō provinces from Kyōto. The development of communications and of exchange business between Edo and Ōsaka indicates that the economic relations of the period were not locally isolated but had close connection among themselves. Thus, the economic system of our country advanced from local to national, especially after the middle of the Tokugawa period. However, when seen from an external standpoint, the period was an era of exclusion which was more and more strictly enforced as time passed. There were various restrictions in economic matters and no progress was made in the nation's foreign trade. Moreover, the foreign trade of the time was one-sidely in favour of imports, so that the production of commodities within the country was made with the demand in the domestic market as the standard ; and the so-called circulation of goods was strictly domestic in character. This is why the Tokugawa period may be called an era of economic exculsion.

The chief feature of society during the Tokugawa period was the existence of feudal classes and this feudal characteristic was often seen in the world of economy. For instance, there was a guild system called *kabunakama* under which

persons engaged in the same occupation had certain privileges ; each *han* issued its own notes
for monetary purposes ; the road and the communication policy also showed the earmarks of
feudalism.   Under this feudal system there was
a long period of peace seldom seen in the history
of the world, thereby enabling the people to pursue
their respective vocations while the Government
authorities directed their efforts toward the development of industries; the result was that,
although no expansion was made in the nation's
foreign trade, various industries were developed
in all parts of the nation.   We may, therefore, say
that our country received the benefits of protected
trade by means of a policy of national exclusion.

The Tokugawa period is known as " an era
of rice economy," because its finance and economy
were based upon rice.   However, the use of money
as the medium of exchange was extensively
developed during this period.   True, it cannot be
said to be a pure currency economy such as now
exists; but the extension of the use of money could
never be compared with those in the previous
periods.   Hitherto, land had been considered as
the only form of wealth, but now gold and silver
also came to be regarded as important forms of
wealth; and although an ideological discrimination was made against money in favour of rice,
the former, in reality, was highly prized and it
was extensively used in cities as well as rural
districts.   This meant a shift from land economy

to money economy.

Agriculture was the most important industry in Japan from the earliest known times and remained the centre of her industrial life during the Tokugawa period. However, there emerged during this same period two other industries, namely, commerce and manufacturing, and this accompanied the rise of the *chōnin* class and the growth of cities. At that time both the Tokugawa Shogunate and the *daimyō* suffered much because of financial difficulties. Accordingly, they tried to meet the situation by developing new rice fields for the purpose of increasing their annual rice revenue, by encouraging industrial activities, by establishing something like monopolies, by recoining money and issuing *han* notes, and more generally by imposing heavy taxes on farmers. But since there was a natural limit to the capacity of these people to bear the tax burden, the Shogunate and the *daimyō* borrowed money from the wealthy merchants of Edo and Ōsaka. They did not hesitate to bow before the *chōnin* in securing the needed money, and tried profitably to arrange their finances with the latter's financial assistance. The '*Chōnin Bukuro*' says: "The entire realm has become the consumer of gold and silver, the change having started almost imperceptibly. Now, gold and silver being largely under the control of the *chōnin*, they were often called into the presence of nobles, and their social position seemed to rise above that of farmers."

In reality, the new *chōnin* class surpassed, not
only farmers, but even *samurai* in point of real
power. The *chōnin* held the power of money
and occupied an influential position in society.
Gamō-Kumpei is said to have declared that the
ire of Ōsaka rich merchants would prove a
terror for the *daimyō* of the land. His words are
sufficient to indicate the real power of the *chōnin*
of the period.

With the development of currency economy
and the rise of the *chōnin* class, the members of
other classes also tried to adapt themselves to the
changed social conditions, took part in the obtaining of economic interests, and became more and
more like merchants. I have already stated that
shrines and temples were engaged in lucrative
undertakings in the middle ages; the same was
true during the Tokugawa period. Some temples
produced particular commodities and sold them;
others carried on the business of money-lending.
The Myōshin-ji in Kyōto, the Kan'ei-ji and the
Zōjō-ji in Edo were particularly notable in this
respect. Some temples even managed the *tomitsuki*, a sort of lottery which took advantage of
people's speculative spirit. Teachers of the arts
and music charged special tuition and other fees.
Blind money-lenders charged outrageously high
rates as they enjoyed a special privilege as
money-lenders. The fact that each *daimyō* established industrial monopolies within his own
territory shows the extent of the commercialisation

of the feudal lords. In short, the power of money
came to replace the power of military force.

Under the feudal system of that time, land
was the principal means of production, farmers
were the only productive class, a privileged class
composed of *samurai* was supported by the labour
of the former class. Unlike those of the Kamakura period, the *samurai* of the Tokugawa period
were detached from the land, were unproductive
as a class and were supported by the farming
class. With the continuation of peace, the people's
standard of living was raised, their habits of
luxury increased and the financial expenditure of
governing the country was expanded, the result
being that both the Tokugawa Shogunate and
the *daimyō* were unable to make both ends
meet and became extremely impoverished. For a
long time the agricultural policy of the feudal
governments was dictated by the idea "that
farmers should pay taxes to the degree that they
might neither die nor live "— the idea being that
farmers should be allowed to retain just sufficient
of their agricultural products to make a bare
sustenance. As time passed, however, the tax
burden of farmers became heavier and heavier
and their living conditions were subjected to un-
told difficulties. In order to escape this hard lot,
farmers tried to leave their farms for the city, or
carry on trade on a small scale in the country,
or exercise a crude system of birth control called
mabiki. All these resulted in a scarcity of labour

power in the rural districts; farms became desolate and the gap between the rich and the poor in agricultural villages more pronounced. Rioting by farmers of the time was their positive method of breaking this deadlock in their daily life. The impoverishment and desolation of farming villages were the indication of the fact that agricultural economic power had come to an utter *cul-de-sac*, and that in consequence it became no longer able to support the *samurai* class and maintain the feudal system in general. On the other hand, there arose besides agriculture (which had long been regarded as the only productive means in the realm) trade and industry, with the consequent development of cities and the *chōnin* class. Thus, it is to be noted that a new economic power made its emergence to stand side by side with the decayed agricultural power. The replacement of land economy by currency economy and the appearance of commercial capital testified to the impossibility of maintaining the feudal system founded upon land economy.

There were now mainly three social classes, *samurai*, farmers and *chōnin*. Many farmers left their farms for the cities where they became tradesmen or hired men. *Samurai* were also hard pressed by economic difficulties and had to pursue material gains by domestic industry or by by-works. Some of them married the daughters of merchants for the purpose of material benefits or adopted sons of *chōnin* for similar purposes. The

status of the *hatamoto* or the *gokenin* was freely
sold, especially after the Kyōho era, and their
values were fixed. Thus, *chōnin* smuggled themselves, as it were, into the *samurai* class; received fiefs by advancing loans to *samurai*; were
allowed to have surnames and wear swords and
otherwise received the treatment of the warrior
class. They also purchased land or developed new
lands, thereby becoming landlords in rural districts. Thus, the *chōnin* class overwhelmed both
the *samurai* and the farmer classes by their sheer
economic power, and there was no clear distinction among the different classes. With the economic change above described, each social class
lost its characteristics and confusion was created
among them. It was evident that the maintenance
of the feudal system which was based upon class
distinction was no longer possible.

We may say then that the changes brought
about in the economic and social aspects of the
Tokugawa period unmistakably pointed out the
inevitable collapse of the feudal system of the
period.

Towards the close of the Tokugawa period,
there were indications of a great economic transformation. In the north, Russia's advance alarmed
the nation, while in the south the arrival of the
"blackships" struck a terror into the hearts of
the people. Important economic and political
changes resulted from the development of the
diplomatic relations of the country, especially after

the years of Kaei and Ansei. Policies which were
absolutely at variance with the traditional policies
of the Tokugawa Shogunate were adopted, and
there were signs on every hand that further
changes in the social and economic conditions
of the nation were inevitable. To give a few
examples, the Tokugawa Shogunate in reality
abandoned its traditional policy of national exclusion and carried on trade activities with
Western countries. New machines as well as
new technologies were imported from the West
and trade establishments similar to companies
were founded; paper money was issued ; and
drastic changes were made in the system of
sankin-kōtai which was one of the sources of
financial embarrassment for local feudal lords.
All of these novel measures, however, were
entered upon rather as experiments and never
were carried out universally. Then the battles
of Toba-Fushimi laid the Edo Government pro-
strate. Both the Central Government and the
advanced feudal *han* realised that the old policies
would not work and that a revolutionary change
of policies was absolutely necessary. The various
economic and financial policies adopted after the
Meiji Restoration corresponded to those already
initiated during the close of the Tokugawa
period ; it is wrong to suppose that the main
policies of the Meiji Government were adopted
for the first time after the overthrow of the
feudal system.

3. CAPITALIST ECONOMY AFTER THE MEIJI RESTORATION

It was during the Genroku era that currency economy began to replace natural economy. While the chief source of the Tokugawa Shogunate's revenue consisted in the natural products of land, the new form of wealth, that is to say, money was concentrated in the hands of the *chōnin*; and with the growth of currency economy, the military power of the *samurai* was gradually superseded and finally replaced by the monetary power of the *chōnin*. The *samurai* of the Chōshū and other *han* who took the prominent part in the Restoration of the Imperial régime succeeded in their gigantic task by utilising the wealth of the *chōnin* class. The campaign funds of the battles that overthrew the feudal régime and the contributions made to the Meiji Government came from the coffers of the wealthy merchants of Ōsaka. It was generally believed at that time that 70 per cent. of the entire national wealth was concentrated in Ōsaka, and the founders of the Meiji Government sagaciously invited the wealthy merchants of this commercial metropolis to take sides with them in the great political struggle. Had they failed to do this, the establishment of the Meiji Government would have been well-nigh impossible.

As has already been stated, the real power

of society during the later Tokugawa period was held by the *chōnin* class and the feudal system was bound to disintegrate. However, the power of the *chōnin* class could not be developed beyond the fixed limit due to the feudal system and the policy of national exclusion, and it was the *samurai* of the lower strata of the warrior class that carried on the work of political transformation in their anti-foreign agitation as well as in their political movements for the overthrow of the Edo Government. These *samurai* of lower station had been discontented because their rise in social status was very difficult under the then existing feudal system. They had long felt the need of making a drastic change in the system, and finally came to establish the Meiji Government. True, behind their political movement lay the awakening of the people as a whole and the financial support of the *chōnin* class. Moreover, the general tendency of the people was towards such a political and social transformation. However, it was these *samurai* of the lower ranks that carried out the actual work of political revolution and after the establishment of the modern Government became either bureaucratic administrators or leaders of the new economic system of capitalism. The members of the *chōnin* class only followed the lead of these *samurai*; they always assumed a passive attitude in the historic political and social movements that culminated in the overthrow of Japanese feudalism.

Although the feudal system of the Tokugawa

period was bound to collapse when considered from the social and economic standpoints, yet the downfall of that system was not actually brought about by the *chōnin* class which held the real economic power of society. It was overthrown by the *samurai* who took advantage of the pressing diplomatic relations of the period. It is also to be noted that the *samurai* class had already become more and more like *chōnin*. Economically viewed, land economy on which feudalism was based was replaced by currency economy, and the nation was forced to open its doors at the invitation of foreign capitalism.

During the Tokugawa period in which Japan enforced a policy of national isolation and exclusion, the Western world was marked by a great material advance, consequent upon the various scientific inventions and discoveries and their utilisation in the means of communications and transportation. In other words, the West passed the period of industrial revolution, while our country lived a self-sufficient economic life within its walls; and she opened her doors in an era of machines and steam power. The Tokugawa Shogunate and the *han* imported Western civilisation towards the close of the Tokugawa period, and it was quite natural that this borrowing of Western systems of political, industrial and social life should be greatly accelerated after the creation of the Meiji Government. During the first ten years of the new régime, the economic conditions of the country were in a state of confusion, due to the break-up of the old system. However, the abolition of class distinctions, the emancipation of people from various feudal restrictions, opportunity offered to men of ability without discrimination, the formation of a unified state, the establishment of monopolies, the encouragement and support of civilian enterprises, the government's direct interference and protection in industry, and the development of companies and corporations — all these prepared the way for the rise of capitalism. In the next ten years, the foundations of the new economy were firmly laid. It made immense progress after the wars with China and Russia, and the modern industrial system came to control our economy. This rapid adoption of foreign capitalism was possible because of the fact that currency economy has been developed during the Tokugawa period and thus our economy was in a position where it could be turned into capitalism. In other words, the germs of capitalism could be found in the economic order of the feudal period. Although some features of feudalism still persisted in remaining in the nation's economy, the so-called capitalistic society made its appearance during the Meiji era. Japan made an abnormal economic development because of the World War and the defects in her traditional economic system were afterward disclosed, resulting in the present movement for its rationalisation and improvement.

Section II

Peculiarities of the Economic Development of Japan

1. WHAT ARE PECULIARITIES OF THE ECONOMIC DEVELOPMENT OF JAPAN?

I wish to study herein whether or not the history of economic development in our country has been marked by phenomena which are not found in those of other countries and which can rightly be regarded as peculiarities in the development of our economic life.

Of course such a study may not have much significance for those who believe that the economic developments of all nations are made along the one and same course. Dr. Takimoto, for instance, declares:

"It goes without saying that different nations have different histories. But the development of the civilisation of the world is one and the human development has been and is following the same course and advancing towards the same direction. In consequence, although different nations manifest different phenomena due to their different stages in civilisation and culture and further because of their complicated internal as well as external relations, the fact remains that, after all, the history of the world is repeating the same things

in these different nations. Accordingly, the experience of an advanced country is followed by
a second country as an example; those which
were once adopted by the second country prove
precedents for a third country, whose course, in
turn, is followed by a fourth country—because
they all are subject to the fundamental laws of
human progress and development. The history of
Japan, therefore, can be regarded as part of the
history of the world's development."[1]

The foregoing assertion is not without truth,
and further it may truly be said that the economic developments of nations are treading the same
course and in the same direction. Needless to
state that it is because the economic developments
of nations have practically the same tendency
that the theory of the economic stages is possible.
Our civilisation itself has been developed in a
large measure by importing and digesting those
of China and Korea, and through them that of
India in the ancient times and that of the West
in the modern times; and thus our external intercourse has had a major part in the development
of civilisation. It is evident then that a study of
the economic development of our country must
be accompanied by that of the world in general,
especially in view of the fact that owing to the
great development of the world's communications,
the interdependence of nations has been extremely

---

[1] Takimoto-Seiichi, ' *Keizai Ikkagen.*'

intensified in recent years.

However, this is only one side of the story. On the other hand, it should be noted that the Occident has customs and tendencies peculiar to itself, while the Orient also has its own peculiarities. Within Europe England differs from the Continental countries; on the Continent conditions in France are vastly different from those in Germany. Although practically of the same race, the economic history of the English by no means shows the same development which is seen in that of the Americans; and this fact is enough to show the vast difference between the economic history of Japan and that of the West.

All countries by no means have the same elementary conditions of economic life such as geography, climate, institutions and customs; there is no guarantee that because certain things were adopted by one country they will also be adopted by others. Nor does communication between different countries remain constant for all times. No nation will be able to disregard utterly its peculiarities or characteristics and to convert them into things universal and common to all. It is only too natural then that, although in outward appearance the developments of nations roughly take the same course, in reality that of each country has special causes or circumstances; and it often happens that those special circumstances in the life of a nation are the important elements constituting its economic development. In such a case it will not be sane to disregard those special circumstances. Of course it is not right to consider isolated facts, but at the same time the peculiar conditions of nations should not be overlooked. The general tendency of the world and the special circumstances in our country are of an equal importance in our minds and what we should do is to evaluate them properly. Such are my views of the economic peculiarities of nations in general, and I do not mean to deny the truth that fundamental tendency of the economic development of the world is universal and common to all.

2. THE PECULIARITIES CONSIDERED FROM THREE ANGLES

In dealing with the peculiarities already referred to, it is possible to consider them from various angles and in divergent degrees; however, it is clear that the viewpoints from which the proposed survey is to be made must be wide enough to cover the entire history of our economic development. Should we point out isolated facts and compare them without order, we would be committing the great blunder of omitting what is important, of being engrossed with trifles, of placing things of unequal importance on the same level, and of misclassifying facts. I shall consider the question from the following three standpoints: the subject of economy, the quality of economy and the form of economy.

By the "subject of economy" I mean the people or the nation who live an economic life. What is peculiar in our economic life is what I call herein the "continuity of the subject of economy." Dr. Uchida-Ginzō[2] has pointed out the following three peculiarities in the national characteristics of our country : the continuity of the form of our State, the continuity of our race, and the continuity of our spiritual culture. The continuity of the subject of economy I have already referred to corresponds to Dr. Uchida's "continuity of our race." Whereas in the case of other countries the principal racial elements of their populations were often replaced by other races, in our country the same race, namely the Yamato race, has continued to maintain its predominant place in the racial composition of our population ever since the dawn of our national history down to this very day. True, the Japanese are the composition of many divergent races which were blended in the ancient time, and during the course of its history new racial elements were also added to it; but their assimilation has been perfect and complete so that today they constitute but one racial stock. Aboriginals such as the Emishi and cave-dwellers called Tsuchigumo have long ago ceased to live an independent life, while naturalised foreigners and their descendants have

---

[2] Uchida-Ginzō, 'Kokushi Sōron oyobi Nihon Kinseishi,' pp. 9–13 & 311–314.

also lost their own characteristics in the great melting pot of the Yamato race which still persists to be the central element of the Japanese race. In consequence there is no need of treating the history of the Japanese economic development in terms of different racial predominances. The history of the Japanese economic development is the history of the economic development of the Yamato race.

Next I shall consider whether or not the economic development of our country has taken place by our own power. In this connection I have already pointed out the fact that our civilisation was much influenced by that of China, Korea and India in ancient times and that of the Western countries in modern times; so much so that had we not borrowed from those foreign nations it is doubtful whether we could have reached the present stage.[3] The development of our handicraft industry in ancient times owed much to the part played by naturalised Chinese and Koreans. We have imported from China under Tang Dynasty the *handen* system by which the Government appropriated and distributed arable lands among the people. The introduction of Buddhism in the thirteenth year of the Emperor Kimmei (552) had the effect of stimulating the development not only of our sculpture, architecture, industrial arts, mining, but also of communication, trade and

---

[3] Tsuji-Zennosuke, '*Kaijō Kōtsū Shiron*,' p. 7 ff.

other phases of our economic life.[4] Generally
speaking, it can be said that our country assiduously copied the Chinese economic and other
systems of the Sui and Tang Dynasties during
two Japanese historical periods, namely, the Nara
and Heian periods (about 400 years and 70 years
respectively); but from the beginning of the
Kamakura period (about 150 years) Japan began
to manifest her own characteristics which were
perfected during the Tokugawa period[5] which
preceded the Restoration of the Imperial rule.
After she entered the family of nations in the
modern era, she borrowed industrial technologies
freely from the Western countries, the result
being a marvelous progress in her economic and
industrial life.[6]

Thus, while it is undeniable that our general
civilisation, including the economic civilisation,
has received a great impetus from the importation
of foreign civilisations, our history cannot be said
to be that of mere imitation; we have not copied
the foreign systems as they were, but took only
those which we thought suited to our special conditions and circumstances, so that those which were
imported from foreign countries contained some
elements which were not found in the countries
which supplied them to us. Our imitation involved

---

[4] Kawada-Shiro and Okamoto-Ichiro, ' *Nihon no Keizai to
Bukkyō.*
[5] Uchida, ibid, p. 314.
[6] Toda-Kaichi, ' *Nihon no Keizai* ' p. 16.

reconstruction and resulted in the special development of the imported systems.   In short, our civilisation is the result of importing foreign civilisations which then were digested, reconstructed, and assimilated to our special conditions of life, and this applies to our economic systems as well. The powerful influence of foreign economic systems can be regarded as one of the peculiarities of our economic development.

Lastly, I shall study the question from the viewpoint of the successive forms marking the several stages of economic development.   According to the theory of the economic stages, advocated by such men as List and Grosse,[7] industrial evolution in general passes the hunting, pastoral, agricultural, commercial and industrial stages in the order as given above.   The primitive Japanese passed the first stage, but generally it is conceded that no pastoral stage ever marked industrial development in Japan.   As to agriculture, it existed in the earliest period of our people and the encouragement of the agricultural pursuit was conceived to be one of the important governmental functions.   Since the time of the Nara period, agriculture became the main Japanese industry, and it was regarded as the foundation of the State.   During the Tokugawa period, and

---

[7] List, 'Das nationale System der politischen Ökonomie,' 1841.   Grosse, 'Die Formen der Familie und die Formen der Wirtschaft,' 1896.

especially after its middle stage, the *chōnin* class increased their power, but still agriculture could be considered as the main industry in our country. Even after a great progress in industry and commerce has been made after the Meiji Restoration, the majority of the people are still engaged in the agricultural pursuit, which is still regarded as the premier Japanese industry.

Some of the Western countries, which have passed the hunting and pastoral stages completely, are nearly passing the agricultural stage. Others have already passed the agricultural stage and are in the midst of the industrial stage. In some countries both agriculture and industry exist side by side, but the former is barely escaping natural decay because of the special protection given it by governments. In others agriculture, commerce and industry exist, but the last named two are more powerful than the first one. Generally speaking, the agricultural stage has already passed and that of commerce and industry is in its place.

However, in the case of our country, agriculture existed in the dawn of our history and it still persists to be the dominant industry even this day. This is traceable to political and geographical circumstances. Though an island nation, Japan had very close communication with the Continental countries in the ancient times, but in the Middle Ages she became seclusive; and in consequence she sought an economic self-sufficiency in her own agricultural industry. (This fact in a large measure also explains why the influence of foreign civilisation upon our systems in ancient times was great while we created our own systems and institutions in the Middle Ages.)

Although agriculture supplied the people with foodstuffs, its very nature, which is conservative, failed to give birth to commerce for whose development active and free spirit is necessary. This state of affairs continued to exist through the Tokugawa period down to the Meiji era. Even after the Meiji era, the importation of industrial technologies from the West have had little effect upon our agriculture. We have made some progress in our industrial life, but agriculture remains the same due mainly to the geographical and other reasons. The fact that Japan is remaining an agricultural country can surely be regarded as one of the peculiarities in her economic development.

3.   SOME AFTERTHOUGHTS.

The three peculiarities mentioned above were produced because of geographical and social reasons. In order to understand the nature of our economic peculiarities it is necessary for us to compare our development with that of other countries, especially those advanced Western countries. Great care should be taken in this comparative study. In making this study we shall find that what are regarded as peculiarities in one country are often found to exist in other countries, though the nature of their development may be vastly different because of differences in time and place.

It often happens that what seems to be identical things in their outward appearance, on an examination of their inner nature it is revealed that they are in reality different things. On the other hand, it also daily happens that what at first are regarded as different things, in actuality are the same things, as far as their inner meanings are concerned. For these reasons it is insufficient merely to point out facts in different countries; but great care must accompany any comparative study of this sort. Not only external appearances of things but also their internal causes and surrounding circumstances should be the subject of careful study.

The Japanese people have been busy adopting the Western civilisation since the time of the Meiji Restoration, and have been unduly neglecting to study their own country's affairs, although such a study is obviously important as well as interesting. The Japanese must first know about themselves, especially their economic questions in the past and present. It is anachronistic to regard history as the autobiography of heroes or as the record of wars and political incidents. The need of a history which treats of the daily life of the people is never more urgently demanded as at present. There is a vast room for such a study as such treatment has been neglected. Virgin soil in which the seeds of scholastic investigation may be sown is seen in every corner of our national history. Of course much difficulty lies in the path of such investigation, but the difficulty itself may prove an incentive for our inquiry.

CHAPTER III
THE FINANCIAL DEVELOPMENT

1. DYNASTIC CHANGES AND THE SHIFTING
OF FINANCIAL POWER

Many changes have occurred in the political and social organisations from the days when a society based on the *shizoku* system prevailed up to the present days of a capitalistic society. When one period shifts to another period, there is always a big political event, which causes a change of dynasty. The change of dynasty is of much greater significance than historians usually ascribe to it. It does not simply mean, as historians would have us believe, the overthrow of the powers that be given by some great men. It is hardly necessary to say that the general trend of social affairs is constantly and gradually changing. From the point of view of the history of finance, it is an important problem to study how the centre of financial power has shifted. The great influence which the Soga family wielded in ancient times, for instance, was presumably due, in large measure, to its control of the financial power of the country through its supervision over the *imikura*, the *uchikura* and the *ōkura*. In the Taika Reform which followed the ruin of the society based on the *shizoku* system, statute labour was abolished in favour of the new system of collecting taxes called *so*, *yō* and *chō*, under which system stable sources of revenue were ensured to put an end to the muddled financial state of the former period. This illustrates the importance attached to financial power in those days. In the Heian period, many *shōen* came into existence. The *shōen* was virtually free from taxation or from intervention of provincial lords; it enjoyed a sort of extraterritoriality. So, many people sought to evade the exactions of Government offices by utilising this privilege. The result was that the Government was denuded of its source of revenue and its coffer became depleted, as the number of *shōen* increased rapidly. In the closing days of the Heian period, the State administration, to say nothing of the local administration, was rendered difficult, and the provincial disturbances gradually spread to the capital. It was only with the help of the warriors that the Fujiwara family was able to suppress these disturbances. In the meantime, the number of *shōen* owned by warriors in various districts went on increasing, so much so that it was said that the manors owned by the members of the Taira family exceeded 500, or about one half of the whole land of Japan fell into their possession. This naturally caused a big decrease in the amount of the tributes to the State with the resulting distress of the State finance. It was, indeed, in the natural order of things that with the gradual loss of financial power, political power gradually passed into the hands of the military caste. On the establishment of the Shogunate at Kamakura by Minamoto-Yoritomo, he replaced the *shōji* and *jitō* (local magistrates) belonging to the Taira family by his own retainers. Further, on the pretext of facilitating the arrest of Minamoto-Yukiie and Minamoto-Yoshitsune, he appointed *shugo* to each province, and more *jitō* to many places. By levying five *shō* of rice on every *tan* of land, he took over the control of land as well as the right of collecting taxes. It was due to the acquisition of financial power through the control of land and taxation, which constituted the most important source of revenue in those days, that the Kamakura Shogunate was established on a firm basis. The financial difficulty of the Muromachi period was the natural outcome of the decentralised feudalism, while the somewhat improved finance in the Oda and Toyotomi periods was due to a better unification of the country, and more especially, to the control of a stable source of revenue from land. Again, the rise of the Tokugawa Shogunate is attributable to its possession of financial power far superior to that of many feudal lords, while its downfall was due to the fact that the financial basis of the Shogunate was shaken as land economy was supplanted by currency economy and also that it proved incapable of controlling the economic power of the rising (*chōnin*) class, these factors combining to reduce the Shogunate to financial straits. The establishment of the Meiji Government was rendered possible because it got control of land in the whole country by replacing *han* by prefectures and possessed itself of economic power of the *chōnin* class. Thus viewed, it will be understood that it is impossible for dynastic changes to take place, in disregard of financial power or independently of economic power.

2. FROM KINSHIP FINANCE AND LOCAL FINANCE TO STATE FINANCE

We often talk of "Japan's finance," but there were very few cases, from remote old days up to the modern age, where finance covered the whole land of Japan. In the days of the *shizoku* system, the revenue from the Imperial land was the principal resource for meeting the expenses of the Imperial Household and the Central Government. People voluntarily paid tributes to the Imperial Court, and of the land tax, statute labour service and tributes collected from private domains, the tributes generally went into the coffers of the Imperial Court, but no taxation was imposed on the people generally. In those days, the Emperor held sway over the Imperial family and the *uji-no-kami* of other families only, no direct ownership being held by him over the land and people of the country. Accordingly, the so-called Japanese finance operated in the limited areas over which the Emperor held direct control. After the Taika Reform, it appeared that the prefectural system was introduced and enforced throughout the country, but soon afterwards, the *handen* system ceased to operate, and there was a revival of aristocracy, many *shōen* being created everywhere. In the middle and latter days of the Heian period, the authority of the Central Government gradually waned, while the local magnates steadily gained influence. The result was that besides the Government fiefs and *shōen* belonging to influential families, there sprang up *shōen* of military families. Kyōto (the Imperial Court) was, in such circumstances, reduced to a position of isolation. In the military régime of the Middle Ages, the Kamakura and Muromachi Shogunates were the financial centres, and they appeared to have extended their right of taxation to the whole country through the collection of rice as military provisions and other imposts, and yet only the fiefs under the direct control of the Shogunate remained the main source of revenue. As the influence of the Muromachi Shogunate declined, the number of fiefs owned by military leaders which refused to obey the Shogunate orders steadily increased. The lords of these fiefs collected taxes from the people in their fiefs, but refused to forward them to the Central Government. Such being the case, the Muromachi Shogunate, though nominally in control of the country, was, as a matter of fact, as powerless as an isolated

provincial lord, and its finance was by no means
on such a scale as merited the name of national
finance.   In the Tokugawa Shogunate also, the
tenryō or the fiefs under the direct control of the
Shogunate formed the chief source of revenue,
and needless to say there were some feudal lords
who owned extensive areas. In short, until recent
times, the finance of our country did not cover
the whole country; it was limited to the areas
over which the rulers held direct sway. Although
national finance in name, it was the finance of
some particular influential families or the Shogunate, to all intents and purposes. It was after
the Meiji Restoration that a national finance
worthy of the name came into existence. Viewed
from this standpoint, it may fairly be said that
Japan's finance has had the three stages of kin-
ship finance, local finance and State finance.

3. FROM SECRETARIAT FINANCE TO STATE FINANCE

As already stated, the finance of our country
was formerly the finance of those in power. It
was governed by the principles of private economy, and offered, no distinction from household
finance. In the reign of the Emperor Richū, it
was divided into *imikura* and *uchikura*, and in
the reign of the Emperor Yūryaku another department called *ōkura* was created.   There is no
doubt that this marked a good step forward in

politics and finance, but it is open to grave doubt
whether a clear line of demarcation was drawn
between the private expense of the Imperial
Household and the State expenditure in respect
of revenue, control and defrayals, or whether
what the Emperor did as the head of the Imperial Family was clearly differentiated from what
he did as the Ruler of the country. As for myself, I am inclined to the view that the establishment of the three *kura*, namely *imikura*, *uchikura*
and *ōkura*, merely shows that there was a big
expansion of finance in those days. The Taihō-
ryō marked another advance in that it provided
an Imperial Household Department for the transaction of Court business, in addition to the People's
Department and the Finance Department. It is
nevertheless very doubtful whether it meant, in
substance, the transition from secretariat finance
to State finance. Even in the military age, State
finance was confounded with household finance.
In the Tokugawa Shogunate, the principle of cutting the coat according to the cloth formed the
nucleus of the financial policy, and the items of
expenditure of the Shogunate clearly show that
the distinction was considerably blurred between
the expenditure of the Shogunate proper and the
family expenditure of the Tokugawas. In short,
the finance of this country in former days, from
the remote old days downwards, was handled as
though it had been private economy, without
regard to one important point of difference exist-

ing between finance and private economy. In the State finance, the expenditure necessary for the execution of the State administration is first fixed and then the ways and means of finding the requisite money are studied, though the capacity of the people for bearing burdens may claim due consideration. In the State finance, therefore, the revenue is regulated by the amount of expenditure. On the contrary, in household finance the expenditure must be fixed within the limits of revenue. It was not until this financial principle was recognised after the Meiji Restoration that the finance of this country was dissociated from household finance.

4. FROM FINANCE IN KIND TO FINANCE IN CURRENCY

The present-day finance consists in the receipts and payments of currency or monetary expedients by the State. In the days when currency economy was undeveloped, however, it was usual for tributes to be paid in kind or labour (corvée) was pressed into service. In the days of remote antiquity, the land tax was paid in sheaves of rice plants at the rate of three sheaves for every 100 *shiro* of land (one *shiro* covering an area of land which produced one sheaf of rice plants). *Mitsugi* consisted of catches and games, cloth, yarn and other products of various districts. For the construction of palaces or for other engineering works, men were recruited from many places, distant as well as neighbouring, as, for instance, recruiting was made of men in Shinano province in the reign of the Emperor Buretsu and in the reign of the Empress Kōkyoku, men were recruited from Ōmi and Koshi provinces for the construction of big temples. There were also cases where men were pressed into service for the building of Imperial Palaces from the districts located between Tōtōmi in the east and Aki in the west. It seems that for ordinary *buyaku* (statute labour), apart from temporary *buyaku*, the men recruited for annual service were at the rate of one per 30 households, as a general rule, in the pre-Taika days. The Taihō-ryō also provided for the land tax, *chishi* (rent in rice plants) and *buyaku*. *Yō* and *chō* embodied tributes to be paid to the capital between the middle of August and the end of the year, according to the distances which separate the provinces from the capital. The men for carrying these tributes to the capital were to be provided by the families from which they were collected. In those days when very little communication facilities were available, the transport of these taxes from distant places involved burdens heavier than the main tax, viz. the land tax. Many of the young men who were chosen for the task of transporting *yō* and *chō* starved to death on the mountains and fields or succumbed to diseases contracted on the way. In order to meet such a situation, relief regulations were enacted, under which these people were supplied with food for their return journey. In the case of those who came up to the capital from distant provinces, it often happened that they could not return home in time for the rice planting season. These were serious inconveniences attending natural economy, and they caused many hardships to the people, though such a system was inevitable in the days when the currency system was undeveloped. In the Nara and Heian periods, coins were minted, as, indeed, we come across references to *yōsen* (tax payments in coins) in many books published in the Tempyō era and afterwards. In an Imperial Edict issued on February 28th of the sixteenth year of Enryaku (797) appears the passage: " The taxes are intended for providing against floods and drought. People cannot live on coins when they are starving. We hear that many officials in the capital collect coins in taxes, but this practice must be done away with, as it ignores the fundamentals of the tax collection. There are, however, poor people, and these do not necessarily keep cereals, and from these people coins may be collected, but the coins collected should not exceed one-fourth of the total amount of taxes." From this Imperial Edict, it may be inferred that the payment of taxes in coins was a device for the protection of poor people. But seeing that this practice of paying taxes in coins was subsequently often prohibited, it seems that with the increased circulation of currency, there developed a tendency to pay taxes in coins in the districts around the Central Government. In the Engi-shiki also, mention is made of the *chō-yō-sen*. At first, the Government conferred Court rank on the keepers of coins as one means of encouraging the circulation of coins, or made travellers carry coins. It also caused people to pay *chō* and *yō* in coins. The amount of coins minted was not, however, large enough to be put into circulation throughout the country. Many coins were kept stored instead of being circulated in the market. There were also cases where coins were privately minted, a circumstance which impaired the credit of currency. Inasmuch as the general economic state was not so advanced as to necessitate the wide use of metal coins in those days, natural economy was prevalent, though coins were in circulation in the limited areas of the provinces around the capital and some other districts. In the Kamakura and Muromachi periods, the land tax was paid either in cereals or in coins, and besides the land tax, there were such taxes as the *tansen* (tax levied on farm land), *munebetsusen* (house tax), *kurayaku* (pawnbroking tax) and *utokusen* (contributions collected from rich families), with the result that tax receipts in coins gradually increased. Especially in the Muromachi period, large quantities of Eiraku coins were imported from China, and there was a larger circulation of coins, resulting in more

widespread payments of taxes in coins. In the
Tokugawa period, coins got into circulation
throughout the country, and they became more
extensively the medium for national finance.
Owing to the fact that whereas rice still formed
the basis of finance and economy, state defrayals
and receipts were made with coins at the same
time, an anomaly arose, with serious effects on
the finance of the Tokugawa Shogunate. In and
after the eighth year of Meiji (1875), economy
in kind was abolished, and finance has been
unified by currency value, while service in labour
such as *buyaku* ceased to be financial revenue.
This marks another advance in the financial
history of the country.

5. DIVERSIFICATION OF SOURCES OF
REVENUE

In the ancient days when land economy ruled
in this country, land was regarded as the sole
source of revenue, and consequently taxation was
levied on land, on farm land especially. At first,
there was no classification of land, the tax being
assessed according to the acreage of land. For
instance, in the days of remote antiquity, three
sheaves of rice plants were collected from farm
land covering an area of 100 *shiro*. Both in the
Taihō-ryo and under the system operating in the
Heian period, a tax was collected at the rate of
about 3 per cent. of the standard yield of rice

per *tan* of farm land, irrespective of the quality of land. With regard to *chishi*, however, farm land was graded according to the degree of its fertility, and from the land of good quality ten sheaves of rice plants per *tan* were collected, from the land of medium quality eight sheaves, from the land of bad quality six sheaves, from that of the worst quality three sheaves. On the whole, the levy was one-fifth of the yield of rice. In the Kamakura and Muromachi periods, the rates of taxation varied, and the rates levied differed with the quality of the land. In the Tokugawa period also, different rates were imposed on different classes of land. It was since the Meiji era that assessment of the tax was based on the value of land. As already explained, taxes were imposed on manufactures of various kinds, besides land, but land remained the main source of revenue all the same. In the days when it became difficult to get sufficient revenue from the land tax, attempts were made to find new sources of revenue in all other directions. What with the very complex relations of rule over feudal territory and what with civil disturbances, it was difficult, in the Muromachi period, to expect a large revenue from the land tax, and new imposts were created such as *tansen, munebetsusen, kanzei* (customs duties), *zayaku* (tax on trade associations), *kurayaku, utokusen, bukeyaku* (tax on samurai) and *hyakushōyaku* (tax on farmers). In the Tokugawa period too, it was found impossible,

owing to the impoverishment of the farming
population, to rely solely on the productive power
of land, and a big source of revenue was sought
from among the commercial and industrial classes
which had come by degrees to possess much
influence. Taking advantage of the spread of
currency also, the Tokugawa Shogunate managed
to increase its revenue considerably by making
use of the privilege of coinage. There are phenomena which are bound to happen in the period
of transition from agricultural economy to commercial economy and from land economy to
currency economy.

6. FROM CREDIT FINANCE TO DEBT FINANCE

In the *Ōchō* period, besides taxes (in a
narrow sense of the word), *suiko* supplied an
important source of revenue, while in the Tokugawa period, *goyōkin* formed a good source of
revenue. These two things make an interesting
contrast with each other. *Suiko* was a system,
according to which *ine* (seed-rice), official and
private, was lent to farmers in spring time, and
farmers were made to pay it back with interest
after the harvest time of autumn. According
to the Imperial Rescript issued in April of the
fourth year of the accession of the Emperor
Temmu (676), farmers were divided into three
classes according to their wealth, and to the
farmers of the middle and lower classes *ine* was

lent. This system was thus originally intended for the relief of poor farmers, but later it was exploited for realising profits to meet the expenditure of the Government offices, so that even rich farmers had to receive *ine* and pay interest on it. The term of the loan was fixed at one year and the rate of interest at 50 per cent. As *ine* was lent out in spring and recovered in autumn or winter, the term was not, strictly speaking, one year. Supposing that eight months were the exact term, the interest it actually bore was 75 per cent. The profits accruing from *suiko* were by their nature designed for meeting the expenses on the making of ponds and channels, and the construction of temples (*kokubunji*), but as a matter of fact they were, in many cases, employed for meeting the expenditure of the Government offices. So, they went to the profit for the *kokushi*, and the evil practice was originated by the *kokushi* of lending out *ine* over and above the stipulated amount in order to realise big gains. In those days, of the levies of *so*, *yō* and *chō*, the last-mentioned two were utilised to pay the expenses of the Central Government, while only a small part of the *so* rice was sent to the capital, and the most part of the rice was kept in local storehouses to meet local expenditure. A large quantity of the rice was used as *suiko* to make profit out of it. The amount of rice lent out as *suiko* was fixed according to the size and wealth of the provinces concerned, but there is no documentary record available to ascertain accurate figures. In the Engi-shiki, the amount of *suiko* is shown, according to which the total amount is given as 42,976,584 sheaves and 1,200 *koku*. These figures do not, of course, represent the total amount of local expenditure in a year, but they may be taken as indicating the basic figures of local finance. In short, the *suiko* system played an important part in local finance. In the closing days of the Heian period, however, *shōen* became numerous and the number of vagrants (*rōnin*) increased in all districts. These evaded their obligations to pay debts and obstructed the transaction of official business. Government officials also were bent on making profits by lending out large quantities of *ine* as *suiko* to feather their own nests. This state of things vitiated the State administration and caused hardships to the people. With the gradual deterioration of official discipline, the *suiko* system seems to have gone out of existence, for no record of its subsequent history is obtainable.

In the Muromachi period, there were already privileged merchants and industrialists on whom special taxes were imposed. In the Tokugawa period, the *goyōkin* system was inaugurated, under which some merchants were ordered to pay monetary contributions to the Shogunate. With these contributions, any deficit in the Shogunate finance was often made up. Unlike taxes, *goyōkin* was of a nature not to be collected compulsorily

by the Shogunate as its proper right. It was by
nature a debt contracted by the Shogunate to a
chōnin from which it was raised, with a promise
to pay it back with interest. From this point of
view, *goyōkin* was not a contribution. The idea
of *goyōkin* was alien to the policy pursued by
the Shogunate in its initial days. As its finance
became difficult in the middle and latter part of
the Shogunate, the system was inaugurated to
tide over the financial difficulty, for the burdens
on farmers were already so heavy that it was
impossible to increase them further to raise the
requisite money, while, on the other hand, the
chōnin class grew more and more wealthy with
practically no burdens imposed on them.

Under the *suiko* system, the State lent *ine* to
people and exacted interest on it, but under the
goyōkin system, the State constituted itself the
debtor to those on whom *goyōkin* was imposed,
pledging itself to pay interest on it. This developed in the Meiji era into the so-called loan
system. That the State passed from the position
of creditor to that of debtor, and that the right
of creditors to the State, which was not sufficiently
secured in former days, became clearly defined,
afford materials of considerable interest to the
study of the history of the origin of public loans
and their developments. It certainly is not im-
pertinent, therefore, to dwell here upon the transition from credit finance to debt finance in the
above-mentioned sense.

7. PERFECTION OF THE SYSTEM

The system and regulations governing taxation have become gradually more elaborate. In the *Ōchō* period, thanks to the importation of various systems from China, which was then ahead of Japan in civilisation, many reforms were effected, and some comparatively detailed regulations were laid down, but in the military age that followed, the regulations were rather simplified as a result of a general regard for simplicity. With respect to the system of imposition and payments of taxes, a fairly perfect system was in operation already from the *Ōchō* period. It is, however, after the Meiji era that a most perfect system and most elaborate regulations were introduced.

Although it was in the Meiji era that all systems relating to budgets, settlement of accounts and finance were put into perfect order, the days anterior to Meiji were by no means devoid of systems governing these matters. There were some rules by which revenue and expenditure were regulated. Even in household finance, it is necessary to know in advance the possible incomes, and if so, it is obvious that such a necessity is much greater in the finance of the State. As far back as the *Ōchō* period, therefore, there was a system governing matters relating to budgets and settlement of accounts. The '*Daikeichō*' in

those days gave the aggregates of the revenue
from *yō* and *chō* to be collected every year, as
well as the number of the households in each
province under the jurisdiction of *kokushi* (provincial magistrate) throughout the country, and the
number of tax-paying and non-tax-paying households. In other words, it embodied the estimates
of revenue accruing to the Central Government
from the provinces. Against this, there was the
book called '*Chōchō*' which recorded the actual
number of *chō*, *yō* and other tax matters. There
was another book showing the settlement of accounts called the '*Shōzeichō*.' In this book was
entered the amount of the cereals paid by people
in taxation and the defrayals made in the previous year. In the Tokugawa period, " The Outlines of the Amount of Expenditure in a Year "
was made public in December of the third year
of Kan'en (1750), In the days subsequent to
the fifth year of Hōreki (1755) also, estimates in
regard to part of the expenditure were drawn
up. The organ for the control of finance called
the *kanjō-gimmiyaku* was also created [from the
second year of Tenna (1682) to the twelfth year
of Genroku (1699) and after the second year of
Shotoku (1712)], though it differed somewhat in
nature from the one which is in existence at
present. Taken as a whole, however, the finance
in the post-Restoration days was not a continuation of the finance of the pre-Restoration days ;
there were marked changes in nature. This was

because the State finance, in the true sense of the term, was not in existence in this country before the Restoration. It is hardly necessary to say that the system and regulations relating to finance were brought to perfection after the Restoration. This development of finance, which is inseparably associated with the changes that came over the political and social organisations in post-Restoration days, was in part due to the introduction of Western civilisation and partly to the progress of financial science.

CHAPTER IV
FROM THE TOKUGAWA PERIOD TO THE MEIJI RESTORATION

1. INTRODUCTION

The Tokugawa period was an age of feudalism. From the economic point of view, feudalism was a system in which land constituted the principal means of production and the farming population formed practically the sole producing class, supporting the privileged class called *samurai*, which ranked above it. Unlike a similar class in the Kamakura period, the *samurai* in the Tokugawa period was an unproductive class; they did not farm the land. They were fed by the farmers.

The Tokugawa period is also known as an age of rice economy, because rice constituted the basis of the finance and economy of those days. As a general medium of exchange, however, money came into wider use in this age. Although it was not an age of currency economy, pure and simple, as the present age is, money was more extensively used in that period than in any of the previous periods. In short, after the middle of the Tokugawa period commerce and industry witnessed remarkable developments and money came into general use. This led to the development of urban districts and to the rise of the *chō-nin* class to a position of influence. The land economy that had prevailed gave way to the currency economy, and a new economic power came into being, side by side with the economic power of the farmer class. These marked economic changes rendered it impossible for the *samurai* class to maintain their livelihood under the old economic system. Nor could the farming population support the *samurai* class any longer. In such circumstances, the *samurai* had finally to bow to the new economic power. They either went to the *chōnin* class for financial aid or converted themselves into virtual *chōnin* or actually adopted *chōnin* ways. On the other hand, the *chōnin* class became predominant in society by virtue of their financial power. Their influence rose above that of the *samurai* class, on the one hand, and made inroads in the agricultural sphere, on the other. In this way, class distinctions became confused and the foundations of the feudal system badly shaken. In its economic policy also, the Shogunate, in its closing days, was forced by various circumstances to adopt many new measures which ran counter to its traditional policy. The new Meiji Administration that supplanted the Shogunate succeeded to many of these measures. It also depended largely on the financial power of the *chōnin* class for the execution of its policy. In the following sentences, I propose to make a general review of these circumstances.

2. THE AGE OF THE RISE TO POWER OF THE *CHŌNIN* CLASS[1]

In the Tokugawa period, currency economy developed as against land economy, but when in that period was it that money came into general use? In the '*Rōjin Zatsuwa,*' we find the passage: "There has been a plentiful suppuly of gold and silver for the past fifty years." The years mentioned refer to the Keichō (1596–1614) and the Genna (1615–1623) eras. In the '*Tamakushige Beppon,*' written by Motoori-Norinaga, there occurs the following remark: "It is since the Keichō era that gold and silver coins have been in wide circulation. Prior to that era, small coins only had been in popular use." In the '*Keizairoku Shūi,*' Dazai-Shuntai says: "In former days, Japan had little gold and silver, and as coinage was unknown, gold or silver coins were very rarely used by people, high or low. In those days, the use of foreign coins only sufficed. In the Keichō era, however, the supply of gold and silver became plentiful. Since Kan'ei coins were struck and put into circulation, it has become the fashion to use gold and silver coins in big transactions and to employ small coins in minor dealings . . . This is, however, an age of gold and silver . . . and money is spent a hundred

---

[1] cf. Chap. IX.

times as much now as in former days." In the 'Seidan,' Ogyū-Sorai also says : "Formerly coins were particularly scarce in rural districts. I remember that in the days when I was still in my native place all things were bought, not with money, but with rice or barley. I learn now, however, that since the Genroku era (1688–1703) coins have been in circulation even in rural districts so that things are now bought with money." All the descriptions quoted above show that gold and silver coins were already in circulation in the Keichō and the Genna eras and that in the Genroku era they were current even in rural districts. The phrase "possessor of gold" or "possessor of silver" was already used in those days in the sense of a wealthy person.

Why was it, then, that money came into such wide circulation in the Tokugawa period? It appears that at the initial stage of the Tokugawa period, the output of gold and silver ore witnessed a sudden increase, which led to the frequent coinage of gold, silver and copper coins and also to the unification of the currency system. Moreover, the sankin-kōtai system (a system under which feudal lords stayed in Edo by turns in the Shogun's service) did much to increase the use of money by the samurai either on their way to and from Edo or during their sojourn in Edo, the seat of the Tokugawa Shōgunate. Also the development of castle towns and the progress of commerce and industry fostered, both among the

samurai class and among the populace, the custom
of purchasing all necessaries with ready money.
Ogyū-Sorai says (in the '*Seidan*'): "The life of
samurai congregated in castle towns is like hotel
life, but these towns are not their fiefs, so they
must buy all things there, no matter how trifling,
not to mention the vital necessaries of life." In
the '*Taiheisaku*' he says: "As in hotel life one
must needs buy all things necessary for living,
money is the most important thing for travellers.
Never in any age since the foundation of the
country has money been so indispensable to life
as during the last 100 years." These descriptions
clearly denote the fact that the economic life of
those days had attained the stage of currency
economy. It may be said that the impression
became general among the people of that time
that money could do anything. Yamakata-Bantō,
in his book '*Yume no Shiro*,' says: "Since the
middle of the Tokugawa period, gold and silver
coins are to be met with everywhere. The
possession of gold and silver means wealth. The
foolish are held to be wise, and the wicked good,
if only they are possessed of gold and silver.
On the contrary, one who has neither gold nor
silver is poor. However wise he may be, he is
dubbed a fool. A clever man with no money is
regarded by the public as a dullard, and a good
man so circumstanced is looked upon as a worth-
less person. Money can restore a ruined family
to former prosperity. As all things, life or death,

success or failure, depend on the possession or non-possession of gold, all people, irrespective of rank or trade, run after gold as the first requisite for existence." Thus, the enormous power of gold and silver came to be generally recognised. In the previous ages land was regarded as the only source of wealth, but now gold and silver became by for the most important. Notwithstanding the fact that the idea of respecting cereals and despising money was assiduously inculcated by some people, money was sought after by all classes, and it found wide circulation not only in urban but in rural districts also.

As already stated, the currency economy developed steadily in those days. In such an age, those who have talent for business can amass wealth and gain much influence. And it was the *chōnin* class which possessed money power. The Shogunate and the *daimyō* which were in financial straits, therefore, either requisitioned money from rich merchants in Edo, Kyōto and Ōsaka, or went obsequiously to them for loans, so that they could balance their budgets satisfactorily. In those days, many feudal lords had warehouses in Ōsaka, Edo and other cities for the purpose of selling rice and other products of their respective provinces. The great majority of feudal lords had their warehouses in Ōsaka. They either sold the products of their fiefs there or with the commodities as security, they borrowed the money they needed. Functionaries of different ranks and with different duties, called *kurayaku-nin*, *kuramoto* and *kakeya* were appointed to these warehouses in Ōsaka. *Kurayakunin*, officials detailed from their respective *han*, at first performed the duties of *kuramoto* as well as their own, but later *chōnin* were made *kuramoto*, whose duties were to take charge of the warehoused goods. The *kakeya's* duties were to receive money for the goods sold and keep it in custody. The *kuramoto* often performed both duties. The *kakeya* in Ōsaka, like the *fudasashi* in Edo, did duties as financial agents for *samurai*. The *daimyō* gave allowances of rice to *kakeya*, and treated them in the same way as they did their *karō* (chief retainers). The influence exerted by *kuramoto* over the *daimyo's* finance was accordingly very great.

Once *samurai* borrowed money from *chōnin*, it was no easy task for them to pay their debts. Very often they became more and more deeply involved in debt until they were obliged to make importunate overtures to their creditors for consent to payments by instalments spread over a long period or to the remission of the interest. In case debtors refused to meet their obligations, they often resorted to the method of boycotting such defaulting *daimyō* by agreement among money-lenders. In the Kyōho era (1716–1735) already, there were cases of reprisals adopted by aggrieved *chōnin* against *samurai*. It often happened in Edo that *chōnin* insulted the *samurai* who had failed either to pay their debts or to pay for articles bought, by planting paper banners or putting up defamatory placards at the doors of the defaulters.

It was at the same time observable that many *chōnin* extended their financial influence to agricultural districts and became extensive landowners. When there were annexations of land or reclamations of land, their influence made insidious advances. Land reclamation works in those days were sometimes undertaken on contract with *chōnin*, a fact which shows that *chōnin* capital was often invested in such works. This does not, of course, mean that the *chōnin* converted themselves into regular farmers, but it means that they acquired the status of landowners in addition to their status as rich merchants.[2]

In short, both the *samurai* class and the farming class had to yield to the *chōnin* class in money power. It must be clear from what I have already described that the *chōnin* class acquired great social prestige by means of the money power which it monopolised.

In bygone ages, it was generally believed that *samurai* formed the governing class, farmers the productive class and *chōnin* the useless class. These class features gradually changed, and in the Tokugawa period the *samurai* class became powerless, the farming class exhausted and impoverished, and the *chōnin* class rose to power.

---

[2] cf. Chap VI.

3. CONVERSION OF *SAMURAI* AND FARMERS INTO *CHŌNIN*

The *samurai* in the Tokugawa period either left their native places to live in their castle-towns or went to Edo in attendance on their *daimyō* in their regular visits to the seat of the Shogunate under the *sankin-kōtai* system. In the case of the direct retainers of the Shogun, they took up their permanent residence in Edo. Large towns were centres of the currency economy where commerce and industry were most developed and where *chōnin* who were possessed of great money power lived. It was but natural that the *samurai* who lived in such towns should have gradually attained higher standards of living until they found themselves unable to support themselves on their regular stipends. To make their livelihood even more difficult, many *han* were driven by their straitened financial circumstances to adopt what was called the *hanchi* (half-stipend) system. Under this system the *daimyō* borrowed part of the stipends from their *samurai*. The amount of reduction in stipends varied; it was not necessarily 50 per cent. In some cases, *samurai* had to give up one-third of their stipends and in other cases one-fourth.

As *samurai* were in such financial straits, they did job-work besides practising economy. Even by such means they could not keep themselves out of debt. They very often contracted heavy debts and put themselves helplessly in the hands of usurers. *Samurai* who used to value honour above all became, by force of circumstances, so degenerate as to put material gains before every thing else. It became the fashion among them not to do anything which did not bring them material profit. The habit also grew on them of taking commission from merchants for articles purchased for, or on behalf of their lords. In many other ways, they tried to realise gains by utilising the offices which they held in their *han*. Even when taking some one into his service, a *samurai* made the go-between offer some money in return. In adopting a child, he made a point of choosing the scion of a rich family. The right of succession in the family of a retainer of the Shogun was actually sold for money. Some *daimyō* in those days made poor *samurai* carry on certain industries with a view to affording them relief. The *samurai*'s pursuit of material gains and their attempts to earn their livelihood by means of industrial work or job-work indicate that, finding themselves unable to support themselves under the economic system then prevailing, they were compelled to alter their modes of living so as to adapt them to the changing economic conditions. Nor was this all. Many gave up their status as *samurai* and converted themselves into *chōnin*. The result is that *samurai* blood runs in a good many famous old families of *chōnin*.[3]

Now as to the farming class. The fundamental
policy pursued to keep farmers in subjection was
to prevent them from raising their standards of
living. For the execution of this policy, various
restrictions were imposed on their clothing, food,
habitation and other phases of life. That such
steps were taken in order to restrain farmers to
their wretched existence is clear from the official
instructions of the Keian era (1649). It was
strictly forbidden for farmers to lead a luxurious
life in imitation of *chōnin* and towns-people. The
agricultural communities were detached from town
life, farmers were segregated from *chōnin* and the
growth of economic knowledge among the farming population was checked. Although farmers
were groaning under the heavy weight of taxation,
they had a natural desire to improve their condition of life. It was impossible to keep them
contented with their wretched life forever. With
the gradual raising of the standards of living
among other classes of people, and especially as
they witnessed the prodigal life of the *chōnin*
class, their natural desire for a better life was
whetted. This rendered their lot only the harder
through the higher cost of living. Motoori-
Norinaga says in his book : " Farmers in dire
distress have been particularly numerous of late
years. There are two chief reasons for this. One

---

[3] cf. Chap. VII.

is the heavy taxes which they are called upon to pay to the lord and the other is their gradual acquirement of extravagant habits in consequence of the general tendency for all classes to live luxuriously.[4]

As already mentioned, it was the policy of the powers that were in those days to prevent the contact of farming communities with town life and keep farmers and *chōnin* apart, but some farmers, enamoured of the life of *chōnin*, settled down in town and became merchants or town labourers. Some formed matrimonial alliances with *chōnin* families. Even those who remained in their villages gave up the plough and turned shop-keepers. It is a fact generally admitted that the expansion of big cities — Edo in particular — was largely due to the settlement there of many people from the provinces. It appears that there was a remarkable development of urban life already in the Kyōho era. Thus, there were, needless to say, many *chōnin* who had been farmers in their earlier life. It is said that there were many Kamigata (Kyōto, Ōsaka and neighbourhood) men — natives of Ise and Ōmi provinces especially — in Edo. It is probable that these Kamigata men included many who, abandoning agricultural life in the provinces, settled down in Edo as merchants.

---

[4] cf. Chap. VIII.

4. ADOPTION OF *CHŌNIN* WAYS BY THE
SHOGUNATE AND THE *DAIMYŌ*

As already described, the *samurai* and the
farming classes gradually developed the tendency
to turn merchants or adopt *chōnin* ways in order
to accommodate themselves to the changes in economic conditions. A similar tendency was also
manifest in regard to the Shogunate and the
daimyō. Tōyama-Kagetaka urged the necessity
of the monetary power being taken over by the
authorities. In his book he says: "If the lords,
the *samurai* and the people generally, are to
be enriched, the money power should not be
left in the hands of commercial men." In the
'*Shūmaiken Jōsho*' also it is urged that the right
of controlling rice should be taken over by the
authorities. These arguments were all advanced
from the desire of extending the financial power
of the Government, so that the authority of the
Government might be firmly established through
the overthrow of *chōnin* power and prestige. In
fact, many instances may be cited where the Shogunate and the *daimyō* acted after the fashion of
chōnin in order to meet the changes that came
over economic conditions. The inauguration of
a system analogous to the monopoly system and
the establishment of the *sambutsu-kaisho* for provincial products are cases in point. In the '*Keizairoku*,' we find the following:

" All high *samurai* and *daimyō* nowadays use money in all transactions, just as merchants do, and so they are bent on possessing themselves of as much gold and silver as they can. They seem to regard the possession of money as the most essential need of the day. The shortest way to get money is to engage in commercial transactions. In some *han* it has been a long-established practice to find the wherewithal to pay the expenses of their *han* by means of such transactions, thereby making up for the smallness of their fiefs. The *daimyō* of Tsushima, for instance, is master of a small province and his fief produces only a little over 20,000 *koku* of rice. He is, however, rich, and is even better-off than a lord with a fief of 200,000 *koku*, because he purchases Korean ginseng and other goods at low prices and sells them at high prices. The *daimyō* of Matsumae has a small fief of 7,000 *koku*, but through the sale of the products of his own fief and of articles produced in Ezo (Hokkaidō), he is richer than a *daimyō* of, say, a fief of 50,000 *koku*. Again, the *daimyō* of Tsuwano, despite his small fief of 40,000 *koku*, has wealth comparable to that of a lord of a fief producing 150,000 *koku* of rice, because much profit accrues to him from the manufacture and sale of pasteboard. The *daimyō* of Hamada follows the example set by the *daimyō* of Tsuwano and encourages the manufacture of pasteboard in

his own fief. This makes him as rich as a
lord with a fief of more than 100,000 *koku*,
though his fief produces only 50,000 *koku* of
rice. Satsuma is, of course, a big *han*, but
its incomparable wealth is due to its mono-
plistic sale of goods imported from Loochoo.
Chinese goods also are imported into Satsuma
through Loochoo, and then sold widely in this
country. Since the *daimyō* of Tsushima, Matsumae and Satsuma have a monopoly of the
importation of foreign goods and sell them to
other *daimyō*, they are much richer than other
daimyō of similar dimensions. As for the *daimyō* of Tsuwano and Hamada, they are rich
because of their sale of the products of their
respective fiefs. The *daimyō* of Shingū has a
fief of only 30,000 *koku*, but as he sells the
land and marine products of Kumano, his
wealth is to be compared with that of a lord
of a fief of 100,000 *koku*."

The monopoly system was already in existence in many *han* in the early days of the
Tokugawa period, but it increased in popularity
after the middle of the period. The *sambutsu-
kaisho*, which were mostly established in and
after the days when Yoshimune was Shogun,
were originally intended for the encouragement of
production, but later many of them assumed the
character of markets for the sale of provincial
products. That is to say, they partook of the
nature of monopoly. For the purpose of regulating

prices, the Shogunate often prohibited cornering operations. In October of the thirteenth year of Tempo (1842), it vetoed the monopoly sale of provincial products in the various *han* of the Kinai, Chūgoku, Saikoku and Shikoku districts. This veto was issued in the year following the prohibition of wholesalers' guilds under the Tempo Reform plan, and it is clear that it had the reduction of the prices of commodities in view. In the closing days of the Tokugawa period, the Shogunate itself attempted to adopt a system resembling monopoly by establishing the *sambutsu-kaisho*. This policy was not prompted by the motive of regulating prices, but was designed to deprive the *chōnin* class of its influence and to replenish the depleted coffers of the Shogunate. Whatever may have been the motive, the fact remains that the Shogunate attempted to do what it forbade the various *daimyō* to do in the thirteenth year of Tempo. This *sambutsu-kaisho* was planned in November of the second year of Ansei (1855), and in November of the first year of Keiō (1865), but each time the plan fell through. That the Shogunate attempted to seize the commercial rights which had been monopolished by merchants shows that the Shogunate itself developed the tendency to engage in commerce. It testifies to a marked change in the spirit of the age.

Besides the above-mentioned plan, many new measures which ran counter to the traditional

policy were adopted in the closing days of the
Shogunate, as, for instance, the importation of
new Western technical arts, the introduction of
the company system, and the issue of notes.[5]
All these measures were necessitated to meet
the economic changes of the times, and they
throw a sidelight on the adoption by the Shogunate and the *daimyō* of commercial ways. It
is noteworthy that these were visualised in the
policy pursued after the Meiji Restoration (1868)
— in the first ten years of Meiji especially.

5. THE MEIJI RESTORATION

As already explained, the *chōnin* class gained
much influence in and after the middle of the
Tokugawa period and the growth of the currency
economy followed. In consequence, the feudal
system, which was based on land economy, was
badly shaken. Even by reason of these internal
circumstances, the feudal system was nearing its
end. The invasion of foreign capitalism which
synchronised with these changes compelled the
opening of the country to foreign intercourse,
culminating in the downfall of the Tokugawa
Shogunate. From the economic point of view,
the age of land economy, on which the feudal
system was founded, was superseded by the age
of currency economy, which was incompatible

---

[5] cf. Chap. XI.

with the former, and then came the importation
of foreign capitalism.

It was not, however, the *chōnin* class, but the
samurai class of the lower grades, that brought
down the Tokugawa Shogunate.   The fact that
the *chōnin* class played no important part in the
overthrow of the Shogunate was partly due to
the imperfect political and economic awakening
of the *chōnin* class, whose influence could not
rise above a certain level because of the feudalism and the exclusion policy that ruled in those
days.   The actual political change was induced
both by the foreign relations and by the movement
launched for the overthrow of the Shogunate
by patriots, and the low grade *samurai* caught a
better chance to participate in the work of the
Restoration.   These low grade *samurai* could not
earn their living under the feudal system, nor
could they give full play to their talents under
it.   This naturally caused much discontent among
them, and they keenly felt the necessity of changing the existing order of society.   When they saw
the opportunity they seized it energetically for
the realisation of their cherished desires.   Disregarding the counsels of upper grade *samurai*,
they managed to establish a stable new Government on the ruins of the feudal system.

The Restoration did not take political power
from the *samurai* class.   The only change that
took place was that power passed from the upper
grade *samurai* to the lower grades.   It was, how-

ever, impossible for all low grade *samurai* who played a part in the Restoration to be put in Government offices. They were therefore given pension bond certificates instead of their former stipends, and had to live as best they could with them in accordance with the dictates of the new currency economy. Some of these *samurai* took to trade but in most cases they failed. Recognising the necessity of removing a menace to politics by providing these *samurai* with regular employment, the Government devised means to give them work. Reclamation works and the encouragement of agriculture were among these measures. It further encouraged and subsidised the establishment of the National Bank, the Nippon Railway Company and other companies. A vigorous policy of protective interference was pursued in order to make them operate their undertakings on the advanced Western plan. The result was that they gradually constituted themselves a new economic influence as the advanced leaders of the business world, far-reaching reforms in the social and economic organisations of this country following. It is an irony of fate that the *samurai* who used to despise money became the pioneers of the industrial world and leading capitalists. The part played by low grade *samurai* before and after the Meiji Restoration was, indeed, very important. It is, of course, true that the great majority of them were swept away by the tidal waves of the Restoration, but some low grade *samurai* who

took an active part in the great political change
seized political power, while some others secured
money power and became capitalists.

It was in the Genroku era that the currency
economy began to encroach on the natural economy of old-world Japan. The main source of
revenue for the Shogunate, which was based on the
feudal system, was from the natural products of
the land. In the meantime, the new wealth in the
shape of money was monopolised by the *chōnin*
class, and with the progress of the currency
economy, the military power of the *samurai* class
gradually gave way to the money power of the
chōnin class. When the Meiji Restoration (1868)
came, the *chōnin* class, which had made much
headway in the Tokugawa period, was deprived of
the privileges and official protection which it had
previously enjoyed, and was compelled to devise
means to support itself in a world of free competition. The *chōnin* class in the Tokugawa
period valued gold so highly that it regarded
wealth as the " pedigree of the *chōnin*." Although
the idea of making money was well developed
among these *chōnin*, they lacked either the enter-
prising spirit or the passion for new enterprises.
In a capitalist society that was ushered in after
the Restoration, therefore, they failed to take the
lead. It was the former low grade *samurai*, such
as Shibusawa and Iwasaki, who played the leading part in the new capitalist society. The conversion of Mitsui into modern capitalists was

due to the able presence of Minomura-Rizaemon, who was formerly a *samurai*, in their management. It would, however, be too hasty a conclusion to say that the *chōnin* class made no contribution to the Meiji Restoration. For, but for the wealth of *chōnin* which they could utilise, the *samurai* from Chōshū and other *han* would have been unable to achieve the stupendous task of the Meiji Restoration. It was by the help of the money supplied by *chōnin* — by Ōsaka *chōnin* especially — that the battles of Toba, Fushimi, Edo and Aizu could be fought by the Imperial Army. They also supplied funds to the Meiji Government and lent financial aid to note issues and other financial measures. Ōsaka was then the virtual treasury of the Government. Indeed, it was said that 70 per cent. of Japan's wealth was in Ōsaka. Such being the case, those who took an active part in the establishment of the Meiji Government acted very wisely in securing the financial aid of Ōsaka merchants. It is doubtful whether the Meiji Government could otherwise have been established so successfully.

The financial straits of the Government at the time of the Restoration were almost beyond imagination. The Government made rich merchants, shrines and temples in big cities contribute money so as to help it to tide over the pressing financial crisis. Donations (*goyōkin*) were often exacted from these rich men for putting the finances of the Government on a stable basis. It was not on a few millionaires only but on many others also that these contributions were levied. In the Government campaign for raising the State financial funds, for instance, 650 people were summoned to the local Government office on two occasions in Ōsaka alone and ordered to donate sums. The list of the donors shows that collections were made from many ordinary citizens as well as from millionaires. The *Dajōkan* notes and other notes also did much to maintain the national finance in the early days of Meiji. Recourse was had to these note issues when it was realised that the Government could not keep on collecting donations interminably and that this policy of raising funds became unworkable. These notes were, of course, inconvertible, and consequently their circulation was attended with great difficulties. Many devices were accordingly invented to put them into circulation. That the finances of the Meiji Government were maintained by the circulation of these inconvertible notes testifies, in a sense, to the financial strength of the people at large. At the same time, it must be noted that their circulation owed much to the credit and efforts of Mitsui and other millionaires who helped in the matter. The same thing may be said of the issue of notes in the closing days of the Shogunate. Thus viewed, it is obvious that the financial power of the *chōnin* class had a great deal to do with the consummation of the Meiji Restoration. It is nevertheless true to say

that the Meiji Government was supported by the
financial power of the public rather than by that
of a few millionaires exclusively.

On the other hand, in the economic world,
the currency economy had already been making
good progress, and, moreover, towards the end of
the Tokugawa Shogunate, new measures such as
have already been mentioned were adopted. The
new Meiji Government came into being just when
the Shogunate had by this means been making a
big volte-face in its policy, in order to meet the
requirements of the new age about to be born.
It too launched various economic enterprises to
cope with the needs of the times and introduced
Western material civilisation. This accounts for
the fact that the capitalist society which followed
the Meiji Restoration was built up not by the
chōnin class but by low grade *samurai* who seized
power in the Meiji Government.

The political transition from the Tokugawa
Shogunate to the Meiji régime did not deprive
the *samurai* class of political power. Power
simply passed from the upper grade to the lower
grade *samurai*. As the economic changes took
place in the circumstances already described,
moreover, the economic development subsequent
to the Restoration embodied nothing but the
gradual growth of the germ which had already
been in existence in the closing days of the
Tokugawa Shogunate. It is not correct to say
that all of the important economic measures

adopted by the Meiji Government were conceived
and carried out after the Restoration. This fact
deserves the attention of all students of the
nature of the reforms effected at the time of the
Restoration.

6. CONCLUSION

In short, the Tokugawa period was a time in
which there was a general tendency for all classes
to become *chōnin*-like. In order to cope with the
changes in economic life, measures were taken
in all quarters to encourage commercialisation.
Such measures became more pronounced as time
passed. The downfall of the Tokugawa Shogunate was partly due to these circumstances at
home and partly owing to the invasion of foreign
capitalism. This capitalism means after all the
development of the policy of commercialisation.
Such being the case, it may be said that the consummation of the Meiji Restoration and the subsequent economic developments denote the fruition
of this commercialisation policy.

The establishment of the Meiji Government
was, in so far as form is concerned, due to the
activity of lower grade *samurai*, and these *samurai* formed the nucleus of the new Government.
The money power of *chōnin* was, however, at the
back of their success. It was because they could
utilise the financial power of *chōnin* that they
could bring the new Government into being. The

money was not supplied by a few millionaires only ; it is more correct to say that the wealth of the people generally was mobilised. It is accordingly noteworthy that the new Meiji Government had the support of the people at large.

PART II

CHAPTER V

THE POPULATION AND ITS PROBLEMS
IN THE TOKUGAWA PERIOD

1. INCREASE OF THE POPULATION

In Japan, even in ancient times, there was an institution for registering the names of numbers of families (*koseki*). In the Taihō-ryō that institution was placed under more exact regulalations. Nevertheless, we cannot learn precisely the exact number of people at that time. In modern times, viz., the Tokugawa period, the number of people before the Kyōho era likewise remains unascertained.

The order to reckon up the population was given by Yoshimune, the eighth Shogun of the Tokugawa dynasty. The two edicts, which were issued in June of the sixth year (1721) and in February of the eleventh year of Kyōho (1726), are of the utmost importance with reference to the problem.

The decrees of the sixth year of Kyōho are as follows :

" Each village and the areas of fields or farms shall be reported on in each district (*kōri*, — a certain administrative area). The number of farmers, merchants, towns-people, shrine-priests, temple-priests, temple-priestesses and other people collected from every domain and fief shall be recorded. But the number of people, who are subordinate to the *samurai*, shall not be required to be recorded. . . ." (June 21st).

" Each village, the areas of fields and the number of people shall be recorded as already ordered. . . .

" The number of farmers, merchants, towns-people, shrine-priests, temple-priests, temple-priestesses and other people shall be recorded. But there is no need to investigate this actual period. The number, which has been already registered in the book, shall be reported. Of course care must be taken to avoid duplication and omission.

" The number of people, whether of this year or of last year, shall be reported with as much detail as possible, and it shall be stated to what year and what age the said number refers. The servants and subordinates, who are not required to be recorded, are those belonging to the *samurai* only. . . ." (June 29th).

The decree of the eleventh year of Kyōho is

as follows :

"As already reported in the sixth year, the farmers, merchants, towns-people, shrine-priests, temple-priests, temple-priestesses and other people shall be fully recorded this year. The whole number in each district shall be given, and recorded from each domain and fief. This time there is no need to report on the area of fields and farms. Only the number of people shall be recorded during the period from April to November. Of course the report must show the month of registration and give the ages. The servants and subordinates, who belong to the *samurai*, shall not be required to be reported.

"Hereafter, even though there were no instructions, in each sixth year (*ne* and *uma* year in the twelve zodiacal signs) the examination and report must be undertaken." (February)

In the earlier decree, there was no order to examine the population and to report the number obtained from this examination. The number reported was only the registered number, which was already known to the officers at that time. But in the later decree, an examination and an actual counting of the people were evidently ordered. Therefore, the former must be the first instance where merely the registered number was reported, and the latter the first instance where the actual number was ascertained.

I may assert that there is one more difference: in the former decree, we find the following words:

"The number of people, whether of this year or of last year, is to be reported with as much detail as possible." Therefore, the number of people reported in the sixth year of Kyōho — failing any evidence to the contrary — consists not only of those of the sixth year exclusively, but also of those of another year. In other words, that number shows merely that of about the sixth year of Kyōho. But the number reported in the eleventh year is the exact number of that year only. Therefore, the opinion that the number 26,065,425, which was reported in accordance with the decree of the sixth year of Kyōho, shows the population of the sixth year of Kyōho is also incorrect.

From these two differences, we can easily understand the number in the eleventh year to be more exact than that of the sixth year; therefore, as our basis, we must take the latter one.

The reckoning of the number of people was carried out every sixth year after the eleventh year of Kyōho. It has been said that this sexennial period was established by our ancient institutions.

In order to know the methods and limits of the examination, we must quote the decrees which were issued in the third year of Kan'en (1750) and the first year of Bunka (1804). These decrees were in almost similar terms.

"The number of people, in the Tokugawa domain must be examined this year by the *daikan* (Governor), in the fief by the lord; from Spring to November, the numbers shall be reported from every province, and in December they shall be collected in each separate book.

"The number of people, who are below fifteen years of age shall be determined according to the previous examinations of each *daimyō*. Therefore, there are some differences in the examined age.

"The number of people, who dwell in the privileged lands, such as *goshuinchi* and the domains of privileged shrines and temples, shall be included in the number of those provinces.

"The number of people, who dwell in the cities, exempt from land tax, such as Edo, Sumpu, Kyōto, Ōsaka, Nara, Sakai, Fushimi, Ōtsu, Nagasaki and other fortress-towns, shall not be omitted from the totals of those provinces.

"Hereafter, even though there were no instruction, the examination and the report must be undertaken every sixth year.

"The servants and the subordinates belonging to the *samurai* shall not be calculated in the number of the people."

If we compare these decrees with that of the eleventh year of Kyōho, we can easily understand the methods and limits of the examination of the population to be as follows:

(1) The Period. As already mentioned, the period of the calculation was every sixth year. But it was not decided in what month it was to be carried out. In some domains it was held in Spring, but in others in another season. From

this fact, the figures did not show the actual number of population at any fixed date, but the round number of the year only.

(2) The Personal Limits. The examination did not comprise the whole people at that time. There were many people outside the examination; namely, on the one hand, the court nobles (peers: —*kuge*), the *samurai* and their subordinates, on the other, the *eta* and the *hinin*, who were not recognised as ordinary persons. Again, those below fifteen years of age could be omitted or counted at the option of each *daimyō*. So the limit was not uniform in the fiefs; in some fiefs were calculated those over one year of age (Shimazu, Date, Tōdō, etc.), in other fiefs those over two years (Ikeda, Hachisuga, etc.) and in the third those over fifteen years (Maeda, etc.). Of course, anyone outside the register of domicile, was left uncalculated.

Why were the *samurai* and their subordinates not calculated? What was the reason for this? One, who thinks that the object of the examination was to adjust the finance, might say it was because the *samurai* and their subordinates were not taxed.[1] But this opinion, I think, is not to the point. In the feudal age, it was always the custom to conceal the numbers of soldiers and their subordinates; thus the actual power of the

---

[1]   Droppers, G., The Population of Japan in the Tokugawa Period (Transactions of the Asiatic Society of Japan, vol. XXII.) p. 260 footnote.

feudal lord was kept secret from other lords. This was the main reason for excluding the number of the *samurai* and their subordinates.

(3) The Local Limits. The examination was held throughout the whole of Japan. But it was usually recognised that the examination was not carried out in the two countries, the Loochoo Islands and Ezo (Hokkaidō). I think these local limits were not always the same. In some cases the numbers of the people in Ezo were evidently examined, — such as in the third year of Kan'en (1750), the first year of Bunka (1804) and the third year of Kōka (1846). In short, we must conclude that the common opinion is not correct as far as Ezo is concerned.

(4) The Process of Examination. The exact and progressive methods now being used in taking the census in civilised countries, were not adopted at that time. The number of the people was calculated from the register-book (*koseki* or *nimbetsu-chō*); or to put it in detail: in every village, town and county the numbers of the people and houses were calculated by the *nimbetsu-chō*, and another book was made up which specified the increase and decrease as against the last time of examination (*ninzü-Zōgen-kakiage-chō*). These two calculations were presented to the central office.

It is not clear whether the process of the examination was strict or not. A famous writer Nakai-Chikuzan says in his great work ' *Sōbō Kigen* ' :

" At the time when the religious registration
was carried out the temple-priests were treated
as if they were register-officers, and it was on
the basis of this registration that the register-
books were complied in towns and in villages,
without actual examination; all was left to the
temple-priests. . . . In the city the temple-site
was very near the houses of the people, but the
priests did not always visit their parishioners,
therefore they could not know how many people
there were in the family.   Accepting the state-
ments of the rich families, they gave the certificates, and the headman in the towns or villages
always trusted them without an examination.
Therefore many mistakes occurred, for instance,
the actual person was not alive, but his name
remained on the register, and sometimes, on
the contrary, the actual person was alive, but
his name was not given: one who came up to
a town had received the certificate from a
temple in his native village and he was also
named in the register of the town; he was calculated as two persons.   The certificates of the
servants were received by the employer and
treated as if of the same sect as he,— in this
case one person was calculated as two persons
and sometimes one person was regarded as
having two sects.   Thus there were a great
deal of complications.   The register-books were
drawn up, without examination, simply from
the certificate.   I dare say there may have

been an excess of two or three thousands in ten thousand of people."

Another writer,[2] of an exactly opposite opinion, has said on the strength of the facts at the Okayama-Han, as follows:

"In modern times, the examination of the number of the people and families was held strictly in accordance with the regulations of each province. In my native country Bizen (Okayama-Han) each temple gave the certificate. But the numbers of the persons and families were examined actually once a year by the headman. Those who lived in other provinces were excluded from the calculation. The process of the examination was as follows: In a town, on a certain date, all the members of the family gathered in certain place in the house. The headman and other officers examined them, comparing them with the register-book. There was no duplication or omission. In a village, the process was also similar. The temple-priests only attested with their signatures the documents presented by the family or the headman. They never took part in the compilation of the register-book. I think that in many other fiefs we could also trace the same circumstances and it was only in a great city that all was left to the temple-priests."

In short, the examination of the people at

[2] Jin-Ikō, 'Sōbō Kigen Tekigi'.

that time was very defective. The whole number of people was left uncertain; the personal
and local limits were not the same every year;
the process also was imperfect. From these facts,
we can say that this examination was inexact,
but it was not merely supposition or guess-work;
it had a reasonable basis. Therefore we must
not ignore this calculation in order to know the
population of the Tokugawa period.

The following table gives the figures for the
population practically calculated every sixth year
from the sixth year of Kyōho (1721) onwards:

Year	Males	Females	Total	Index Number
Kyōho 6 (1721)	—	—	26,065,425	98.17
,, 11 (1726)	—	—	26,548,998	100.00
,, 17 (1732)	14,407,107	12,514,709	26,921,816	101.02
Enkyō 1 (1744)	—	—	26,153,450	98.51
Kan'en 3 (1750)	13,818,654	12,099,176	25,917,830	97.24
Hōreki 6 (1756)	13,833,311	12,228,919	26,061,830	98.16
,, 12 (1762)	13,785,400	12,136,058	25,921,458	97.25
Meiwa 5 (1768)	—	—	26,252,057	98.88
An'ei 3 (1774)	—	—	25,990,451	97.51
,, 9 (1780)	—	—	26,010,600	97.57
Temmei 6 (1786)	—	—	25,086,466	94.49
Kansei 4 (1792)	—	—	24,891,441	93.71
,, 10 (1798)	—	—	25,471,033	95.93
Bunka 1 (1804)	—	—	25,517,729	96.11
,, 13 (1816)	13,427,249	12,194,708	25,621,957	96.50
Bunsei 11 (1828)	14,160,736	13,040,064	27,201,400	102.45
Tempo 5 (1834)	—	—	27,063,907	101.93
Kōka 3 (1846)	13,854,043	13,053,582	26,907,625	101.35

As already mentioned, these figures do not include the number of the court nobles, the *samurai*, their subordinates, the *eta*, the *hinin*, and those outside the register of domiciles. Sometimes the populations of Ezo and the Loochoo Islands were also omitted and those below fifteen years of age were calculated or omitted at the option of each *daimyō*. Of course the method of examination was inexact. There would be a great deal of omission and duplication. I think it very likely that the actual number of the pupulation would exceed the figures given. If so what number must be added to the total? Many learned men have endeavoured to give the closest approximation to the total population of Japan in those days. From the fact that the number of people in the Loochoo Islands, Hokkaidō, and the court nobles, the *samurai*, their subordinates, the *eta* and the *hinin* at the beginning of the Meiji era was about 2,620,000. Mr. Komiyama has added this figure to the number in the fifth year of Tempo and has estimated the whole number of the population at the time of Tempo to be about 29,680,000: he has disregarded the number of persons outside the register of domicile, because there is no method of calculating such persons.

Mr. Droppers says as follows:

" Count Katsu, an excellent authority, puts the number of *samurai* at 350,000, and the average number of servants to each as three. Thus the whole number of servants omitted would be not far from 1,050,000, and we may consider this figure as approximately correct. Again, the same authority states that there were only two *daimyō*, who omitted the children under fifteen from the census. One of them was Matsudaira-Kaga-no-Kami, whose domain consisted of Kaga, Noto, Etchū, and part of Ōmi. His subjects numbered 576,734, and as we know that children under fifteen years of age in Japan are about 30 per cent. of the whole population, the number omitted must have been about 240,000. The other exception was Matsudaira-Ōi-no-Kami, *daimyō* of Bizen. His subjects numbered 396,500. He omitted all the children under two years of age, and if we take these to be equal to about 5 per cent. of the population, the number omitted cannot be far from 20,000. Some writers, moreover, add that the *eta* and *hinin* classes were also omitted from this enumeration, but on this point authorities conflict. We are therefore in doubt at to the precise number of the population that were not counted. But as the number omitted was a fairly fixed proportion of the number rendered, the mistake cannot be serious. The object of this paper is not as much to get the absolute population of the Tokugawa period, as the relative growth or decrease from year to year. As the omissions, whatever they were, were uniform, the number given in the government register must be considered on the whole prefect for my purpose. To this number Count Katsu would add 1,860,000,[3] a number which I consider too small. It would be much nearer the truth to double this figure, say 3,720,000, and add it to the number returned in the registers. For those who are interested in discovering the precise population of Japan in the Tokugawa period, it is clearly necessary to add from two millions to three millions and a half to the official figures, but as already stated, it is unimportant for the purpose of this paper."[4]

All these theories are only guesswork; there are still many omissions. Let us consider first Mr. Komiyama's theory; as above mentioned, he has already added the number of five classes, but we must add also the number of children under fifteen years of age who have been omitted. Secondly, the numbers of court nobles, the *eta* and the *hinin* are still omitted in Count Katsu's account. Not only in Kaga and Bizen, but also in Awa (Matsudaira-Awaji-no-Kami) the number of children over two years of age was merely calculated, and I am afraid such examples may be found in other fiefs also. Finally, Mr. Droppers in his enumeration, without any good reason,

---

[3] According to Count Katsu's calculation, 1,660,000 must be added ; while Mr. Droppers putting the number at 1,860,000, the total came to 3,720,000 instead of 3,320,000.

[4] Droppers, ibid., pp. 261–262.

considers that Count Katsu's estimate is too small
and that he must double it. There is, however,
no method of correcting the omissions and dupli-
cations which occurred through the defectiveness
of the process of reckoning. Therefore at the
present time it is surely impossible to estimate
the exact number of that distant period. We
must content ourselves with round figures from
the theories which already prevailed. I dare say
that we should add two or three millions to the
calculated number, that is to say, the population
in the latter half of the Tokugawa period was
perhaps in round figures, from 28,000,000 to
30,000,000.

What was the rate of increase and decrease?
If we take the number in the eleventh year of
Kyōho as the standard number, only in four examined years we find an increase of population :
—viz., the seventeenth year of Kyōho (1732), the
eleventh year of Bunsei (1828), the fifth year of
Tempo (1834) and the third year of Kōka (1846).
Now, if we take the number in the eleventh year
of Bunsei, which showed the largest total of the
period, and compare it with that of the eleventh
year of Kyōho, we find an increase of only 652,-
402 persons in 102 years, so the ratio of increase
was only 0.24$^{0}/_{00}$ in a year. Bearing this rate of
increase in mind we may say generally that the
population in the latter half of the period, was
almost stationary, not showing a rapid increase
as at present.

Then, what are the circumstances in the former half? We can not know the number of the whole people in that half, because no examination had been made at that time.

Shogun Yoshimune, taking much interest in the increase of the people after the report of the number in the sixth year of Kyōho, for purposes of comparison, ordered the ten great *daimyō*, whose fiefs gained more than 100,000 *koku* a year, and had not changed their domains for over 80 years, to submit reports on the number of people in their dominions 70 or 80 years before. These reports were sent in by nine *daimyō*[5] and are summed up in the next table.

By this table we can see that only in one case was the population diminished. In all other cases, the number had increased. The ratio of increase however is very different and we can not infer the whole population of Japan at that time from these few cases, but if we set aside the actual number given above and dwell upon the marked tendency, we dare say that in the former half of the period the ratio of increase was greater than in the latter half, and also that in these examples of the nine *daimyō*, the ratio in the earlier period was greater than in the latter.

From these observations, I think it is not unreasonable to state that the population in the

---

[5] No report was received from one *daimyō* Sakai-Sanuki-no-Kami. In this fief, the population was calculated every year, but documents were not preserved.

Daimyō	Fief and Annual Yield	Year Examina-
Matsudaira-Kaga-no-Kami (Maeda)	Kaga, Etchū, Noto and Ōmi More than 1,020,000 *koku*	Kyōho "
Matsudaira-Mutsu-no-Kami (Date)	Mutsu, Hidachi, Shimōsa and Ōmi More than 620,000 *koku*	Genroku " Kyōho
Matsudaira-Ōsumi-no-Kami (Shimazu)	Ōsumi, Satsuma and Hyūga More than 600,000 *koku*	Genroku Kyōho
Matsudaira-Ōi-no-Kami (Ikeda)	Bizen, Bitchū More than 340,000 *koku*	Jōkyō Hōei Kyōho
Tōdō-Daigaku-no-Kami	Iga, Ise, Yamashiro, Yamato and Shimōsa More than 320,000 *koku*	Kambun Genroku Kyōho
Matsudaira-Awaji-no-Kami (Hachisuga)	Awaji and Awa More than 250,000 *koku*	Kambun Genroku Kyōho
Sakai-Saemon-no-jō	Dewa More than 140,000 *koku*	Genroku Kyōho
Niwa-Sakyō-Daibu	Mutsu More than 100,000 *koku*	Jōkyō Genroku Kyōho
Nambu-Shuri-Daibu	Mutsu More than 100,000 *koku*	Kambun Genroku Kyōho

of tion	Age Examined	Popula- tion	Increase $\triangle$ Decrease	Ratio of Increase in a Year $^0/_{00}$
5 (1720)	Over 15	551,754		
17 (1732)	,, ,,	576,734	24,980 in 12 years	3.77
3 (1690)	Over 1	599,241		
15 (1702)	,, ,,	617,323	18,082 in 12 years	2.51
17 (1732)	,, ,,	647,427	30,104 ,, 30 ,,	1.62
11 (1698)	Over 1	260,961		
17 (1732)	,, ,,	339,955	78,994 in 34 years	15.66
3 (1686)	Over 2	185,043		
3 (1706)	,, ,,	207,215	22,172 in 20 years	5.34
17 (1732)	,, ,,	223,959	16,740 ,, 26 ,,	2.87
5 (1665)	Over 1	252,061		
3 (1690)	,, ,,	284,126	32,065 in 25 years	4.52
17 (1732)	,, . ,,	287,242	3,116 ,, 42 ,,	0.26
5 (1665)	Over 2	308,880		
1 (1688)	,, ,,	385,751	76,863 in 23 years	10.82
17 (1732)	,, ,,	470,512	84,761 ,, 44 ,,	4.98
7 (1694)	Over 1	126,383		
17 (1732)	,, ,,	131,164	4,781 in 38 years	0.97
11 (1685)	Over 1	73,351		
15 (1702)	,, ,,	76,130	2,779 in 17 years	2.14
17 (1732)	,, ,,	70,614	$\triangle$5,516 ,, 30 ,,	—
9 (1669)	Over 1	245,635		
16 (1703)	,, ,,	306,142	60,507 in 34 years	5.81
17 (1732)	,, ,,	322,109	15,967 ,, 29 ,,	1.70

former half of the Tokugawa period probably increased fairly rapidly.

We may therefore conclude that, though the population in the latter half was almost stationary, in the former half it showed a fair increase.

We admit the existence of such a difference. Therefore, as a matter of course, we must investigate the reason why such a difference occurred. The period of the Tokugawa régime was distinguished for its peaceful character. For several hundred years previously, Japan had been the theatre of civil wars and tumults. In such an age, horrible warfare raged and swayed hither and thither. Blood ran in streams and corpses lay in heaps. Thousands of the strongest and most efficient men went to battle, setting their lives at naught for the sake of loyalty to their lords. Not only the surplus population, but even the necessary and effective members of the nation were killed off either directly or indirectly by wars. At such periods we can never expect any marked increase in the population.

But the Tokugawa régime, after this time of war, took hold with the strong hand, and restored the whole land to order, and peace reigned for about two and a half centuries, a matter of rare occurrence in the history of the world. War became then scarcely more than a memory, and armour, weapons and military organisations were retained only by means of an elaborate etiquette. At such a time, the people were well content,

since their days were filled with peace and they
had ample leisure to cultivate the industrial and
other arts, and to develop the wealth of the
country. We cannot, therefore, be surprised at
the increase of the population under such circumstances. This is the reason why the increase
was fairly rapid in the former half of the Tokugawa period. Of course this is not the only example of such an increase in the world. There
are many such examples of populations increasing
rapidly in peace-time after wars, and many scholars also have recognised this fact.[6]

The development of industry and the increase
of population mentioned above, could not make further progress after attaining a certain limit. Why?

At home after enjoying an excess of the bless-
ings of peace, several evils made their appearance :
ease and absence of progress in general characterised society, people lived in idleness and luxury,
the agricultural districts were in an exhausted
condition, commerce and industry, in which many
guilds were organised, relied too much upon their
privileges : therefore there was not enough competition, no endeavour to progress, and in particular no great manufacturing industry to ab-
sorb many workers. In such conditions life was
difficult.

As regards international relations, our country
was almost wholly closed to foreigners from the

---

[6] Mayo-Smith, ' Statistics and Sociology,' 1910, p. 73. Droppers, ibid., p. 262.

reign of the third Shogun Iemitsu. The few Dutch and Chinese, who engaged in trade, were strictly confined to particular places. No outlet existed in the shape of foreign emigration for the increase of population. No foreign trade was permitted to give scope to new forms of industry, or to stimulate activities for which the country had peculiar advantages. Cut off from all foreign intercourse, Japan did not even suspect the existence of a more progressive civilisation.

These conditions at home and abroad, kept the population from increasing beyond a certain limit.

In addition to this general tendency, famines, epidemics and other visitations were frequently reported from several quarters of the country. A great many lives were lost by these calamities. The heavy burden of taxation, the influence of exaggerated ideas of thrift and diligence, and the struggle for life : all this made the people shrink from an increase of population. Moreover, the frightful practices of abortion and infanticide were almost universal. These so-called preventive and positive checks interrupted the increase of the population, and these are the reasons why the population did not increase in the latter half of that period.[7]

---

[7] Mr. Droppers enumerates many other checks. He says : a) "Beside famines there were other calamities. . . . Among others we may mention earthquakes, fires, floods and epidemics " (p. 265). (b) " Sumptuary laws of this kind, I believe, must have had an effect upon the growth of population. They must have tended to stop marriages and all kinds of festivities " (p. 277).

Of course, we must admit that even in the former half of the period there were famines, epidemics, natural calamities and the practice of abortion and infanticide. But the influence of these checks upon the population is very different in a society which has a tendency to increase rapidly and in another where it is already impossible to feed more than a certain number of people.

The abhorrent practices of abortion and infanticide infected the whole land in consequence of the fiercer struggle for existence in the latter period; and the three great famines of that time occurred also in the latter half. We may venture to say that these catastrophes and customs severely checked the increase of popula-

---

(c) " The severity of punishment during the Tokugawa era was at least a minor check to the growth of population " (p. 280). (d) " In many parts of Japan, notably Satsuma and other parts of Kyūshū, a *samurai* never married before the age of thirty, and it was considered degrading to have a family of more than three children. . . . The doctrines of Confucius taught that the sexes ought to be separated early in life. . . . The same rule extended to the richer class of farmers and merchants, who accepted the doctrines of Confucianism instead of Buddhism " (p. 280). (e) " One other cause which may have helped to retard the growth of population was the practice of pederasty. It existed chiefly in the south-western parts of the Empire " (p. 281). (f) " Certainly during the last century of the Tokugawa régime sexual morality was at a very low ebb in Japan, at least in the large cities. Prostitution was practised far more openly and widely than it is at the present time " (p. 284). It is very doubtful whether these causes were so powerful that they had a great effect upon the birth and death rate of that time. They can not have been so powerful as famines and epidemics. In any case I think the question is open to discussion.

tion in the latter half of that period.

Some words must be added here about famines. The influence of a famine has more effect on the increase of population than that of the other checks already mentioned. In the lean years, there is not only the heavy death-rate which is directly accounted for by starvation and the plague due to it, that is, after a famine, the economic circumstances of the people become worse, the strength of the human body is exhausted, goods and resources run low. The people can not recover their former life. Therefore, the rate of increase in the population is very slow.

Let us compare famines with epidemics. The influence of the latter is only temporary. After the epidemic is stamped out, on the one hand many strong people survive, and on the other, materials are more abandant than before, being inversely proportional to the decrease of the population. Owing to the scarcity of labour, wages rise. Generally the economic condition becomes good. The population recovers very quickly. But in the case of famine, the circumstances are different. There is not only a heavy death-rate but famine also exerts a permanent weakening influence upon the population.

These are not theories merely, but in the actual number of the people of the Tokugawa period, we can distinguish these facts clearly. For example, the number of the population in the sixth year of Temmei (1786) was 920,000 less than that of the nineth year of An'ei (1780), and the number in the fourth year of Kansei (1792) was less by 200,000 in comparison with that of the sixth year of Temmei (1786). In these two cases the decrease amounted to about 1,100,000. This marked decrease was due to the great famine from the third to the seventh year of Temmei (1783–87). In the tenth year of Kansei (1798) the number of the population exceeded that of the sixth year of Temmei (1786), but was less than that of the nineth year of An'ei (1780). The decrease in the first year of Enkyō (1744) was due to the famine of the seventeenth and eighteenth years of Kyōho (1732–33) in the western provinces. The number of the third year of Kōka (1846) was less than that of the fifth year of Tempo (1834). This shows that the diminished population had not yet recovered from the famine of the seventh and eighth years of Tempo (1836–37).

From what has been already said, it will be seen how terrible is the influence of famine, directly and indirectly, on the population. The effects of famine in diminishing and weakening the population were greater than those of epidemics and of all other so-called positive checks combined.

The above observations are in regard to fluctuations in the population of Japan, as a whole, and it must be noted that somewhat different circumstances obtained in respect of

different provinces and districts. In some provinces, an increase was recorded even after the
Kyōho era (see Note 1). This increase was due
not only to the general causes already described,
but in no small measure, to the movements of
the people from one district to another. As for
those migrators or seasonal labourers (see Note 2),
who made periodical visits to other places in
quest of work, they did not affect the sum total
of the population of any particular district, but
with regard to those who left their native provinces for good in order to settle down in other
provinces, their migrations, needless to say, reduced the population of their native provinces.
These deserters mustered in prosperous cities
such as Edo (now Tōkyō), Kyōto and Ōsaka,
where they worked either as day-labourers or as
servants. The abandonment of the plough by
these people led to the impoverishment of agricultural villages ; while, on the other hand, the
population of big cities — Edo in particular — witnessed an enormous increase by their influx, as
was pointed out by many scholars at the time.

Note 1. In the leap-month April of the ninth year of
Tempo (1838), the *kanjō-bugyō* (a magistrate in the days of the
Tokugawa Shogunate), acting under instructions from Lord
Mizuno-Echizen-no-Kami, addressed inquiries to the *gundai* and
daikan as to the increases or decreases of the populations
within their respective jurisdictions. The reports submitted by
these officials in reply to these inquiries throw some light on
fluctuations in the number of inhabitants in various districts.
I quote below a few reports out of many :

(a) Teranishi-Kurata, the *gundai* of the Saikoku district, reported that in the district under his jurisdiction, namely, Buzen, Bungo, Hyūga and Chikuzen provinces, where rice was produced to the quantity of 117,000 odd *koku*, there was an increase exceeding 8,400 in the population as compared with that of the first year of Kansei (1789).

(b) Soeda-Ichirōji, a *daikan*, reported that the region under his jurisdiction, consisting of 194 villages of Settsu, Kawachi and Harima provinces, where the production of rice exceeded 67,200 *koku*, there was a decrease of a little more than 70 a year on an average during the ten years between the ninth year of Bunsei (1826) and the sixth year of Tempo (1835). In 108 villages of Ōshū and Hidachi provinces, where rice was produced exceeding 58,600 *koku* per annum, there was a decrease of some 310 persons a year on an average during the ten years between the fifth year of Bunsei (1822) and the second year of Tempo (1831). In 91 villages of Dewa province with a rice yield of 69,900 *koku*, a yearly decrease of 230 on an average was recorded during the ten years between the eleventh year of Bunsei (1828) and the eighth year of Tempo (1837).

(c) Ōi-Tatewaki, the *gundai* of Hida province, reported that in his province there had occurred an increase of some eight or nine thousand in population as compared with the Kyōho era (1716–1735). In Echizen and Mino provinces, however, there was a marked decrease in population as compared with the Kyōho era.

(d) Matsuzaka-Saburōzaemon, a *daikan*, reported that in Echigo province which was a fief of 56,000 *koku* of rice, and over which he had jurisdiction, there was a decrease of more than 600 in population during the ten years between the eleventh year of Bunsei (1828) and the eighth year of Tempo (1837), but that there was no tract of land which was allowed to go waste because of a shortage of farm hands.

(e) Kobayashi-Tōnosuke, a *daikan*, who had two hundred villages of Yashiro and Koma districts of Kai province under his jurisdiction, a fief of 56,600 *koku* of rice, said in his report that the houses in these villages totalled some 19,100 with a population of 87,600 in the eighth year of Tempo (1837), which showed an increase of about 2,900 in the number of houses and of 11,700 in population.

(f) Nomura-Hikoemon, a *daikan*, in his report said that there had been a gradual decrease in population in Shimozuke, Hidachi, Shimōsa and Mutsu provinces.

Note 2. In the case of seasonal labourers who migrated from Echigo and Shinano to Edo and other cities, and from Tango and Tajima to Kyōto and Ōsaka, they usually left their villages in October and returned home in March of the following year. This migration was due to the lack of occupation at home in winter. If some of these seasonal labourers remained in the cities whither they had gone in quest of temporary work, it was because they found life in such cities much easier, and not because they had any positive reasons for the desertion of their native villages.

2. THE RUSH OF PEOPLE INTO BIG CITIES

The population of Japan in the Tokugawa period was in the state as already described, and in those days the rush of people into big cities and birth control formed two most important phases of the population problem.

Let me, first, deal with the concentration of people in urban districts. Some farmers in those days abandoned the plough and went to big cities, where they became either tradesmen or day-labourers. This naturally led to an increase in the population of these cities. The farmers of those days were treated as though they were machines for producing taxes, and their lot was a very hard one.[8] It was quite natural that

---

[8] cf. Chap. VIII.

there should have been a big influx of people into towns when farmers, who were leading a miserable life, found life in towns free and easy. The fact is generally admitted that the expansion of big cities — Edo in particular — was due largely to the influx of the people of other regions into them. As far back as the Kyōho era (1716–1735), town life was in a state of good development. Ogyū-Sorai, a famous scholar, in one of his books, says: "There has been a daily increase in the number of peasants, who, after coming to Edo to find temporary work as servants, decided to settle down permanently here either as day-labourers or as hawkers, with the result that the city has expanded to the extent of five *ri* (12.5 miles) with a great density of houses." In a memorial submitted to the authorities in the seventh year of Temmei (1787), Uezaki-Kuhachirō said: "There has lately been a tendency among the farmers to show indifference to their agricultural pursuits and contract luxurious habits. In the case of farmers in easy circumstances, they leave the tillage of the soil to their servants, wear fine clothes and indulge in citified pleasures and amusements. When once they visit Edo, they become dazzled by the bustle and splendour of the metropolis and their mode of life becomes more and more depraved. Many small farmers also regard farm work as drudgery and develop and inclination to leave their villages. So far as girls are concerned, their parents send them out to domestic service in Edo, in order to satisfy their wish to see Edo and the life there. At first, these girls sigh for their homes and tearfully regret that they had ever been engaged to work in a strange city, but they soon come to imitate the manners of the Edo people and to detest life in their own native provinces. The example find many followers and all vie with one another in despatching their daughters to Edo. Thus, there is a steady increase in the number of people who prefer life in Edo to that in their native provinces. The result is that farm work is largely abandoned and the supply of rice falls off. As no restrictions are put on the free emigration of people to Edo, the city finally be turned into a reservoir of the population from all parts of the country. Although it may appear at first sight that the prosperity of the city increases with the increase of its population, serious consequences may gradually arise because of the abandonment of agriculture, the mainstay of the country, by many people in favour of pursuits of lesser importance (commerce and industry were in those days regarded as of secondary importance), as the rice fields run waste and the roads in the provinces fall into disrepair." In the ' Seji Kem-monroku,' a book written in the thirteenth year of Bunka (1816) also, the eagerness with which people sought city life is described at length, and the writer makes the remark: " In the provinces, the population falls off, but hardships remain; while in the prosperous cities, new hardships are created by the increase of their inhabitants."

What measures, then, did the Shogunate adopt to meet this concentration of people in urban districts? In the days prior to the establishment of the Tokugawa Shogunate, restrictions were often set on the freedom of movement on the part of farmers, and these restrictions were enforced more rigidly in the Tokugawa Shogunate. Under that régime, all feudal lords jealously kept their fiefs and with a view to maintaining their military strength on an efficient basis, to keeping the conditions prevailing in their own fiefs from being made known to those outside their fiefs, to preserving peace and order within their own feudal domains or to increasing tax revenues, ruthless restrictions were put on the outgoings of *samurai*, farmers and *chōnin*, and on the incoming of deserters, *rōnin* (lordless *samurai*) and questionable characters. In August of the twentieth year of Kan'ei (1643), the Shogunate issued orders to all villages that those who came on the parish by neglecting their farm work or those farmers who left their native places to settle down elsewhere should receive condign punishment. Notwithstanding this, there was a remarkable increase, from the middle period of the Shogunate and downwards, in the number of people who, abandoning the plough, went to live in cities, resulting, as before, in the decrease of the population of the provinces and in the waste of arable land. This state of things excited much comment and discussion among the scholars of the day. In May of the sixth year of An'ei (1777), further restrictions were enforced on the number of people going out of their own provinces in search of work and service, and on the period of their service in other provinces. Shortly afterwards, the disastrous famine of the Temmei era overtook Japan, and there was a marked decrease in the population of Mutsu, Hidachi and Shimozuke provinces. This led to prohibitory orders being issued in these provinces in December of the eighth year of Temmei (1788) against the outgoing of inhabitants in quest of work, permission being given only in cases where their going out to Edo did not cause a decrease in the population of their villages or where it did not interfere with farm work. In such cases, they had to get written certificates from the *daikan* or the *jitō*. Not only was the outflow of people prohibited in this way but the return of migrators to their agricultural pursuits was encouraged. In the second year of Kansei (1790), the policy was framed for encouraging the general return of local people working in Edo again to take up farm work in their native places. This policy was not, however, very successful, as can be inferred from an order issued in the leap-month April of the ninth year of Tempo (1838) in which it was mentioned that the earnest endeavours made by the Shogunate at heavy cost since the Kansei era to encourage the return of provincial people working in Edo to the agronomy of their earlier days could not arrest the decrease of the population in the provinces near Edo, where the areas of waste lands increased, while the population of Edo was steadily on the increase.

The above-mentioned policy of encouraging the return of those who had once evaded the strenuous life on a farm to take up again their pristine existence was chiefly prompted by apprehension lest the farm villages should be improverished by the desertion of farm work by many people. In the Reform of the Tempo era, which was carried out by Mizuno-Echizen-no-Kami, who modelled after the administration of the Kansei era by Matsudaira-Rakuō, however, a similar policy framed and pursued by him had another object in view, namely, to reduce the population of Edo. The Order, issued in March of the fourteenth year of Tempo (1843), prohibited the migration of provincial people to Edo. Even those who were actually in Edo at the time this Order was issued, were forced to return to their respective homes, except those who had been carrying on their trades in that city for many years and had their families and relatives to support. As to those farmers who went to Edo in quest of temporary employment, they were allowed to stay there only for a limited period, and on the expiry of this term they were compelled to return to their village work in their respective localities. A strict control was also exercised over those, such as Buddhist or Shintō priests, fortune-tellers, pilgrims, etc., who travelled from province to province. By these means the authorities tried to check any diminution in the population of farm villages, by way of encouraging agriculture, but their policy was evidently a failure, though it had the effect of reducing the number of migrators for a time. The following figures show that although there was some decrease in the number of migrators to Edo, there was practically no decrease in the population of Edo:

	Apr., Tempo 13 (1842)	July, Tempo 14 (1843)	Sept., Tempo 14 (1843)	Apr., Kōka 1 (1844)
Total of the towns-people in the quarters under the jurisdiction of city officials and those in the precincts of temples and shrines.	551,063	553,257	547,952	559,497
Migrators.	—	34,201	29,745	24,092

In short, the policy followed by the Shogunate for checking the concentration of people in cities, which was negative at first, assumed a positive character in the end. At first, it confined itself to affording facilities to those who desired to return to their native provinces, but afterwards, or, to be more exact, in the fourteenth year of Tempo (1843), it adopted the positive policy of forcing the return of migrators to their respective homes, enforcing rigorous measures of control in other directions also. Neither policy yielded the desired result, however. In the '*Tamakushige Beppon*,' written by Motoori-Norinaga, the author rightly remarks: "In all villages there has been a gradual decrease in the number of households, the fields have been left to go waste, and the poverty of the villagers increased. In some provinces, regulation have been enacted strictly prohibiting farmers from leaving their villages, but these prohibitory regulations do not work well, as they are tantamount to attempting to purify a stream which is muddy at the source."

3. POPULATION CONTROL

Another point worthy of special note in connection with the population question is that the evil practice of abortion and infanticide prevailed almost everywhere in the country in those days. The big cities of Edo, Kyōto and Ōsaka were no exceptions to the rule, though in Ōu provinces, Kazusa, Shimōsa, Kōzuke, Shimozuke, Hidachi, Tosa, Kyūshū provinces and other rural districts it was particularly rife. Either drugs were used or medical treatment was obtained to effect abortions, or new-born babies were stifled to death. This infanticide was called *mabiku*, or *kaesu* or *modosu* in those days. *Mabiku* means thinning. People of those days thought on more seriously of infanticide than of rooting out vegetables or herbs.

Satō-Nobuhiro says: " Many women become pregnant, but they can not nurse their children. They murder their babies or procure abortion. By travelling around our country, I know this custom prevails. It is a very terrible fact that in a village consisting of ten houses, every year over two babies are killed." " This custom is most prevalent in the provinces of Ōu and Kantō. In Chūgoku, Shikoku and Kyūshū abortion is universal. Even in the provinces of Dewa and Ōshū alone every year about sixteen or seventeen thousand babies are killed. But no one is startled by this deplorable custom."

In a memorial submitted by Ro-Tōzan, of the Sendai-Han, to the Shogunate authorities, (about 1754) the following remarks were made: " Up to fifty or sixty years ago a couple of farmers used to bring up five or six or even seven or eight children, but in recent years it has become a fashion among the farmers not to rear more than one or two children between a couple, though it is not clear whether this is due to the luxurious habits that prevail among them or some other causes. As soon as a baby is born, its parents put it to death. All this is ascribable to their poverty. They prefer leading as best a life as they can without encumbrances to bringing up many children to hunger and penury, and restrict the number of their children to two or three. Even rich families are contaminated by this evil custom, and deliberately restrict the number of their children. In my opinion, the prevalence of this usage is partly responsible for the waste of agricultural fields." In the fourth year of Meiwa (1767) an official order was issued prohibiting such evil practices. The official order said in part : "We understand that in some provinces farmers who have already many children put to death new-born babies immediately after their birth. This is a very inhuman act. Village officials must see that no such crime is committed in their villages, while farmers themselves should keep watch upon one another in order to prevent such crimes." In Kyūshū, there was a custom to kill two of five children born to their parents. In Tosa province, one boy and two girls were considered the maximum number of children to be brought up in one family. In some other districts, practically all the babies, whose births were reported to the local authorities, were boys. Hardly one out of every ten children reported was a girl. Again, in Hyūga province, only the first-born was allowed to live, all other babies being killed as soon as they were born. It was even thought better to buy children from traffickers in children popularly called *hitokai-bune*, who came to sell boys and girls whom they had kidnapped in Kyōto, Ōsaka and other places, as this could save them much of the trouble of bringing them up.

It seems that the *samurai* class in the provinces was not free from the above-mentioned custom. In the ' *Sōbō Kigen,*' Nakai-Chikuzan says : " There are an exceedingly large number of poor people in the out-of-the-way districts who refuse to bring up their children. Indeed, this custom has become so widespread that people regard it as if it were a matter of course. This usage is specially noticeable in Hyūga province. I have often heard that this evil practice has spread even to the *samurai* class. If a baby is born in a *samurai* family, for instance, the friends of the family make inquiries among themselves as to whether the baby is going to be brought up. They do not visit the family to congratulate the parents until they are sure that the newly born infant is going to be brought up. If they learn that it is not going to be of the living, they pretend to know nothing of the matter, and leave it severely alone. Most families do not take the trouble to bring up any except the first-born. If any family chooses to bring up two or three children, it is held up to ridicule by others. This is simply outrageous."

In formulating its policy for dealing with this practice of population control, the Shogunate used a good deal of care. It vetoed the practice and punished the delinquents. This policy achieved some good results in some districts, but it apparently failed to meet with general success. It is also noticeable that some *han* made earnest endeavours to stamp out the evil custom. As one example of this, let me describe the policy pursued by Lord Matsudaira-Rakuō for increasing the population. As already stated, the bad custom of abortion and infanticide prevailed in the Ōu and other provinces, and the Shirakawa district was no exception to the rule. Lord Rakuō often issued instructions to the inhabitants in his fief dwelling upon the evil nature of the practice. In the fourth year of Temmei (1784), he laid down a rule that one bale of rice should be awarded to the couple who, in spite of their poverty, kept aloof from the evil custom and brought up more than five children. In the Shirakawa district, the male population was out of proportion larger than that of females in those days, and it was, in such circumstances, impossible for young men to marry women unless they were rich enough to make the parents of their future wives monetary gifts. This led to the decrease of births and the gradual dwindling of the population year after year, with the result that areas of waste farm fields increased every year. On the other hand, in Echigo province, which was Lord Rakuō's branch fief, the population was on the increase and women had industrious habits. Being informed of the fact that their adherence to the Ikko sect prevented the inhabitants of Echigo from committing infanticide, Lord Rakuō caused many women of that province to migrate to the Shirakawa district, supplying them with travelling expenses. They were, moreover, given a house and a tract of land, and helped to get husbands so that they could settle down to the cultivation of the soil and make it their life work. Recognising also the fact that the prevalence of the custom of abortion and infanticide was due, after all, to poverty, the *daimyō* made a new order in the second year of Kansei (1790), under which a monetary grant except for the first-born, was made to each married couple to whom a child was born, towards the expenses, of its bringing up. It was also arranged that pregnant women should be officially registered, that births should be duly reported to the proper authorities and that the babies born should be officially inspected. Thanks to these measures, a capitation taken in the fourth year of Kansei (1792) showed an increase of more than 3,500 in the population of his Shirakawa fief as compared with the fifth year of Temmei (1785). New farmers were also created and new farm villages formed brought into existence at Iizawa and other places, and a striking increase in the production of rice in many places. Besides the Shirakawa-Han, the *daimyō* of Mito, Shōnai, Tosa, Yonezawa, Sendai, Akita, Kagoshima, etc. devised various remedial measures for these various ills. In the writings of the scholars of those days we find frequent references to the necessity of eradicating the evil custom by means of a grant of money for bringing up children, or by other means.

As another example, I will give the record of Tomita-mura in Kazusa province. Tomita-mura was a village which produced some 1,382 *koku* of rice. About the Genroku era (1688-1703) it possessed 196 households on an average, with a population of about 1,000, but in the second year of Ansei (1855), the households were reduced to 112 in number while the population diminished to 517, showing a decrease of 84 in households and of 483 in population. The figures given of the births and deaths of infants in the fourth year of Ansei (1857) show that the total of the children born in this year, numbering 26, thirteen grew up, while the rest died. The following classification gives further details :

Births.	Heirs.		Others.	
	Brought up.	Died.	Brought up.	Died.
26	10	4	3	9

It will be seen from the above table that whereas in the case of heirs, the deaths represented about 30 per cent. of the total, the percentage of deaths was 75 in the case of the others. Referring to the four dead among the heirs, the recorder mentions that had the necessary instructions been given during the pregnancy of their mothers or medical treatment been given during the illness, two or three of them might have been saved. Again, with reference to the nine dead in the other lot of infants, he says that although he was told that three had died of various diseases, and six were either born dead or died of illness soon after they were born, it was difficult to ascertain whether it was really so. In these cases also, the recorder says, if strict injunctions had been given, seven or eight of them might have been saved. Regarding the three that were brought up, he says that it was on the earnest persuasions of many that their parents finally consented to bring them up. The above remarks clearly show that the practice of infanticide prevailed. The percentage of infanticide was comparatively small in the case of heirs, but it was very high in regard to other children. If it was only on the advice of many people that the parents of the three more fortunate children decided to bring them up, it is obvious that it was rather exceptional that the babies who were not heirs should have been allowed to live. Things were greatly improved, however, in the fourth, fifth and sixth years of Ansei (1857, 1858 and 1859) and the first year of Man'en (1860), as can be seen from the following table:

	Births	Live	Dead	Percentage of the Living
Ansei 4 (1857)	26	13	13	50
„ 5 (1858)	26	17	9	65.3
„ 6 (1859)	29	22	7	75.8
Man'en 1 (1860)	31	23	8	74.1

From the above it will be seen that not only did the number of births increase but there was a considerable increase in the number of children brought up.   This betterment of the conditions was presumably due to the efforts of leading villagers, as can be gathered from the following remark appearing in the record : " Humble and ignorant as I am, my constant advice to my fellow-villagers has gradually had its effect upon them, and they have come to bring up their children."

The causes of birth control in towns and in agricultural districts were not exactly the same. In urban districts, besides poverty, fornication, and adultery, fecundity, the coincidence of preg-nancy in a mother and her daughter-in-law, and the selfishness of parents, were among the causes, while in agricultural districts, birth control was almost exclusively due to the difficulty of living, which prevented people from rearing many children.

4.   ADDENDUM

In those days the freedom of the farmers was drastically restricted.[9]   They were treated as though they were tools for producing taxes, and were groaning under the heavy burdens put upon them.   To make matters worse, bad crops or famines occurred at frequent intervals.   In the meantime, there was a gradual levelling up of the standards of living, as the times progressed. These causes combined to make the life of the

---

[9] cf. Chap. VIII.

farming population particularly wretched. As farmers could not afford to meet death by starvation with folded arms, they chose to resort to this means or that in order to ward off their difficulty of living. A variety of means were adopted by them for this purpose, and among the negative methods adopted may be mentioned birth control, migration to big cities and setting up as *chōnin*. Farmers' riots may be described as a positive means adopted by them to better their wretched mode of living. Thus, there was a steady inflow of the rural population into cities, on the one hand, and the general practice of infanticide, popularly called *mabiki*, on the other. The latter course naturally checked the increase of the population. Even those who remained in their native places did not necessarily pursue agrestic pursuits in earnest, and that were cases where farmers took to other occupations. The shortage of farm labour was the natural outcome of this state of things. These causes, combined with others, brought about the due waste of agricultural fields and the impoverishment of agricultural districts.

In the feudal system of the Tokugawa Shogunate, land formed the main factor in production and the farming population constituted the only productive class, the privileged class called *samurai* being supported by the farmers. The conditions of living among the farmers became so distressing in the middle period of the Tokugawa Shogunate and after, as has already been described, that they could not afford to support the *samurai* class. The result was that the maintenance of the feudal system was rendered very difficult.

Furthermore, commerce and industry gradually developed, and currency found general circulation. With the development of the urban districts, the *chōnin* class came to exert greater influence, and currency economy gradually took the place of land economy, while commercial capital came into active play. In this way, the *samurai* class, which could no longer depend upon the old economic system for support, had to bow before the rising economic power, with the result that the *chōnin* class came to wield predominant influence in social life.

In short, the various phases of economic change in the Tokugawa period indicate that the feudal system of those days was predestined to disintegration. The population problem, when considered in conjunction with the agrarian question, can be regarded as constituting an important factor in the collapse of the Tokugawa Shogunate.

CHAPTER VI

THE CHANGES OF SOCIAL CLASSES DURING THE TOKUGAWA PERIOD

1. INTRODUCTION

The Tokugawa period is noted for its centralised feudal system. Historians agree that the feudal state in our country reached its perfect form during that period. Feudal society in general has certain characteristics such as the strict relation of loyalty between master and servant, firm distinctions between different classes, the static positions of all social elements, and reverence for special privileges. These characteristics were fully developed in that period. In political relations, for instance, "strict adherence to the ancient laws," and "prevention of new rules" were regarded as the guiding principles of political conduct. Human actions were strictly circumscribed by the perfection of ceremonial rules and social status. Freedom of expression was not recognised, and nothing was more abhorred than open discussion of public affairs by men not in government service.

On the social side, there was a strict discrimination among the four classes of society. Each trade had its guild and no one was allowed to become a member unless he had first become an apprentice and after a certain period been allowed to become a full-fledged master artisan and to engage in his particular trade. In all other branches of human endeavours — learning, the martial arts, as well as light accomplishments — the old forms were strictly preserved; and any one who disregarded the rules of his school would be regarded as a renegade. The relations of master and servant existed, not only among lords and *samurai*, but also among employers and employees and among teachers and pupils. Thus, all society was feudal in nature.

The ranking of the social classes of the time was indicated by a popular expression "*shi-nō-kō-shō*" which means *samurai*-farmer-artisan-merchant, arranged in order of social status importance. Thus, the *samurai* occupied the highest rank, the farmer came next, followed by the artisan and merchant. Of course, there were several other classes, for instance, the court nobility, the Shintō priests, Buddhist priests, scholars of the Chinese classics, and a body of social outcasts called *eta* or *hinin*. But the classes of importance were those of *samurai*, farmers and *chōnin* (including artisans and merchants).

In the beginning of the period, the preservation of the distinctions dividing these three main classes was regarded as one of the principal policies of the Feudal Government, and in fact the distinctions were so firmly maintained that it was impossible for those of one class to get into another class. Moreover, there were various class distinctions within a class itself which, also, were strictly maintained. However, with the lapse of time, it became impossible to keep up these distinctions, owing to the transformation which was brought about in the social and economic conditions of the country. In other words, each class gradually lost its inherent characteristics, which sometimes became possessed by another class ; some of these characteristics were shifted from one class to another. It is the purpose of this article to point out the social and economic transformations which gave birth to such changes in the feudal system of the period.

2. THE EXISTENCE OF CLASS DISTINCTIONS

The *samurai* class was at the head of the four social classes and occupied a position which was totally different from those of the farmers and the *chōnin*. The *samurai* were regarded as the centre and pattern of society — so much so indeed that an insult even upon the lowest grades of the *samurai* by farmers and *chōnin* was punishable by death. It seemed as though the farmers and *chōnin* were allowed to exist only in return for their service in supplying the subsistence of the *samurai* class.

Class distinctions were strictly maintained even within the *samurai* class itself. The rank

of each class from the Shogun to the lowest
grade of *samurai* or *chūgen* or *ashigaru* was fixed
according to its standing. *Daimyō* were classified
according to the ranking of their houses into the
gosanke (the three families of Kii, Owari, and
Mito), the *gokamon* (the Matsudaira families of
Echizen, Matsue, Tsuyama, etc.), the *fudai* (those
who were the subordinates of the founder of the
Tokugawa Shogunate) and the *tozama* (those who
were the subordinates of other feudal lords and
who had been subjugated by the founder of the
Tokugawa Government); and according to extent
of territory into the following : the *kokushu* (those
whose territories comprised more than one province), the *jun-kokushu* (those who possessed territories next in size to those of the *kokushu*), the
jōshu (who possessed castles of their own), and
the *yūshu* (who possessed military camps of their
own). The direct retainers of the Tokugawa Government were classified into the *hatamoto* and
the *gokenin* ; the former was comprised of those
who received a hereditary annual stipend under
10,000 *koku* of rice and who were above the rank
of *omemie* ; those direct retainers of the Government who were below the rank of *omemie* were
grouped into the *gokenin*. In each group, there
was a great difference in official rank and social
position between the *fudai* (hereditary retainers)
and the *okakae* (temporary retainers). There were
strict rules as regards the promotion of their official
ranks, their seats in the Shogun's castle, the forms

of their residences, their costumes, the arrangement of processions and implements carried during journeys, the order of processions when paying visits to the Shogun's castle, the nature of offerings to the Shogun, and that of grants made by the Shogun or other superiors. Appellations were also strictly fixed; the Shogun was called by the honorary title of *uesama*, while his consort by the title of *midaisama*. His concubines also had different appellations according to their respective rank. The forms of the documents issued by the Shogunate were also strictly determined; there were seven different ways of writing the word *on* according to the rank or degree of relationship; there were the same number of ways of writing such honorary appellations as *dono* and *sama*. A strict regard for the exact values of all these distinctions was required. There were strict regulations as regards the manner of ceremonial greetings. Those having the rank of *omemie* or above could enter the main gate when paying a visit to the *rōjū* (one of the high administrative officials of the Shogunate) and when they reached the *genkan* or the antechamber, an usher would come out and meet them. But those of the ranks below *omemie*, had to go through a small side gate and must get to the antechamber and offer greetings instead of waiting for an usher to come out. Members of the former class could disregard even one of the *gosanke* who might happen to pass on the way at the head of

a procession; but those of the latter class had
to squat down by the roadside as soon as they
saw the lances at the head of such procession,
and if the door of the palanquin (in which the
daimyō was seated) should happen to be left
open, they had to bow their heads to the ground.
Thus, within the *samurai* class itself there was
an extreme amount of ceremony and discrimination at every turn.

Thus, the order of ranks was perfected, but
it was devoid of real substance. Except in the
early years of the Tokugawa period, the relations
of master and retainers were historical, based
upon the facts of two or three generations before;
and there was no real tie existing between the
two in later times. True, the formal relations of
master and retainers were perfected because of
the policy of the Feudal Government to maintain
order in time of peace, through a military class;
but the spiritual tie of the actual relationship of
master and retainers became weaker and weaker
in inverse proportion to the perfection of their
exterior form.

Various class distinctions also existed among
farmers. In the first place, there was a distinction between ordinary farmers and village officials
such as the *shōya*, the *kumigashira* and the
hyakushō-dai. In the case of the *shōya* (village
headman), he was sometimes elected but ordinarily
was a hereditary official, his family being of high
official or social standing. Farmers who were

pioneers of big landlords occupied a higher social position than ordinary farmers; while sad was the social position of tenants who were regarded as much inferior in social standing to regular farmers and who had to take their seats at the lowest end of the room at village meetings.

Among merchants and artisans there were strict distinctions between the *oyakata* (master), the *shokunin* (journeyman) and the *totei* (apprentice). There was also a great difference between house owners and tenants, the right to take part in public affairs of districts being limited to the former. Thus, there were also various distinctions with the *chōnin* class whose spirit was freer than those of any of the other classes; and these distinctions were strictly preserved.

In short, there existed strict distinctions within all classes particularly in the *samurai* class; farmers, merchants and artisans had rules, precedents and regulations of their own; all these proved hindrances to their activities at every turn. The outward forms of these regulations were perfected but their substance was void. In fact the perfection of their outward forms caused their real failure.

3. THE DECLINE OF CLASS DISTINCTIONS

In the very old days, there was no distinction between *samurai* and farmer. The *samurai* tilled the soil in time of peace, and took up arms when war prevailed. However, as the result of changes in the methods of warfare, the *samurai* forsook the country in which they had lived and went to live in castle-towns. They thereby ceased to be farmers and received annual grants of rice from their lord for their military service. Thus, the separation of *samurai* and farmer took place, and the former came to form a class of their own. After this, they no longer tilled the soil and became an unproductive or consumptive class.[1] When they had secured the political right, they occupied the highest position in society, monopolised all rights, treated the farmers and *chōnin* like slaves, and even enjoyed the right of slashing them with edged weapons like dogs whenever an act of insult was committed or thought to be committed by the inferior. But during the eras of Genroku, Bunka and Bunsei, these unproductive warriors experienced considerable difficulty in living because of their luxurious habits of life which were out of proportion to their incomes; and they could no longer exercise their special right of cutting down the people of the lower classes even when they were provoked by the latter. In the third year of Bunkyū (1863), the Feudal Government issued a warning to the *samurai* class stating that the Government would not enforce the law providing the ending of the family of a *samurai* who was killed by a *chōnin*

---

[1] cf. Chap. VII.

as the result of the former's attempt to slash the latter for some effensive act. (The basis of this law was that it was regarded as a gross dishonour for a *samurai* to be killed by a *chōnin*.) In agricultural districts also, that farmers after the middle of the period no longer obeyed the authorities unconditionally; on the contrary, there were frequent insurrections and uprisings by tenant farmers; the authorities often had to submit to their demands, and thus the real power of the Government was openly questioned.

Both the Feudal Government and all the *dai-myō* suffered because of their extreme financial difficulties. Nearly all *daimyō* and *samurai* had to bow before *chōnin* in order to borrow money from them and managed to make both ends meet through the financial assistance rendered by the wealthy merchants of Edo, Kyōto, Ōsaka and other principal cities. The *daimyō* and *samurai* met the financial stringency for the time being through the extortion of taxes and loans from merchants. The '*Keizairoku Shūi*' says: "It was the facts of the eras of Kambun and Empō that Kumazawa-Banzan declared that the total amount of the debts of all *daimyō* was one hundred times the total amount of money the whole country possessed. Now that seventy years have passed since that time, the amount must be a thousand times greater." The fact that the '*Chōnin Kōkenroku*' treats of the Kyōto merchants who became bankrupt because of the loans they extended to *daimyō* and other *samurai* during a period of fifty or sixty years around the Genroku era, indicates that *daimyō* depended on a loan policy even at comparative early days of the Tokugawa period. Loans to these *daimyō* were not easily redeemed; interest gave birth to interest thereby adding to the amount of the principal; and, when the debtor's burden had become too unbearable, he asked for a long instalment plan for paying the money back, or for the cancellation of the interest. Some *daimyō* failed to pay back any part of his debts, and the creditor *chōnin* financiers resorted to a boycott by way of retaliation, thereby not infrequently holding such *daimyō* in submission. Sometimes the finances of a *daimyō* might be controlled by a certain money-lender who loaned money to a *daimyō* with rice as security; an example may be cited of the Sendai-Han whose finances were controlled by a *chōnin* in Ōsaka called Masuya. Even the Feudal Government sought the financial aid of wealthy *chōnin*. Thus, in matters of finance, the Shogunate and the *daimyō* did not possess any real power as the ruling class over *chōnin*.

Nor was the economic distress limited to the Shogunate Government and the *daimyō*. There are many facts showing the extreme poverty of the *samurai* class in general after the middle of the Tokugawa period.[2] To cite few instances,

---

[2] cf. Chap. VII.

military equipment such as swords and armour which were regarded as representing the spirit of the *samurai* were pawned and left unredeemed; many *samurai* had to take their ceremonial robes out of some pawn-shop whenever they had to attend some public affair in the castle; and would return the robes to the pawn-shop upon their return from the castle. The great majority of *samurai* had to borrow money in various ways in order to meet their financial obligations for the time being. A written memorial presented by Inoue-Saburoemon in July, the sixth year of Kaei (1853), points out the economic poverty of the *hatamoto*, and describes the manner in which they were placed in financial distress by money-lenders in the following words:

" The manner of loan contraction has become objectionable in recent years. When a loan certificate expressly bears the interest rate to be one *bu* ¼ *ryō*) for every 25 *ryō*, it in reality is one *bu* for every 20 *ryō* each month. Moreover, a fee of 10 per cent. is paid to the creditor as a token of gratitude, in addition to various presents which the debtor makes to the creditor. If a person borrows 100 *ryō*, he first pays a gratuity of 10 *ryō*, the yearly interest is 15 *ryō* : pays the compound interest at the end of every four months when the certificate is renewed. Moreover, as dinners are given by the debtor to the creditor at the times of negotiation, the total yearly amount of expenses would be something like 30 *ryō*.

Debtors realise that all this is outrageous, but unless they follow the custom they would not be able to secure loans. If a debtor is unable to repay his debts for some years, the total of the principal and interest will reach an enormous amount and his entire revenue would not cover it, so that his service to his master can no longer be continued." Ogyū-Sorai spoke the truth when he said in the 'Ginroku': "In these days the property of the samurai was absorbed by merchants."

These facts indeed disclosed the distressing condition of the samurai class whose outward high position in society was not accompanied by any real power. The samurai in fact had ceased to possess the real power of a ruling class. This state of affairs is referred to by the 'Chirizukadan' in the following words: "Although in form the samurai govern and the merchants obey, in reality it seems to be an age when the chōnin hold sway."

I shall next consider the farmer class. Viewed from an economic standpoint, the feudal system of that time was based upon land as the principal means of production, with the farmers as the only productive class which supported a specially privileged class known as samurai. This is the main reason why agriculture was placed above both trade and industry in ranking; agriculture was indispensable for to the existence of the samurai class. But after the middle of the Tokugawa period, the farmers were subjected to an

extreme economic difficulty; the population of
rural districts moved to the cities; a crude method
of birth control known as *mabiki* was resorted
to, thereby preventing the natural increase of the
rural population.[3] Nor did all those who remained
in the villages engage in farming; on the contrary,
the change of vocations resulted in a scarcity of
agricultural labour.   This and other reasons naturally caused desolation to fields and furrows.
The upshot of all this was that the farmers became no longer able to support the *samurai* class
as they had done formerly, and in consequence
the latter class no longer could depend on the
farmers alone for its subsistance.   True, the
farmers had been a productive class; but viewed
in the above light, it became incapable of sustain-
ing the *samurai* class; and thus a great difficulty
arose for the maintenance of the feudal system.

What was then the condition of the *chōnin*?
In the eyes of the Feudal Government, the *chōnin*
were quite different from both the *samurai* and
the farmers, inasmuch as they had no ancestors
who had performed some meritorious services;
they did not produce foodstuffs for the benefit
of the State like farmers; on the contrary, they
engaged only in an unproductive pursuit with
abacuses in their hands and living an easy life,
thereby stimulating luxurious methods of life
among the people.   Profit-making enterprises at

---

[3] cf. Chap. V and VIII.

that time were regarded with utmost contempt, hence the *chōnin* was placed at the very bottom of all the social classes. " Merchants and artisans can be dispensed with. . . . Efforts must be made in order to increase even a single farmer, and to lessen the number of merchants as much as possible." Commerce and industry were regarded as insignificant enterprises, and special efforts were made in order to prevent the dissemination of the spirit of the *chōnin* among the farmers. In short, the *chōnin* class was regarded as unnecessary as a social element.

The continued peace in the feudal society of Japan, however, brought about many social changes. The *samurai* became accustomed to peace and luxury; they put away their arrows, allowed their lances to remain undusted; war was only an old tale; muscular strength became useless and was replaced by the power of money. While the *chōnin* class increased its real power with the progress of time and unmistakably became a powerful social class, agricultural communities were greatly impoverished, the *samurai* class was placed in economic distress. *Samurai* had to bow before the *chōnin* whose financial assistsnce enabled them to meet their economic needs. Gamō-Kumpei is reported to have said: "The anger of the wealthy merchants of Ōsaka has the power of striking terror into the hearts of the *daimyō*." His words truly indicate the real power of the *chōnin* of that time. The *chōnin* class which had once been regarded as unnecessary had become necessary even for the existence of the *samurai* class itself.

In the beginning, the *samurai* were regarded as the ruling class, the farmers as a productive class and the *chōnin* as an unnecessary class; but after the middle of the Tokugawa period their class characteristics underwent changes; the *samurai* class became impotent, the farmer class impoverished and the *chōnin* class rose to social ascendancy.

4. THE TRANSFORMATION OF CLASS DISTINCTIONS

As has been pointed out, the distinctions among different classes gradually became lost, and some of the members of one class were changed as if they were those of some other class; while some members smuggled themselves into class not originally theirs.

(a) **The *samurai* became like *chōnin*.** The *samurai* of the old days regarded money-making as contemptible. During the Genroku era a *samurai* did not hesitate to cut down his comrades because of insults received over some money matters. With the lapse of time the *samurai* fell into extreme poverty, and they would do nothing which did not bring them economic returns; when they bought provisions for their lord from *chōnin*, they wrangled for commissions in various dishonest ways; they accepted every possible sort of bribe. Finally, the *samurai* insisted on loans when they hired retainers, and the amount of money possessed by the boy's parents became an important factor when adopting the son of a stranger as his heir by a *samurai*. Some *daimyō* encouraged their *samurai* to engage in domestic industries, the most general as well as the most successful being cotton spinning. The *Gunnai-ori* of Kai province and the *Yonezawa-ori* of Uzen province were notable silk textile products. The Lord of the Kumamoto-Han encouraged the production of silk textiles among the wives of his men, while Lord Shirakawa also encouraged the production of silk crêpe among the *samurai* in his own feud. These are notable historic incidents during the feudal period. This phenomenon together with the side works of *samurai* indicate that the unproductive *samurai* class attempted to engage in industrial production in order to adapt themselves to the changing economic condition of the country; they also show that the *samurai* could no longer make a living under the prevailing system of economy: and provide an example of the acquisition of the characteristics of *chōnin* by *samurai*.

(b) **Samurai join the chōnin class.** Not only did *samurai* acquire the characteristics of *chōnin*, but also many of them actually joined the latter class, by giving up their status of *samurai*. According to the ' *Edo Machikata Kakiage* ' compiled during the Bunsei era (1818-1829 , of 250 merchant families, about 48 families had ancestors who were either regular *samurai*, or *rōnin-samurai* (masterless *samurai*) or *gōshi* (special country-*samurai*). Again, the '*Chōnin Kōkenroku*' points out that the following *chōnin* of Kyōto had their ancestries among *samurai* of one kind or another : Ishikawa-Jian, Takaya-Seiroku, Hirano-Yūken, and Miki-Gondayū. Of course some of their ancestors had ceased to enjoy the status of *samurai* long before they actually became *chōnin*. However, it is undeniable that many of those noted old *chōnin* families had *samurai* ancestors.

(c) ***Chōnin* and farmers became *samurai*.** The *Buke-hatto*, promulgated in the seventh year of Hōei (1710), says : " It is a contemporary custom to regard the amount of property as more important than blood relationship in fixing on one's heir." Thus the custom of adopting another's son as heir with the object of economic gain prevailed even as early as the Genroku and Hōei eras (1688-1710). Some *samurai* purposely put aside his eldest son from the heirship to his family property, and adopted the son of some other man with a large amount of property, and family inheritances were actually bought and sold. Nor was this limited to *samurai's* sons ; on the contrary, *chōnin's* and farmers' sons were also adopted as heirs of some *samurai* families. The '*Seji Kemmonroku*' says : " Thus, the family inheritance of the *hatamoto* in reality was bought

and sold; and in consequence, *samurai* adopted
as their heirs the sons of some *samurai* who
were engaged in the occupation of accountancy
or of physicians and even of servants who were
not of *samurai* rank.   Thus the adoption of the
sons of others was in vogue and all families lost
much of their ancestral blood." During the reign
of Shogun Yoshimune, the sale of the *samurai*'s
status was prohibited, but it continued to be
carried on so that in the course of time it became an ordinary practice. The ' *Seji Kemmonroku* ' on this point says: " Those who bought
the status of *samurai* were, sometimes, *samurai*
of low rank, and sometimes sons of low-class
chōnin ; relatives of money-lenders who were in
the habit of charging outrageously high rates of
interest ; sons of the blind ; those who had fled to
Edo after committing some crime in their home
towns; those who had offended their original
daimyō or master; those excommunicated priests
who had become laymen ; sons of priests who had
violated their religious vows ; and even those
who belonged to the class of *eta* or *hinin*." Mr.
Kobayashi says : " Some of those who purchased
the positions of such low-grade *samurai* as *yoriki*
or *kachi* rose to the position of *hatamoto*, through
their own endeavours, especially towards the end
of the Tokugawa régime.   An example may be
found in the case of Kusu-Sado-no-kami-Sukeaki,
one of the very powerful *samurai* during the
time when Mizuno-Tadakuni held the office of

rōjū; Sado-no-kami was first in the province of Shinano, but through the purchase of the position of *samurai*, he rose to fame and power eventually occupying the office of *kanjō-bugyō*. His son, Suketoshi, was also known as Sado-no-kami and was appointed to a high office in the city of Ōsaka."[4] This was true of many other *han* where the positions of low-class *samurai* were freely bought and sold. A more recent example may be found in the case of the family of the late Prince Itō-Hirobumi, one of the founders of modern Japan, whose father, originally a farmer of good lineage, purchased the position of a *samurai* called Itō in the castle-town of Hagi, the capital of Chōshū province.

According to the report made by Inoue-Saburoemon in June, the sixth year of Kaei (1853), the money-value of the positions of *samurai* during the last years of the Tokugawa period was as follows: 50 *ryō* per every 100 *koku* of annual revenue of rice for the adoption of a son while a *samurai* is in his normal condition; anywhere between 70 *ryō* and 100 *ryō* for the adoption of a son in urgency. According to the report made by another person, Yamamoto-Motoshichirō, in July of the same year, the price for the adoption of a son in urgency or for an inheritance in urgency, was 100 *ryō* for every 100 *koku* of rice revenue and 1,000 *ryō* for every 1,000 *koku* of

---

[4] Kobayashi-Shōjiro, '*Bakumatsushi*' p. 38.

rice revenue.

Thus, the sale and purchase of the position of *samurai* among all classes of men — *samurai*, *rōnin*, farmers, and *chōnin* — having property as the central factor, have resulted in the loss of the *samurai* blood in the *samurai* families through the mingling of the blood of *chōnin*.

(d) **Farmers turn into *chōnin*.** The policy of the Government authorities of that time was to keep rural districts intact from the influence of cities and maintain a similar independence between farmers and *chōnin*. However, farm families near cities were influenced by urban life; some of the farmers held the life of city people as their life's goal: others were hired by *chōnin* or became tradesmen in cities; some married into city families; while some of those who remained in the village ceased to be farmers and engaged in small trade. The ' *Keiseidan* ' says: "Farmers wished to become *chōnin*, and in offering their daughters and sons in marriage would prefer *chōnin* to those of their own class vocation. Some of them would give up all their family inheritance in favour of their younger brothers in order to live in a prosperous city or port; while those who remained on the farm for their whole life would imitate the *chōnin* in the matters of hair-dressing and of *kimono*-designs, and of other phases of the luxurious life of *chōnin*." In consequence, there were many people in agricultural villages who did not exclusively

engage in farming. The report made by Ro-
Tōzan, of the Sendai-Han during the Hōreki
era, says: "Of 100 farmers, about 50 entrust
the work of farming to their wives and children,
and themselves engage in trade and industry.
The remaining 50 engage both in cultivation and
other trades. There is not a single farmer who
is exclusively engaged in farming." His report
should not be regarded as exceptional, but as
having universal reference to all other parts as
well. While there is no doubt that the number
of the *chōnin* who were originally farmers was
not small, the '*Edo Machikata Kakiage*' mentions
19 such *chōnin*. I am of the opinion that the
real number was much greater than that. It is
said that many of the merchants of Edo came
from the two provinces of Ōmi and Ise. Some
of them must have been farmers before they
came to Edo.

(e) **The transformation of the *chōnin* into
samurai.** I have already mentioned the fact
that *chōnin* overwhelmed the *samurai* through
their financial power. The following practices
placed *chōnin* practically on the same level as
the *samurai*: "Some *samurai* would ask the
financial assistance of the farmers in their fiefs
as well as of the *chōnin*. Such farmers and
chōnin often made financial plans on behalf of
samurai. The *samurai's* rewards for *chōnin*
and farmers were given in accordance with the
amounts of loans or contributions. They were

also given official costumes and annual grants of rice; received permission to carry swords and to bear surnames; they were also granted the status of *samurai.*"

The *kakeya* of Ōsaka and the *fudasashi* of Edo were the financial organs for *daimyō* and *samurai* in these days. *Daimyō* gave annual stipends of rice to those *kakeya* and accorded them the same treatment as was given to the principal retainer of a *daimyō*. A notable example is found in the person of Kōnoike-Zen'emon who acted as *kakeya* for the five *daimyō* and whose total annual stipends of rice amounted to 10,000 *koku*. This is an example of the transformation of merchants into *samurai*.

(f) *Chōnin* became landlords. On the other hand, it was a matter of common observation that the financial power of *chōnin* extended into agricultural villages and their social status was greatly increased by virtue of their becoming landlords. Their financial power was best manifested at the time of the concentration of lands or the development of uncultivated lands. The financial power of *chōnin* was one great factor in the development of uncultivated lands in these days. The development of new rice fields at Fukano undertaken by the Branch Temple of Hongan-ji at Namba, Ōsaka, in April, the second year of Hōei (1705), was participated in by many *chōnin* of Ōsaka; and about the seventh year of Kyōho (1722), the northern half of the fields had become the possession of the Kōnoike family and the southern half, that of the Hirano family. The rich fields of Masanari, Owari province, cultivated in the sixth year of Bunsei (1823), later fell into the hands of some wealthy merchants of Nagoya. All these facts indicate that *chōnin* came to possess the status of farmer, in addition to their being *chōnin*, although they did not actually engage in farming. The manifesto issued by Ōshio-Heihachirō in part says: " The wealthy *chōnin* of Ōsaka in recent years have been exploiting *daimyō* by putting them under vast pecuniary obligations, and thereby getting an enormous amount of money and annual stipends of rice. They have been living like princes. Despite their being *chōnin*, they would be appointed *karō* or *yōnin* by *daimyō*. They possess fields and newly cultivated lands of their own, and are living in a very luxurious manner."

In short, the *chōnin* through the power of their money smuggled themselves into the *samurai* class; receiving the same treatment as *samurai*; enjoying the status of farmers. A man was *samurai* one day and *chōnin* the next. It was an era of sweeping changes.

4. CONCLUSION

I have endeavoured to point out the fact that the social classes of the Tokugawa period were neither fixed nor unchangeable throughout the

whole period, but that their nature underwent a
transformation with the flux of time; and that
confusion was brought about in the distinctions
among different social classes. Now what does
this transformation signify? In the first place,
the feudal system of that time was a social
system in which a privileged class called *samurai* dominated the rest of the social classes as
a ruling class and the *samurai* were supported in
their economic life by the farmers. Gradually,
however, there arose trade and industry existing
side by side with farming (which had been regarded as the only means of production). Money
came to be extensively used, cities developed
and the *chōnin* class made its emergence. These
phenomena unmistakably indicate the coming into
prominence of commercial capital and of the
money economy which replaced land economy.
As the result of this change, the *samurai* became
unable to maintain their economic life; the farmers also became unable to support the *samurai*
as before. Both the *samurai* and farmer bowed
before the economic power of the *chōnin*. They
depended on the latter for capital; transformed
themselves into *chōnin*, or smuggled themselves
into the *chōnin* class.

On the other hand, the *chōnin* class came to
possess the real power in feudal society, dominated the *samurai* class and extended its grasp
over agricultural communities. In other words,
each social class gradually lost its old characteris-

tics as the result of economic changes ; members of a high class degraded to a class below theirs, while those of the lower grades climbed up into the class above them ; thereby giving rise to much confusion in social distinctions. Inasmuch as the maintenance of class distinctions was an indispensable characteristic of the feudal system, this confusion inevitably shook the very foundation on which the system was based. The final overthrow of the feudal system in this period was very natural and to be expected in view of the facts I have pointed out.

CHAPTER VII

THE DECAY OF THE *SAMURAI* CLASS IN THE TOKUGAWA PERIOD

1. THE CAUSES OF THE DECAY

As already mentioned, in the very old days, there was no distinction between *samurai* and farmer. The *samurai* tilled the soil in the time of peace, and took up arms in the field of battle. The separation of the two was brought about because of the change in the method or warfare and in the consequent concentration of *samurai* in cities and towns. Since the Ashikaga period, the individual method of fighting in which swords, bows and arrows played a conspicuous part, gradually ceased to be an important factor, infantry-men and foot-soldiers who used spears and guns became the central factor of armies ; the castle was built at a convenient place, not in a natural fastness. The old farmer-soldier, in consequence, ceased to exist ; and the *samurai* who had lived in the country were concentrated in castle-towns for the purpose of drill and to familiarise them with other measures for the defense of their lord's castles. When a *samurai*, after reaching a castle-town of his feudal lord, began receiving the annual grants of rice for his military service, he was no longer a farmer-sold·er; he ceased to till the soil; his sole task was that of a simple soldier; and he lived on the rice which his lord gave him in the form of annual grants. Formerly, the retainers of a *samurai* constituted a productive class — they tilled the soil. After the separation of *samurai* and farmer, those retainers also ceased to be producers; they became an unproductive class of people whose subsistence was maintained by the rice granted to them annually by their master. Later, some *samurai* dismissed their retainers and employed day-workers as their servants — a fast bearing witness to the unproductivity of retainers.

Let us now study the significance of this separation of *samurai* and farmer and of the fact that the *samurai* class ceased to be a productive class, becoming a consumptive class.

At the time of the change under consideration, the economic system of our country was being developed from local to national and from natural economy to money economy. While rice was the foundation of the finance and economy of the time, the use of money made such a great advance as had never been seen in previous ages. Now, the *samurai*, by that time, had to convert the great portion of his grants of rice into money for his daily living (living in towns, as they did where no economic self-sufficiency was possible). Moreover, the amount of their annual revenue was fixed for all years regardless of the condition of the rice crops. In consequence, the *samurai* class suffered greatly because of the fluctuations of the price of rice. In other words, the *samurai* tried to sit on the stool of rice economy and on the stool of money economy, and between the two he fell down. This indicates that they could not adapt themselves nor their method of living to the economic system of the time, hence their fortunes were ever exposed to extreme unstability.

As was stated, the *samurai* assembled in cities, some of them going to Edo with their lords on an official duty known as the *sankin-kōtai*; and the direct retainers of the Shogun lived permanently at Edo, the seat of the Shogunate Government. But the cities were the centre of money economy and were inhabited by the *chōnin* who had become wealthy with the development of commerce and industry. It was only too natural that the living standard of the *samurai* in the cities should become higher and higher and their revenue, in consequence, inadequate. What an enormous amount of money was wastefully expended by those *samurai* who were in Edo either temporarily or permanently is evidenced by the following account given in Gamō-Kumpei's writing:

"Those *daimyō* who lived in Edo built their houses in various parts of the city and employed many servants both men and women all of whom performed almost no real services. The number of those servants in Edo constituted one-fifth of the whole number of servants; while the sum of the living expenses in Edo amounted to seven-tenths of the total aggregate expended in the fief."

Lastly, the poverty of the *daimyō* involved that of the *samurai*. The feudal lords were confronted by a severe financial crux arising from the fact that while their revenue was usually fixed for all time, their expenses steadily increased; and this crux compelled them to adopt a practice known as the *hanchi* system by which a certain percentage of the annual grants of rice to the *samurai* was held back. The amount thus retained was nominally borrowed by *daimyo* from their followers but, since it was borrowed practically permanently, no term being specified it, in reality, amounted to a reduction of the *samurai's* grant of rice. There is no question that the *samurai's* poverty was greatly intensified because of this practice. The term *hanchi* literally means half-stipend, but in actual practice, the reduction was not necessarily one-half; it was sometime one-third or one-fourth. An old writing[1] on the economic condition of the Tokugawa period says: "Of recent times, the *daimyō*, both small and great are suffering because of their poverty. They are borrowing from *samurai* the sum amounts anywhere between one-tenth and six-tenths of the *samurai's* annual grants of rice."

---

[1] Dazai-Shundai, ' *Keizairoku Shūi.*'

At any rate, the separation of, *samurai* and farmer was the indirect cause of the poverty of the *samurai* class; but the extension of money economy, the development of the standard of living, and the reduction of its revenue, were the direct and proximate causes.

2. THE FACT OF THE POVERTY

That *samurai* were after the middle of the Tokugawa period subjected to an extreme financial difficulty can be supported by many facts, and I shall here point out only a few of them. Such military equipment as swords and armours which were regarded as representing the spirit of the *samurai* were pawned and unredeemed, thereby falling into the hands of strangers. Perhaps such equipment were not needed in times of peace, of course, but such a procedure on the part of a *samurai* would have been unthinkable at any previous period, when *samurai* were comparatively wealthy and economically self-sufficient. Many *samurai* had to take their ceremonial dresses out of pawn whenever they had to attend some public affair in the castle; and would again return the dresses to the pawn-shops on as soon as they got back from the castle. Some *samurai* were not wealthy enough to employ domestic servants, and in consequence the members of their families had to do the general housekeeping, and sometimes did some profitable work on the side at home.

But the poverty of the *samurai* could be only little alleviated by such things as private work or thrift. Many *samurai* fell deep into debt owing to the pressure of circumstances, borrowing money right and left. The following account is given by a writing on the condition of the time :

" *Samurai* had to borrow money from the Feudal Government and from *chōnin*. . . . They also borrowed from the blind who received special protection from the Feudal Government. In all cases, the rates of interest were very high, but *samurai* took pride in their ability to borrow money at all risks, sometimes even mortgaging their annual grants of rice."[2]

Because of the extreme difficulty of living, the *samurai* of that time would do nothing which did not bring them economic returns, thinking that *samurai* ethics and honesty ought to be given the go by in these days. When they were asked to do a service for some one, they would agree in accordance with the nature of the gifts they received. They cared little whether they were fitted to do the work they were about to take up, and while serving one lord would seek another master who might give them a better material return. They would allow themselves to take bribes. When they bought provisions for their

---

[2] ' *Seji Kemmonroku.*'

lord from *chōnin*, they wangled commissions in various dishonest ways.

As was already stated, *samurai* replaced hereditary retainers with temporary ones, who were hired on the condition that they would loan money to their master, and to whom the master entrusted the whole task of managing his financial affairs. When it was necessary to adopt a son, the amount of property possessed by the family of the prospective heir formed the deciding factor, and even the status of a *samurai* was bought and sold. This was practised even as early as the Hōei and Genroku eras; the regulation regarding the general conduct of *samurai* promulgated in the seventh year of Hōei (1710) has a reference to the *samurai*'s love of money and of other worldly matters. Some *samurai* adopted the sons of wealthy commoners as their heirs. Sometimes even those who had sons of their own specially adopted a boy from another family because this family possessed great wealth. In later periods, new regulations on inheritance were established under which the *samurai* who adopted a son had to surrender his substance and the headship of the family to the adopted son, himself drawing special grants of rice for his own living.

The *samurai*'s practice of adopting the sons of others for their heirs and of selling the status of *samurai* to some wealthy commoners — a practice having economic return as its main purpose

— resulted in debasing the purity of the blood which the *samurai* had carefully preserved from generation to generation since the time of their remote ancestors; the practice also created an opportunity for the blood of commoners to find its way into the veins of *samurai*.

3. REMEDIES FOR THE POVERTY

I shall now dwell on several remedies which were instituted by the Shogunate Government and the *daimyō*. As I have already pointed out, the *samurai* suffered greatly because of the fluctuation of the price of rice which was their only revenue; this was due to the fact that, while rice formed the foundation of the social and economic organisations of the time, the use of money had become extensively popularised. Consequently, the Shogunate endeavoured to regulate the price of rice — to maintain it at a reasonable rate. This remedy was one way of meeting the poverty of the *samurai*. I have discussed this point more fully elsewhere. I shall here only mention that it did not prove a successful remedy.

Another remedy was thrift. This was a policy which was adopted by the founder of the Tokugawa Shogunate, and various edicts were issued to urge *samurai* to exercise thrift; the law governing the conduct of *samurai* which was enacted in the early part of the Tokugawa period also had provisions regarding thrift. Edicts on thrift promulgated during the eras of Kan'ei, Kansei, and Tempo are famous. Although these edicts were not intended for the *samurai* class alone, it was evident that its necessity in the case of the *samurai* was greater than that in any other class because of their failure to adapt themselves to the economic conditions of the time; limitation of their consumption was surely an important means of relieving their poverty. The successive Shoguns urged *samurai* to observe two things: martial accomplishments and thrift; but it is doubtful whether they observed either of them to any appreciative extent.

The Shogunate also granted loans to its direct vassals and retainers in times of natural calamities and other emergencies. Although this cannot be placed in the same category as the regulation of the price of rice or with the edicts on thrift, it also can be regarded as a means of relieving the poverty of the *samurai*. In the first year of Bunkyū (1861), loans were granted to *samurai* according to the amount of their annual revenue. A loan of 25 *ryō* was granted to a *samurai* whose annual revenue of rice was 300 *koku*; 20 *ryō* for 200 *koku*, 15 *ryō* for 100 *koku*; and from 5 to 10 *ryō* for revenues under 100 baler of rice. The loans were redeemed in ten-year instalments.

By far the most drastic method adopted by the Feudal Government by way of relieving the poverty of the *samurai* was the repudiation of debts, which was called *kien*. The direct vassals of the Shogun who had rice fields of their own, could demand that the tenants make advance payments of their taxes, or force them to shoulder extraordinary expenditures. But some of those ordinary *samurai* who received annual revenues from *daimyō* borrowed money from *chōnin* with the greater part of their revenues as security; and the Feudal Government had no other way than to cancel their debts in order to relieve them financially. The Government also issued many orders for the purpose of placing limitations on the interest rate; and the Order of repudiation of debts issued in the first year of Kansei (1789) was intended to eradicate all evils resulting from the debts of the *hatamoto* and *gokenin* of the Shogun who had mortgaged their annual revenues for a term of years according to the size of the debt. By this order all debts incurred prior to the end of the fourth year of Temmei (1784) were entirely cancelled, while those incurred after the beginning of the fifth year of the same era were redeemed in instalments, regardless of the sum total of the loan, the rate of the instalments being one per cent. for every 50 *ryō* per month. 3 *ryō* in cash for every 100 bales of rice was paid back in annual instalments. As a result of this order, the *fudasashi* lost old loans amounting to something like 1,187,800 *ryō*. Naturally after such a disaster, *fudasashi* became unwilling to extend loans to *hatamoto*, who were compelled to employ

rōnin or masterless *samurai* or others who had
vim and vigour and eloquence, for the purpose
of negotiating with the *fudasashi*. In some cases,
these negotiators had to resort to force in order
to secure loans. The repudiation of debts thus
gave rise to those negotiators who were called
kurayadoshi. The *fudasashi* also employed such
negotiators in order to meet the *hatamoto's* demands. Fear of an order for the repudiation of
debts caused great unrest in society in general.
This is why at the time of the failure of the
rice crop, the Government promised that it would
not issue any order for the repudiation of debts.
When, some fifty years later, Mizuno-Tadakuni,
rojū of the time, carried out the Reform of the
Tempo era, he attempted to grant public loans
to the *hatamoto*, with the stipulation that they
would not be required to pay back any principal,
provided they paid an annual interest of 7 per
cent. for a period of 25 years. The plan was
intended to make the *hatamoto* pay back their
debts to the *fudasashi*, but it was never fully
carried out. In December, next year, the fourteenth year of Tempo (1843), the Feudal Government issued an order making all debts, both old
and new, redeemable in annual instalments, without interest; and all secured loans were to be
paid back by the borrowers at the rate of 5 *ryō*
annually in case of debts above 100 *ryō* and at
the rate of 5 per cent. in case of debts below
100 *ryō*. It is said that one-half of the *fudasashi*

closed their doors, indicating the drastic nature of the measure.

The practice of *kien* was also adopted by *daimyō* in their own territories. As already stated, some of those feudal lords encouraged *samurai* to carry on domestic industries. They were all intended to relieve the poverty of the *samurai* who were unable to adapt themselves to the existing economic conditions: it indicates that *samurai* were unable to make a decent living under the then prevailing economic organisation of society.

The foregoing measures were taken by the Shogunate and *daimyō* to relieve the *samurai* from their extreme poverty. But there are moreover several measures of minor importance which had the same intention. But none of them had much success, as far as the relief of the financial difficulties of the *samurai* was concerned, due mainly to the fact that the very foundation of the life of the *samurai* class had become unsteady. We shall next consider this foundation.

4. THE FOUNDATION OF THE *SAMURAI*'S LIFE

The foundation of the *samurai*'s life, in a word, was based upon the fact of allegiance, both in its spiritual and material phases. Spiritually, feudal lords, vassals, and retainers, trusted one another and formed a permanent tie of personal loyalty; materially, the life of the *samurai* was

sustained by the annual grants of rice which
were given to them by their respective lords,
the feudal lords, or *daimyō*.

We shall first consider the spiritual side.
The relation of loyalty, that is, of the *samurai* to
his lord, was formed several generations prior to
the foundation of the Shogunate. But in course
of time, the tie seemed to have lost much of its
vigour, it only existed as a historical relationship.
Its outward expression was perfected through
the Shogunate's effort at maintaining the military
hierarchy. There were various classes within the
same class and the distinction between them was
strictly maintained by various outward forms,
such as the different ceremonies and greetings
required at entering the gates of a castle or residence, or the nature of the honorary addresses
used in public documents, etc. But the spiritual
tie based on personal loyalty was weakened as
the outward form was perfected. The descendants
of great ancestors often proved persons of weak
characters or of meagre capacity, while successors
to the *samurai* house were also in many cases
inherited by adopted sons, who would not dare
to sacrifice their own lives for the sake of their
lords. Especially, as *samurai* began to hire temporary paid retainers, this personal tie almost
became extinct.

Temporary, paid retainers were wage workers.
A master hired retainers for a fixed sum for a
certain period of time. Their relations in con-

sequence were simply a matter of contract; they were devoid of the personal sentiment of love and fidelity which marked the tie between a master and his hereditary retainers. Ogyū-Sorai mentions in his treatise on politics,[3] written during the Kyōho era, that the hereditary retainers had been entirely replaced by hired retainers and that even great farmers had very few hereditary servants. We may then suppose that there were a great number of temporary hired retainers by the middle of the Tokugawa period.

As I have already pointed out, the hereditary retainers became unproductive after the separation of *samurai* and farmer, as they no longer tilled the soil of their master. The *samurai* no longer became able to support their hereditary servants. Moreover, hired retainers were superior to those hereditary ones in that they knew more about Edo than the former as they were denizens of the capital. But the hiring of those paid retainers put an end to the personal tie which had existed between the *samurai* and his servants. On this point Ogyū-Sorai says:[4]

"In these times of peace, all *samurai* hire paid servants. As those servants are hired for the period of one year, their relations to the master are like those between men in the street. Whenever some trouble arose, the master would

---

[3] *'Seidan.'*
[4] ibid.

call the one who acted as go-between in hiring them, and discharge them in his presence. The master thought that this summarily ended his relation with such discharged servants. The servants, on the other hand, regarded all *samurai* in Edo as their masters. Thus the loyalty existed only in name. . . .

" The hereditary servants of *samurai* when the latter lived in the country where rice was produced, were a sort of farmers. Though rustic, they were true. But those paid servants whom *samurai* are employing in the castle-town do not usually stay long in any one place ; and, in consequence, are irresponsible and reckless. . . . The replacing of hereditary retainers by hired ones has had a demoralising effect upon the ethical conduct of the *samurai* class in general."

Great *daimyō* who held extensive territories did not employ paid retainers, but lesser *daimyō*, *hatamoto* and small *samurai* had to employ them in great numbers. The spiritual tie was thereby lost.

Let us now consider the material side of the question. After the separation of *samurai* and farmer, it seemed as though the *samurai* who moved to cities were a leisure class without definite means of subsistence, receiving annual stipends because of the military service of their ancestors. They, however, received those grants of rice for their loyalty to the lords ; because of these grants, *samurai* would be ever ready to expose themselves to danger for the sake of their lords. They had no other source of income, and their patience was extremely tried when they pretended to be satisfied even though their revenue did not allow them to make a decent living. Nor was it an honourable thing for them to be satisfied with a revenue insufficient for their subsistence. Moreover, the poverty of the *daimyō* compelled them to reduce the fixed annual stipends of the *samurai*.

The following is extracted from the '*Shōhei Yawa*':

"The adoption of the system of annual grants of rice for the pay of *samurai* was the fundamental cause of the decline of their prestige. Reductions of the grants of rice came into being because of this very system. The reduction of a *samurai*'s revenue had no justifiable ground whatever. . . . There is absolutely no reason why the rightful revenue of one who has committed no wrong should be cut by one-half. There was no such custom in the ancient times. True, as *samurai* were expected to sacrifice their very lives for the sake of their lord they should be ready to give up their entire revenue for his sake, if only there were some great necessity for it. But if the lord himself should break promises, seek selfish ends and have no compassion for the sufferings of his subordinates, the latter cannot but entertain discontent. Discontent breeds disobedience. There is no guarantee that in times of great emergency, the *samurai* would not foresake their master and flee."

It was only too natural that the material relations between the feudal lord and his *samurai* could not remain pure and true as they had been before the separation of *samurai* and farmer. Under the new condition, *samurai* were expected to be ready to sacrifice their lives for the sake of their master, and they would often complain of their hard lot. This complaint indicates that their material relations with their master were not sufficient, and that the foundation of their economic life had become greatly weakened. After the middle of the Tokugawa period, this foundation became extremely unstable; *samurai* were exposed to great poverty; and the very existence of the *samurai* class was threatend with extinction.

CHAPTER VIII

THE AGRARIAN PROBLEM IN THE TOKUGAWA PERIOD

1. THE LIFE OF FARMERS

In the days of the Tokugawa Shogunate, rice formed the basis of the country's finance and economy, and as the country's population had to be fed with the rice produced at home, the cereal was held as particularly precious by the people. Inasmuch as the country owed the production of this important commodity to agriculture, special regard was naturally had for agriculture, which was popularly called the mainstay of the country. Most scholars of those days regarded agriculture as the principal pursuit and looked upon industry and commerce as subsidiary occupations. They held that only by promoting the principal pursuit and by holding the subsidiary ones in check could the country be properly ruled and the happiness of the people advanced. Even Yamakata-Bantō, who was a merchant in Ōsaka, says in his book entitled the '*Yume no Shiro*': "Agriculture should be encouraged, while commerce should be discouraged. Farmers are the essence of the country. They are more important than any other class of people. Farmers cannot be dispensed with, though we can do without merchants and artisans. Efforts should be made to increase the number of farmers and to reduce that of merchants. It is the pre-requisite of statesmanship to advance the interests of the farming population by encouraging agriculture at the expense of the townspeople."

The life of farmers in those days was, however, very wretched. Their freedom of action was most ruthlessly restricted. Their lot was, indeed, so hard that they appeared to exist simply for the purpose of paying taxes.

The fundamental policy of dealing with farmers in those days was to keep them to a low standard of living. Efforts were made to prevent them from improving their miserable mode of living in any way, or sharing in the bliss of civilised life, so that they might be contented with a life which was little better than that of dumb animals forever. "Agriculture is the mainstay of the State" was a popular saying, but the fact was that while agriculture was held in regard, the farmers were treated with scant respect. In other words, the saying simply denoted the principle of basing the country on agriculture, but not the principle of putting the interests of the farmers before those of any other class of people.

The famous official notice of the second year of Keian (1649) describes farmers as a class of people who have neither wisdom nor prudence. From this notice it is clear that official inter-

ference thrust itself, not only into the management of the farmer's business, but even into
matters relating to the private life of the farmer
himself. As the policy of the authorities in those
days was to keep farmers down to their low
standard of living, it was considered a most de-
testable thing for farmers to lead a luxurious life
by imitating merchants or townspeople. Villages
were, therefore, dissociated from towns and farmers were isolated from townspeople. Furthermore,
attempts were made to prevent the growth of
economic knowledge among the farming population, so that they might be contented with the life
of serfdom all their life through. Many scholars
in those days held views supporting such a policy.
For instance, a book entitled the ' *Hyakushō
Bukuro* ' contains the warning: " Farmers should
by no means imitate the mode of living of towns-
people."   In the ' *Kashoku Yōdō* ' appears the
following advice : " Farmers should not wed their
children to those of townspeople," while the
' *Keizai Mondo Hiroku* ' mentions : " It is a good
farmer who does not know the prices of cereals."
It was considered the sole duty of farmers to produce, regardless of the market price, the cereals
with a single-eyed devotion, so as to be able to
pay as much tax as possible. It is a well-known
fact that taxes were exacted with the utmost
severity. In the ' *Jikata Ochibo-shū*,' farmers are
compared to well-water, saying : " If moderately
drawn, a well can supply sufficient water to a

farmhouse, for moderate drawing gives time enough for water to flow out. There will be, then, an inexhaustible supply of water for all times. If, on the contrary, the well be drawn on too abundantly, the supply would soon be exhausted, and what water that could be obtained would be too muddy to be drunk. In levying imposts upon farmers this truism must be kept in mind, for if farmers are taxed in the former way, they will not suffer much and the taxes will continue to flow in from generation to generation." This only shows the severity with which exactions were made. In short, farmers were, so to speak, a kind of productive machinery which was worked to an excessive extent. In the '*Minkan Seiyō*' it is said : " A class of people known as farmers are groaning under maladministration, heavy taxes, and exacting service, and yet they have no means of airing their grievances. Their hard lot causes many to go bankrupt, to sell their wives and children, or to suffer severe losses or lose their lives, but they must put up with it, suffering without complaint the abuses heaped upon them and the thrashings meted out to them at all times. However cruelly they may be treated, they cannot protest against their treatment. Officials, however petty, lorded it over farmers, who winced under their minatory stare. Some petty officials were formerly farmers themselves, and yet they treat farmers with harshness. It is like burning dried bean plants in order to boil beans. The overbearing attitude of these officials may be likened to that of a cruel driver of a horse or a cow. He puts a heavy burden on the animal and beats it mercilessly. When it stumbles, he gets all the more angry and whips it with greater violence, cursing it viciously. Such is the lot of farmers too." The above description is a true picture of the wretched life which farmers were forced to lead in those days.

The burdens under which farmers were groaning were so excessively heavy, that, being made of flesh and blood like other men, they could not be expected to remain contented with a life which was little better than that of the beasts of the field forever With the general levelling up of the standard of living for all people, and especially when they saw the luxurious life which townspeople were leading, their desire for a better life received a stimulus, and their costs of living grew in consequence. The farmer who formerly used straws in tying their hair and who were contented with their shabby clothes, came gradually to prefer Edo (Tōkyō) *motoyui* (paper strings for tying the hair) and to use aloes-wood oil, into the bargain. It is hardly necessary to say that this made their living even more difficult. According to a few books in which the economic life of farmers in those days is described, most farmers, middle-class and downwards, could not earn enough to support their families by following the agricultural pursuit only.

To make matters worse, what with the crude
state of agriculture then prevailing and the imperfect means of communication available, there
were frequent visitations of famine, which wrought
complete havoc with the life of many farmers.
In short, it is quite clear that farmers were in
great distress at the best of times, a fact which
was, indeed, widely recognised by most scholars
in those days. It must be admitted at the same
time, however, that some big landowners among
the farmers were quite comfortably off, so farmers were presumably divided into rich and poor.
In the ' Seji Kemmonroku ' it is noted that " the
disparity between the rich and poor has grown
very marked, and for one man who makes a
fortune, there are twenty or thirty farmers who
are reduced to penury." Mention is also made
of the fact that one man could live in luxury at
the expense of a multitude.

2. THE IMPOVERISHMENT OF THE FARMING CLASS

I have already explained the great distress
of the farmers in those days. Their difficulty of
living produced its effects in various directions.
To sum up, it brought about the impoverishment
of the farming class.

(a) **The population problem.** As one phase
of the impoverishment of the agrarian class, the
population question must, in the first place, be

dealt with. In the latter half of the Tokugawa period, conservatism and retrogression ruled in all fields of activity. The country's population was also, on the whole, stationary. In those days, the evil custom of abortion and infanticide prevailed all over the country, and this greatly hindered the increase of the farming population. It is on record that in the fourth year of Meiwa (1767) an official order was issued prohibiting such evil practices. Many examples can be cited to illustrate how infanticide prevailed in those days.[1] Infanticide was then called *mabiki* (thinning), a fact which shows that people thought no more seriously of this shocking deed than rooting up vegetables. It seems that the urban districts were not entirely free from this evil custom, but things were not so bad there as in the rural districts. Needless to say, this was a custom which arose out of the difficulty of supporting many children and it throws much light on the very distressful life which the farmers were leading in those days. The decrease of the farming population resulted in a shortage of labour power, which, in turn, brought about the decline of agricultural interests.

The influx of farmers into towns was another contributory cause of the decrease of the farming population. The life of farmers being so wretched as has been described above, many farmers, finding it unbearable, forsook the plough and moved

---

[1] cf. Chap. V.

to towns, where they either turned tradesmen or became day-labourers. It is quite natural that there should have been a marked inflow of country-folk into towns, once it was discovered that they could live in a freer atmosphere in towns and that it was easier to earn a living there. The fact is generally admitted that the expansion of big cities — Edo in particular — was due largely to the influx of country-folk. There is no denying the fact that this influx of farmers into towns reduced the farming population.[2]

Due note must at the same time be taken of the fact that rural life gradually took on much of the aspect of urban life. Although it was the policy pursued by the authorities in those days to dissociate the rural districts from the urban districts and to isolate farmers from townspeople, farmers living near towns gradually got into the habit of imitating the life and manners of the town. Some farmers made it their aim to live the life of towns-people for which they had been yearning. Some married their children to those of townspeople, while others gave up the plough and set up small shops. Thus it seems that there were many inhabitants of farm villages who did not follow agriculture as their sole pursuit.[3]

Thus, the farming population fell off by processes both natural and artificial. All who remained in their native villages did not follow the

---

[2] cf. Chap. V.
[3] cf. Chap. VI.

plough. This naturally caused a shortage of labour power, with the result that farms were allowed to go to waste and the farmers became impoverished. This is the most important phase that calls for attention in considering the question of the impoverishment of the agrarian class.

(b) **The land question.** During the Tokugawa régime, the sale of farms owned by farmers was prohibited in order to prevent the bankruptcy of farmers and the annexation of land. It was with the same object in view that restrictions were put on the division of land by farmers among their children. It was laid down that unless they owned land covering over 1 *chō* (2.45 acres) which yielded rice amounting to over 10 *koku* (some 50 bushels) of rice, farmers should not divided their land among their children, because it was feared that if the division of land were allowed unrestrictedly there would be created numberless poor farmers who could not manage to pick up a livelihood. As a matter of fact, however, it seems that this prohibitory rule was not strictly enforced. Various devices were invented to elude the prohibition to sell farms. Farms frequently changed hands also in the form of pawns forfeited, and there actually occurred many cases of annexation of land. Inasmuch as the farmers in those days were reduced to such straits, as already explained, many had to pawn their land in order to raise the money necessary for paying taxes and obtaining means of sustenance, and as there was no alternative but to turn to rich people for financial aid, land inevitably passed more and more into the hands of the rich. According to the ' *Seji Kemmonroku,*' all good farms fell into the possession of the rich, the poor owing only such farms as could produce but little. In some districts, the practice was widely resorted to by poor farmers to under-rate the quantity of rice produced in the fields which they intended to sell and to over-rate the rice yield for the fields which they wished to retain, for the express purpose of selling their fields at as high a price as possible. The result was that rich farmers could obtain good farms on which light taxes were imposed at comparatively low prices, while poor farmers had to cultivate bad fields burdened with heavy taxes. Those who were unfortunate enough to part with even their bad farms sank to the status of tenant farmers. The lot of tenant farmers was a very hard one. They had to drudge on the farms of big landowners, handing all the rice produced thereon over to their landowners as rent, themselves retaining only chaff, bran, straw and the like. Not a moment of rest or comfort could they get all the year round. The rich, on the other hand, went on amassing wealth, increasing their land every year. They created branch families, each of which lived in grand style. On the contrary, the poor grew poorer and poorer. They parted with their farms, disposed of their estates and, in many cases, their homes were scattered.

Thus for one farmer who became wealthy, there were twenty or thirty farmers who were reduced to distress.

Another phase of the land question is presented by the waste of land. As already stated, the desertion of their villages by poor farmers caused large areas of land to go to waste. For other reasons also, land was let run waste. For instance, farmers gradually learned by experience that it was foolish to do any work earnestly from which they could derive little profit. Some concluded that it was more advantageous to earn a living by selling firewood or doing manual work as day-labourers than to waste much energy in putting barren land under cultivation for a pittance, and gave up the plough. Some went in for a retrogressive life and neglected their farms, because of their desire to be relieved of the troublesome procedure of cultivation and tax-paying. Owners of good farms also found the taxes levied upon their land so heavy that there was no margin of profit, despite their indefatigable labour. They, therefore, vied with one another in giving their land away to poor people. In some extreme cases, they had to give some money together with their land, as, otherwise, they could not induce poor people to accept it. This anomalous state of things was particularly marked in Mito and district, and it had the grievous effect of transforming many fertile farms into waste land. Of course, the work of reclaiming land for cultivation purposes was going on in many places in those days, and, generally speaking, there was an increase in the acreage of land under cultivation, while improvements were also made in the methods of cultivation. On the other hand, however, there were cases where old rice fields were damaged by the process of creating new rice-fields. The taxes levied upon farmers were very heavy or the methods of collection adopted were extremely exacting. Finding themselves unable to stand all this, many farmers abandoned their villages to complete ruin, and large tracts of land were left to go to waste in the Ōu and Kantō districts, and many other localities.

Another cause of the waste of land was the *sukegō* system. In those days there were agents at the post-towns on the five Highroads and other roads, who kept men and horses in readiness for service. As traffic grew heavier, these men and horses were found inadequate to meet the demand, and what was called the *sukegō* system came into being in consequence. Under this system a certain number of men and horses were commandeered from neighbouring villages according to their size. It often happend that the agents tried to put larger part of service on villagers, or that they kept men and horses commandeered from villages all day long without any work, letting them go home towards evening. Some villages from which men and horses were very frequently requisitioned were obliged to ask the agents to undertake the task for them by paying exorbitant compensation at the rate of 700 *mon* per head and 1,000 *mon* per horse. This added greatly to the distress and complaint of the villages. It is obvious that this *sukegō* system interfered with the farming business and caused land to go to waste and farmers to become impoverished in many cases.

(c) **The farm tenancy problem.**[4] The farm tenancy system prevailed in the Tokugawa régime. There were two kinds of farm tenancy. One referred to the tenancy of the land belonging to landowners, which was called *myōden-kosaku*. The other kind, which was termed *shichiji-kosaku*, referred to the tenancy of the land in pawn. Ordinary tenancy was that where big owners of land rented their land to small farmers to cultivate. When the period of tenancy was fixed at over twenty years, it was called *eikosaku* (permanent tenancy). The permanent tenancy system, was often adopted so as to facilitate the recruitment of tenant farmers for the cultivation, for instance, of rice fields newly reclaimed. The labourers who were employed on the reclamation work were often made permanent tenant farmers. *Shichiji-kosaku* was also divided into two kinds. One was that the owner of the land in pawn became the tenant of it and this was called *jiki-kosaku* (direct tenancy), while the other kind,

---

[4] cf. Chap. I.

which was known as *betsu-kosaku* (separate tenancy) was that the creditor rented the land in pawn to a person other than its owner.

Tenant farmers are a class of people who, owning no land of their own to cultivate, till the land which they rent from others. The social position of such farmers was accordingly very low. They were not qualified to take rank with landowning farmers. When, on some occasions, villagers met together, they always took the lowest seats. The same marked disparity in social position as existed between landlord and tenant in towns subsisted between landowner and tenant farmer. In towns, landlords were privileged to take part in the discussion and settlement of public matters relating to their towns or streets, but such rights were absolutely denied to tenants.

I have already described the pitiable life of the farmers generally. If the lot of common farmers was a very hard one, the life of tenant farmers was positively wretched. In a book entitled the '*Minkan Seiyō*,' we find the following: "Landowners know perfectly well that tenant farmers can hardly find their account in farming and wonder how they can manage to pay their landowners their rents in rice, as stipulated. Yet landowners think it politic not to betray what is in their minds." Instances are also quoted where landowners took their tenant farmers to task, because taxes and other public imposts on their land increased in proportion to the increase in the yield of rice, thanks to the assiduity with which tenant farmers cultivated the land. Tenant farmers found themselves in a dilemma, for their energetic cultivation only earned for them the displeasure of their landowners, while, if they went about their work in a sluggish way, they could not earn enough to keep body and soul together.

It would appear at first sight that it was to their mutual interest that those who had no regular occupation should take to tenant farming, while owners of extensive tracts of land should rent their land to tenant farmers. As a matter of fact, however, the interests of landowner and tenant farmer were often at variance, and there were evidently many cases even in those days where the two classes — the landowners, the oppressors, and the tenant farmers, the oppressed — were at daggers-drawn. As I have already mentioned, there were some tenant disputes in the Kyōho era (1716-1735), in the fifth year of Meiwa (1768), in the second year of Kansei (1790), and in the Kōka and Kaei eras (1844-1853).[5]

(d) **Farmers riots.**[6] Farm tenancy disputes mean trouble between landowner and tenant farmer, or, in a sense, hostile rivalry between two classes of farmers. In some cases, however, groups of farmers in certain villages rose in re-

---

5) cf. Chap. I.
6) cf. Chap. I.

volt against their feudal lords or the agricultural officials. Thus these disputes lead to farmers riots. If the birth-control measures, and the abandonment of the plough already referred to were negative steps taken by the farmers to extricate themselves out of the difficulty of living, the farmers riots were the positive measures to better the distressing conditions of their existence.

Farmers riots broke out frequently during the latter half of the Tokugawa period. They occurred most often when there were excessive exactions, or when the authorities failed to take appropriate relief measures in famine years. The discontent and irritation which farmers entertained towards their liege lords and the agricultural officials at other times found violent vent on such occasions. The farmers who were similarly circumstanced rallied round the ring-leaders and advanced in large bodies on the castle-towns to make direct appeals to their feudal lords, running riot at the same time. The ring-leaders were condemned to death in such cases, but the demands of the rioters were generally accepted. Towards the closing days of the Tokugawa Shogunate, those riots grew very complex in nature, and some of them hardly fall within the domain of agrarian problems. However that may be, the farmers riots generally occurring during the Tokugawa period clearly constituted important agrarian problems as embodying the positive revolt of farmers against their rulers.

3. THE POLICY TO RELIEVE AND ENRICH
THE FARMING CLASS

I have dealt with the more important phases of the agrarian problem, and next I propose briefly to state the measures taken by the authorities of those days in coping with the situation then prevailing.

(a) **The population policy.** So far as the policy for the prevention of abortions and infanticides is concerned, the Shogunate gave it a good deal of attention, and its policy in this direction seems to have been productive of some good results in some districts. But, on the whole, it was not very effective. Efforts were also made by *daimyō* to reform these evil customs. Lord Matsudaira-Rakuō, for instance, took much pains in order to eradicate them. Hearing that while there prevailed such evils in his chief fief of Shirakawa, Echigo, his branch fief, was quite free from them, the inhabitants there being industrious and having a strong aversion from infanticides because of their firm religious faith, he caused Echigo women to settle in Shirakawa. He saw to it that these women were supplied with houses and land, got married, and engaged in farming and weaving. He also kept the registers of pregnant women, and ordered the people to report births to the proper authorities. The system of official inspection of newborn babies was also adopted. To the poor parents of babies money was given towards the expense of bringing them up. Thanks to these measures, the calculation of the number of people taken in the fourth year of Kansei (1792) showed that the population within the fief of Shirakawa increased by more than 3,500 since the fifth year of Temmei (1785). Some new villages were created and there was an increase in the production of rice in many places. In the Sendai, Shōnai, Mito and other *han* also, the system of supplying infant-rearing funds and other kindred methods were adopted. Many scholars in those days urged in their books the need of such methods for the reform of the bad customs and for the increase of the population.[7]

By way of preventing the influx of countryfolk into the urban districts, the Shogunate pursued the policy of inducing these people to go back to farming. The Shogunate decree issued in March of the fourteenth year of Tempo (1843) prohibited the settlement of farmers in Edo. Even in the case of those who had already settled in Edo, steps were taken to make all, except those engaged in permanent occupations or having their families with them, return to their native villages. With regard to those farmers who went up to Edo in search of work, a certain period was fixed for their residence there, and they were ordered to go home at the

[7] cf. Chap. V.

end of this period. Strict control was also exercised over Buddhist and Shinto priests, fortunetellers or pilgrims who frequented Edo. These measures did not meet with eminent success, however. They had the effect of reducing the farmers in temporary employment in Edo for a time, but they did not bring about any tangible result.[8]

(b) **The land policy.** That the Shogunate pursued the policy of preventing the annexation of land, as far as possible, is obvious from the fact that permanent sales and purchases of land and similar transactions were vetoed. This policy was not successful, as I have already noted, as transfer of landownership took place in the form of the forfeiture of land or estates, held as security for mortgages, etc.

The waste of land caused much concern to the Shogunate, which often issued instructions ordering farmers to engage in farming with diligence. In the preface of the ' *Goningumi-chō* ' we find the injunction not to allow even a patch of land to go to waste. In October of the eighth year of Temmei (1788), instructions were issued to Mutsu, Hidachi, Shimōsa and Shimozuke provinces, under which rich people were ordered to take into their service those farmers who might be contemplating leaving their provinces to seek fortune elsewhere, and put them to farm work.

---

[8] cf. Chap. V.

It is also mentioned that the Shogunate was willing to give allowances to poor farmers to help them put waste land under cultivation. In some other *han* too, similar steps were taken. Lord Uesugi-Harunori, of the Yonezawa-Han, appropriated a certain sum as an agricultural encouragement fund, which was employed for the promotion of the cultivation of land and the settlement of people in his fief. He is also said to have seen to it that new farmers were supplied with funds and that reclaimers of waste lands were exempted from taxes. Earnest endeavours were made to increase the productivity of old farms, and when it was feared that old farms would be damaged by the reclamation of new fields, such reclamation work was not permitted. As a matter of fact, however, it seems that there were many cases where the productivity of old farms was affected by reclamation works.

In the Tokugawa period, there was what was called the land allotment system (*jiwari*). At every stated interval, land was divided into many parts, each of which was allotted to the villagers, re-allotment taking place at the end of each period. This system operated over quite a wide extent of our country. So far as has been ascertained up to the present, it was in operation in the provinces of Iwashiro, Hidachi, Kaga, Noto, Echizen, Etchū, Echigo, Owari, Shinano, Mino, Ise, Tango, Iyo, Tosa, Chikuzen, Bungo, Hizen, Hyūga, Satsuma, Iki, Tsushima and Okinawa (Loochoo).

Various causes may be assigned for the coming into being of this system, but the main cause was, when it was applied to old farms, a desire to make the incidence of taxes on the villagers as fair as possible, so as to prevent the waste of land. Where floods were frequent this system was operated in order to equalise profits and losses for the villagers so that all villagers could be saved from ruin. When it was applied to newly reclaimed land, it was due to the joint reclamation of land, or for the purpose of equalising profits and losses for the farmers in flood-time. Thus, this land allotment system may be regarded as one device to avert the annexation of land, to prevent the flight of bankrupt farmers from their villages, and to avoid the waste of agricultural land.

(c) **The policy of providing against famine.** Famines were frequent in the Tokugawa period, and this rendered the life of farmers all the more difficult. These times of dearth sometimes dealt a fatal blow to many farmers. The miseries caused by the famines which overtook the country in the Kyōho, Temmei and Tempo eras were enough to make one's blood run cold. Needless to say, various relief measures were then projected and an earnest study was made of substitutes for rice and barley. Moreover, there had been in general operation a system of providing against famines. For instance, the Shogunate and all feudal lords had their warehouses for the storage of cereals to be used in time of emergency. In Edo, Ōsaka and other places also, storehouses of a similar kind were provided against the day of need. But for this storage of cereals, which served the good purpose of relief, the effects of the famines would have been far more disastrous.

         ✲   ✲   ✲

      ✲   ✲

The difficulty of living of the farmers was mainly due to the excessive burden of taxation and therefore there was no doubt that the lessening of this burden was a most desirable thing. But the rulers were so circumstanced that they could not carry on unless the farmers were taxed heavily. In such circumstances, good feudal lords, their wise vassals and scholars, who might have been cognisant of the necessity of lessening the burden on the farmers, probably found that nothing short of a radical reform of the political, social and economic systems then ruling would enable them to carry out their wishes.

The population policy, the land policy and the policy of providing against famine, which have been explained above, may well be looked upon as measures adopted for a solution of the agrarian problem, but it is not likely that these measures were adequate to solve it. Seeing that the question of lightening the grievous burden on the farmers, which was the nucleus of the whole problem, was beset with such supreme difficulties as already stated, an effectual settlement of the agrarian problem could not be expected to be achieved, if all other measures, which were, after all, of secondary importance, worked well. Indeed, a successful solution of this basic problem was an utter impossibility unless the political and social organisations of those days in which the *samurai* class was predominant and the farmers and *chōnin* subservient were changed. It must be remembered that, just as the agrarian question to-day is due, after all, to the essential nature of agriculture and the present-day economic system, the agrarian problem in the Tokugawa period sprang from the political, social and economic systems of those days.

CHAPTER IX
THE *CHŌNIN* CLASS IN THE
TOKUGAWA PERIOD

1. THE SOCIAL STATUS OF THE *CHŌNIN*

Of the four social classes that constituted the social fabric of the feudal period of Tokugawa, namely, *samurai*, farmer, artisan, and merchant, the last two made up what was generally termed *chōnin* or commoners, in contradistinction to the higher social class of *samurai*. In the eye of the authorities of the Feudal Government, the social status of commoners was much inferior to that of both the *samurai* whose ancestors had rendered very meritorious services to the State and the farmers who were engaged in the ceaseless toil of producing the main foodstuff of the nation. The commoners were viewed as a class of people who indulged in the despicable enjoyment of life; who were shamelessly devoted to a life of profit-making through exchange of goods; and who would resort to any dubious method in order to coax others to buy high-priced goods, thereby stimulating a habit of luxury, the demoralising effects of which were greatly feared by the authorities. The commoners, in short, were considered a good-for-nothing and unproductive class of people. In the opinion of the *samurai*, the commoners should be grateful for their being allowed to engage in their vocation, and were expected to make monetary contributions as *myōga* and *unjō* to the ruling class. Thus, the feudal authorities never seriously thought of imposing any formal tax on the commoners.

The feudal authorities exercised much interference in the daily life of the commoners as in the case of farmers. The use of articles of daily necessity such as head and foot gear and even such things as umbrellas was strictly circumscribed by law. Both commoners and farmers were prohibited from using silk clothes. Strict control was also exercised regarding the consumption of various commodities : sale of articles of novelty was prohibited ; sale of vegetables produced before their proper season of harvest was also prohibited ; raise of labour wage as well as of commodity prices following some great natural calamity was barred. The manufacturers of *tōfu* would be scolded by the authorities for their failure to lower the prices of their product, when the price of beans, raw material used in the manufacturing of *tōfu*, dropped. Various intricate methods were also adopted by the feudal authorities in order to regulate the prices of commodities, especially rice.

Although commoners were subjected to various interferences by the feudal authorities in their daily life, their treatment was vastly better than

that which was accorded to farmers, when the nature and degree of the interferences are taken into
consideration. This may become clear when the
following two sets of official notices issued in the
second year of Keian (1649), one for farmers and the
other for commoners, are compared. The notice
issued for commoners were directed to prevent
them from indulging in extravagance and luxury
and all insulting remarks were carefully avoided
in its wording. Commoners were simply told
" not to wear silk dress," " not to make gold
lacquered furnitures," " not to use either gold or
silver in house decorations," and " not to build
any three-storied house for themselves." The
notice for farmers, on the other hand, told them
in no uncertain terms that " they had no discre-
tion in their daily conduct nor any purpose in
life." Moreover, their daily life was subjected to
a stricter regulation than in the case of commoners. For instance, they were urged to cultivate a habit of early rising and were prohibited
from drinking *sake* and tea as well as from smok-
ing. They were ordered not to eat rice and to
eat other cereals and urged to divorce lazy wives.
Thus, the notice implied a recognition of farmers'
mental and educational inferiority. However, in
social rank commoners were regarded as being
inferior to farmers chiefly because the former
were engaged in the despicable practice of profit-
making for private ends (in the opinion of the
feudal authorities); and, as has been already

pointed out, the commoners often made monetary contributions to the authorities in token of their gratitude for their being allowed to engage in business. The fact is to be noted, however, that the superiority of their standard of living and of their economic power was unquestioned. Commoners were allowed to form industrial guilds among themselves for the purposes of their common solidarity and monopoly, and enjoyed self-government to a certain extent.

2. THE FINANCIAL POWER OF THE *CHŌNIN*

I have dwelt on the social status of the merchants of the Tokugawa period in its formal aspect. This period was marked by the wide prevalence of rice economy and the gradual development of money economy which finally came to replace the former in the course of time. Those who had financial and economic knowledge were in a position to amass wealth and to attain an economic power of great magnitude. The long reign of tranquillity in the land had brought changes in the life of the *samurai* who constituted the ruling class of the time. They had put away weapons of fighting, and wars and battles only remained in their memories. People had gradually acquired the habit of luxurious living and the *samurai* had no occasion to use the military power, which had been replaced by the power of money. Now, it was the commoners who had command over this new power. At first both the Feudal Government and many *daimyō* often exacted forced contributions called *goyōkin* from wealthy commoners of Edo, Kyōto, and Ōsaka, but later they had to bend their knees in order to borrow from them. It was with the financial help thus rendered by the wealthy merchants that the *samurai* could barely succeed in making both ends meet. In the '*Keizeiroku*,' Dazai-Shundai says : " Present-day *daimyō*, both big and small, bow before wealthy commoners in order to borrow money from them and depend on the merchants of Edo, Kyōto, Ōsaka, etc. for their continued living." The foregoing quotation is sufficient to indicate the great extent to which the *samurai* class depended on the financial assistance of wealthy commoners whose economic power over the entire realm had so greatly expended. Another record of the time entitled '*Chōnin Kōken-roku*' written by Mitsui-Takafusa, an ancestor of the Mitsui Family, throws a flood of light on the financial relations between some fifty wealthy commoners of the time and the *daimyō* during a period of about sixty years in and around the Genroku era (1688–1703). The book gives an account of the bankruptcy of these fifty families whose financial downfall was caused either by forced contributions or their own extravagant living. This record unmistakably proves the fact that the *daimyō* borrowed a vast amount of money from the wealthy commoners of Kyōto.

The list of *daimyō*-debtors includes the Lords of the following provinces : Kaga, Satsuma, Sendai, Higo, Hiroshima, Tottori, Nambu, Owari, Kii, Tsuyama, Chōshū, Tosa, Saga, Yonezawa, Fukuoka, etc. These powerful *daimyō* managed to patch up their finances with the financial aid of wealthy merchants.

The majority of *daimyō* had their *kurayashiki* or warehousing quarters at Ōsaka or Edo, in order to facilitate the sale of their rice and other products raised in their respective territories. The *daimyō* of Northern Japan had their *kurayashiki* mostly at Edo, while those of Central and Western Japan including the Kantō district had their warehouses at Ōsaka, where the products brought there were either sold or mortgaged.

The warehousing official called *kurayakunin* was in charge of each *kurayashiki*. He was sent by the *daimyō* who was the owner of the warehouse and he represented his lord. At first he also acted as *kuramoto* or the keeper of the warehouse, but the later period the *kuramoto* was assumed by a merchant of great wealth. He was in charge of the receiving and delivery of warehouse goods. There was another official in the *kurayashiki* who was in charge of the accounting of the transactions of warehouse goods and who was known by the name of *kakeya*. This position was also often assumed by the *kuramoto*. The *kakeya*, like the *fudasashi* at Edo, was a financial agent for *daimyō* and *samurai* in general. He

was usually given an annual grant of rice and
treatment similar to that which was given to the
chief retainer of a *daimyō*. The foremost *kuramoto* at Ōsaka was called Kōnoike-Zen'emon, who
was in the service of the many *daimyō* including the following: Kaga, Hiroshima, Awa, Oka-
yama and Yanagawa. He was also in the special
service for the Lords of Owari and Kii, and his
total fief amounted to 10,000 *koku*. Some of the
branches of his family received an annual grant
of rice sufficient to support some 70 men. Thus,
such wealthy merchants as Kōnoike-Zen'emon,
Hiranoya-Gohei and Tennōjiya-Gohei lived as
extravagantly as a *daimyō*.

Naturally enough, the *kuramoto* possessed a
powerful influence over the finance of the *daimyō*
he served. For instance, Masuya-Heiemon, an
Ōsaka merchant, exercised an almost absolute
power over the finance of the Sendai-Han in
the capacity of its *kuramoto*. He was described
by Kaihō-Seiryō, a noted writer of the period, as
" having taken over unto himself the management
of the household finance of the Lord of Sendai."
The Sendai-Han engaged several merchants acting as its *kuramoto* over a long period of time,
but none of them was as powerful as Masuya-
Heiemon.

The settlement of loans advanced to *daimyo*
by merchants would often drag for many years.
With the passing of years, the former would find
themselves in deeper waters, and they would

frequently demand settlement by instalments or
exemption of interest. Such a demand was usually accepted in case the merchants were in the
capacity of *kuramoto*, because they were in a
position to secure interest, receive annual grant
of rice, and often received various gifts from the
daimyō whom they served; so that the principal
could be returned in a period of ten years or so.
On the other hand, the merchants harassed by
the repressive measures of irresponsible *daimyō*
knew how to deal with them. The merchants
pledged among themselves not to make further
advances to such *daimyō* in the future, and this
refusal often had electric effect. For a defaulting *daimyō* would invariably make an apology to
the creditor, to whom gifts would be presented
and the promise made that the repayment of the
debts would be made so that future advances
would be made by the merchant. "*Samurai* were
fired with anger (at the indignity of being hard
pressed by merchants), but they forebore the in-
solence of merchants, and were even ready to
give up *bushidō* in their attempt to court the
goodwill of the commoners, for the sake of their
Lord (who had to borrow from the commoners)."
A writer of the period called Shingū-Ryōtei wrote:
"Shameless and regrettable is the flattery shown
by the high retainers of *daimyō* to the commoner-
creditors. They would proceed at the head of
a suite of scores of attendants to offer respects
to their commoner-creditors, as if the latter were

their own lords, and would flatter the shop clerks in a most despicable manner."

Retaliatory measures against *samurai* who failed to settle debts were adopted by commoner-creditors as early as during the Kyōho era (1716-1735). One of the common practices adopted by them was to place a paper flag or to paste a paper in front of the *samurai*'s house in case the latter failed to repay his debts or make payment for some goods. In December, the fourteenth year of Kyōho (1729), a decree was issued by the Edo Government, providing that any commoner who committed such an act of misdemeanour against a *samurai* would be severely dealt with.

The commoners also extended their financial arm over to the farm districts where there was an unmistakable tendency of concentration in land. We may naturally conceive, therefore, that transactions in land and borrowing of money for other agricultural purposes were no longer limited to farmers themselves, for merchants gradually came to participate in them to a great extent. Many merchants possessed concentrated lands and newly developed lands. Many commoners took an active part in the enterprise of developing new lands for agricultural purposes.

The *samurai* class, in short, was under the financial sway of the commoners. '*Chōnin Bukuro*' says: " No one knows when the practice of using gold and silver originated, but it made its development steadily. As the commoners had sway over

gold and silver, they would be allowed to be in
the presence of nobles. Thus, they came to be
superior to the farmers in point of personal appearance." Nay, they are superior not only to
the farmers but also to the *samurai* class in respect of economic power. They hold in a firm
grip the economic power of the realm and constitute a powerful force in feudal society.

3. THE PRIVATE LIFE OF THE *CHŌNIN*

The commoner class attained full development
during the Tokugawa period. There lived many
commoners who were as rich as Crœsus and who
would spend money like water. Some of them
led lives which were more luxurious and extravagant than those of *daimyō*. At Edo, Kinokuniya-
Bunzaemon and Naraya-Mozaemon amassed fabu-
lous fortunes, and their life of unparalleled dis-
sipation and extravagance in the gay quarters of
the metropolis has become proverbial. Naka-
muraya-Kuranosuke and Naniwaya-Jūemon both at
Kyōto and Yodoya-Tatsugorō at Ōsaka astounded
the people of their time by the grandeur of their
residences, the splendours of their dress and their
princely dinners. Their extraordinary life, indeed,
represented the luxury and extravagance of the
commoners of the period.

The following story of a foolish competition
in extravagant display of women's dress presented
by the wives of two wealthy merchants, one at

Edo and the other at Kyōto, during the Empō era (1673-1680) is truly illustrative of the spirit of extravagance among the wealthy commoners of the Tokugawa period. This curious competition developed on the occasion of a visit paid by one Ishikawaya-Rokubei, a noted millionaire at Edo, to Kyōto. His wife who accompanied him was attired in such an expensive costume that the people of the ancient capital were greatly amazed. This provoked the competitive spirit of the wife of a Kyōto millionaire called Naniwaya-Jūemon. In order to show that her husband was richer than Ishikawaya, she walked through the streets of Kyōto, wearing a *kimono* made of silk satin and on which were embroidered the scenic views of the ancient city. Not to be outdone by her dress, Ishikawaya's wife also walked through the streets of the capital, wearing a rich *kimono* made of black *habutae* silk with a design of the nandin. At first people thought that the Kyōto woman had a more expensive costume than the Edo woman, but they later found, to their great astonishment, that every red fruit of the nandin was made of expensive coral. Accustomed to expensive costumes as the populace of Kyōto had been, they could not but express their great surprise at the extravagant dress of the woman from Edo.

The following account of the extravagant life of Yodoya is contained in the '*Genshō kan Ki*': "Yodoya built a bridge in front of his shop and

gave it the name of his family, Yodoya. His forty-
eight warehouses were full of treasures collected at
an enormous cost. He received the title of *chōja*
(millionaire) because of his great wealth. Yodoya
is the name of his establishment and. his family
name is Okamoto. The Yodoya reached the zenith
of its glory during the life time of Okamoto-Saburo-
emon, who, after his retirement from an active
business career, assumed the name of Koan. He
built stages around his house which was magnificent beyond description. The parlours are gilded
with gold and the gold gilded screens bear the
paintings of the flowers of all seasons drawn by
famous artists. His garden has a splendid pond,
bridges spanning it, as well as trees of all descriptions gathered from all places in Japan and
China. The so-called Summer Chamber has *shōji*
(sliding door) made of glass. There were glass
cases lining the upper part of the walls just below the ceiling which are filled with water in
which gold fish can be seen swimming. No chamber even in the Imperial Palace can compare with
Yodoya's magnificent dwelling. His tea room is
decorated with gold and silver, while the *ramma*
(transom window) of his reception chamber are
engraved with the flowers of all seasons. The
rails of the spacious hallway are lacquered red.
All these are so magnificent and grand that no
residence of any *daimyō* or other noble can be
compared with the Yodoya residence. All the
rooms and chambers — the vestibule, the clerks'

room, and the kitchen — are very large and each of them is watched over by a superintendent. So many persons are found within the house that it rather resembles a market place, rather than a private house. It is the master of this very house that is in financial service for the *daimyō* of thirty-three provinces in Western Japan. No *daimyō* in the western part of the mainland of Japan and Kyūshū is free from the financial assistance of Yodoya. His great money power forces the *daimyō* to make presents to him and their chief retainers bow before him. Nobles of high rank and *daimyō* with extensive feudalities must show the utmost respects to Yodoya."

4. CULTURE AND LEARNING OF THE *CHŌNIN*

Education had much advanced during the Tokugawa period and learning was no longer a monopoly of the nobility and the clergy. Primary education was given through the medium of the so-called *terakoya*. The commoners were no longer satisfied with the sordid task of money-making : they also pursued learning to a great extent. The progressive and active commoners demanded a fresh and practical philosophy of life, and it was to meet this new requirement by a rising class that *shingaku* came to be popular among the merchants. It outlined the way of the merchant and was a philosophy for the commoner class in general. It

was originally propounded by a scholar at Kyōto
named Ishida-Baigan, and was later expounded
by his pupils such as Tejima-Sho'an, Wakisaka-
Gidō, and Shibata-Kyūō. Their head-quarters at
Kyōto was called Meirinsha. There were established at Edo two lecture halls called Gorakusha and
Jishūsha where *shingaku* was taught, but it never
flourished at that city as it did at Kyōto and
Ōsaka. Great was the influence which this particular line of learning exercised on the minds of
the common people. Besides the scholars who
taught *shingaku*, there were in the Kyōto-Ōsaka
district many others who taught similar studies.
For instance, Motoori-Norinaga, a great scholar
of national classics, was born of a commoner at
the town of Matsusaka, Ise province. Itō-Jinsai,
a great exponent of the Confucian classics, was
born of a merchant at Kyōto. Ishida-Baigan, the
propounder of *shingaku*, also was a son of a
merchant. Two noted Ōsaka scholars, Yamakata-Bantō and Kusama-Naokata, were also commoners. Bantō was the head-clerk of an exchange
shop, namely, Masuya-Heiemon. He is the author
of a great work called '*Yume no Shiro*.' Kusama-
Naokata was first in the service of the Kōnoike
Family and later opened an exchange shop of his
own. He also wrote a book called '*Sanka Zui*.'
There was a lecture hall at Ōsaka which was
called Kaitokudō. It was founded by two scholars,
namely, Miyake-Sekian and Nakai-Shūan. Here,
lectures were given to commoners and artisans.

Two Nakai brothers, namely, Chikuzan and Riken, outlined economic theories of considerable importance. Bantō was also a pupil of these two brothers. The foregoing account shows some of the notable examples of the learning which was popularised among the commoners of the Kyōto-Ōsaka district.

5. CONCLUSION

During the Tokugawa period, especially in its later half, the commoner class not only had already come to control the financial power of the nation, but also had participated in the nation's culture and learning. The commoners really shouldered the destiny of the land in its practical phases.

CHAPTER X

THE FINANCE OF THE TOKUGAWA GOVERNMENT

1. INTRODUCTION

During the Tokugawa period, Japan had a feudal system of centralisation. The existence of such a system presupposed that political power was unified to a certain degree; it also showed that financial power was simillarly gathered at the centre. One may say that, unless the suzerain possessed predominant financial power over the other lords, it would have been impossible for him to occupy a position of political preponderance in the nation. The necessity of having immense financial power for securing general obedience is only too obvious.

The Tokugawa Family possessed not only a powerful feudal lordship, it also possessed a financial power of stupendous nature over other lords. The area of its fief was as large as one-fourth of the areas of all the country and was scattered over some 47 provinces. Moreover, the Tokugawa Shogunate had command of all territories of political importance and cities of vast commercial significance, as they were all situated in these 47 provinces. It is undeniable that the Tokugawa Government constituted a Central Government the like of which had never before existed in Japan. The Muromachi Shogunate, for instance, could never be compared with it in point of power and prestige, as it was an isolated local power devoid of any faculty of centralisation, political or otherwise.

2. CHANGES IN FINANCIAL CONDITION

Plenty was the salient characteristic of the financial condition of the Tokugawa Shogunate during its early stage. When Tokugawa-Ieyasu, the founder of the Feudal Government, retired from active service and went to the town of Suruga, he gave 30 000 pieces of gold, and silver amounting to 13,000 *kan* to his son and successor, addressing the following instructions to his old retainers who had assumed important posts in the Feudal Government:

"You must not use the money I now transfer for your daily expenses. You must regard it as a public trust and increase its amount as much as possible. You must make it a rule to balance your budgets in the financial administration of the Government. By exercising utmost thrift, you must store your gold reserve for the following main purposes: for possible military campaigns, for relieving people in times of calamity, and to provide against crop failures."

Ieyasu succeeded in enriching the treasury of his Government by means of a negative policy of thrift and retrenchment and by a positive policy of monopolising mines and of expanding foreign trade. His mind was occupied with the problems of public finance even after his retirement from active service, and when he died he is said to have left something like 2,000,000 *ryō* of gold, which he had saved at the town of Suruga.

His son, Hidetada, the second Shogun, was content with keeping and maintaining his legacy ; but his successor, Iemitsu, who was a man of lofty ambitions, poured out treasure in undertaking public works such as the building of the Nikkō Shrine. He also increased the fiefs of his retainers, and spent much in the suppression of the Shimabara insurrection. And yet, all that had no evil effect on the financial condition of the Tokugawa Government.

From the time of the fourth Shogunate, the Tokugawa Government began to feel the pinch of financial scarcity, and there were several causes for this. The great fire of the Meireki era, which reduced the greater portion of Edo to ashes, imposed upon the Government a great financial burden. The construction of Imperial Palace on two occasions also cost the Edo Government an enormous sum of money. However, its financial difficulties were not of a serious nature during this stage, and it was not till after the commencement of the Genroku era which was noted for its luxurious mode of living, and its spirit of decadence that the finances of the Government became extremely encumbered.

During the reign of the fifth Shogun, Tsuna-yoshi, the impoverishment of the Edo Government became more and more pronounced. He was a lover of luxury and extravagance and spent a stupendous amount of money in charity, music and public works. To aggravate the financial embarrassment of the Edo Government, there were frequent earthquakes and conflagrations, requiring the expenditure of a vast amount of money for the relief of their victims and reconstruction works. The output of silver and gold production had decreased by that time ; while the specie of the country found its way abroad. The personal corruption of the officials in charge of the financial administration of the Government increased its difficulties. In order to escape from the imminent bankruptcy, the Government re-coined money and imposed new taxes on *sake* and foreign trade. The first-named expedient, in particular, was frequently resorted to, and during the seventeen years between the eighth year of Genroku and the first year of Shōtoku, money was re-coined four times. Re-coinage, in fact, was the main method of financial relief during this stage.

During the administration of the sixth and seventh Shoguns, namely, Ienobu and Ietsugu, comprising eight years, Arai-Hakuseki, the great historian and economist, tried to adjust the financial condition the best he could, but before he was able thoroughly to solve the various problems, the eighth Shogun, Yoshimune, came to hold the reins of Government. He was one of the most remarkable Shoguns and instituted and carried out many reform measures in order to put his Government in the former position of financial abundance. Following the example set by the founder of the Shogunate, Yoshimune issued decrees for the purpose of enforcing thrift among the people ; revised the system of *sankin-kōtai* ; established new systems of *agemai* and *tashidaka* ; improved the method of tax collection ; did his utmost to adjust the price of rice ; developed new rice fields ; and re-coined money. In the sixteenth year of Kyōho (1731), there was a surplus of 35,654 *koku* of rice and 127,557 *ryō* of gold and silver. At the end his fourteen years' rule, there was a surplus of 792,000 *koku* of rice and 1,216,-000 *ryō*. All this shows that Yoshimune made a stupendous success in view of the miserable financial condition at the time he became a Shogun.

However, what he had built up was largely pulled down by Ieshige, his successor, within less than ten years after his accession, for in the fifth year of Hōreki (1755) the financial policy established by Yoshimune was " slackened and the amount of the Government's revenue decreased while its expenditure increased." Thus, the Edo Government was again faced by immense financial difficulties. It was then decided to fix a part of the Government's expenditure for three years, and to exercise strictest thrift thereafter.

The period of financial disorder commences from the time of the next Shogun, Ieharu, whose administration was in greater part carried on by Tanuma, a Minister, who exercised a sort of despotic power. Such things as the kitchen management, stationery expenditure and the repairing of the house mats were prescribed in detail, so as to forestall any over-expenditure in the household management of the ruling family. Under the sway of this Shogun, new money was coined; the Imba-numa and Tega-numa Lakes in the province of Shimōsa were reclaimed to be made rice paddies; new mines were worked; guilds and a kind of credit organ (*kashikinkaisho*) were created. But after Matsudaira-Sadanobu replaced Tanuma under the succeeding Shogun, Ienari, these financial measures were completely abolished. And it is said that as the result of his wise financial policy, the surplus of the Shogunate treasury at the end of his ten years' administration, from the first to the tenth year of Kansei (1789–1798), was estimated at 338,000 *ryō*. However, his policy of thrift and retrenchment was not welcomed by the masses who had become accustomed to a life of luxury and extravagance. Up to the Bunka era (1804–1817) the total revenue of the Shogunate from various sources was estimated at one million *ryō* per year, and this was about sufficient for its expenditure. After this era, however, the expenditure of the

Government steadily increased. This was especially true after the Tempo era (1830-1843). The
expenditure was increased to 1,500,000 *ryō* at the
commencement of this era ; it rose to 2,000,000
ryō in the seventh year, and again to 2,500,000
ryō in the eighth and ninth year, thus showing an
increase of 250 per cent. when compared with
the figures at the beginning of the Bunka era. All
this rapid increase in the expenditure of the Government was not accompanied by a corresponding increase in its revenue, the result being a
deficit in the Government finance every year.
This deficit was barely met by loans and the re-
coinage of money. Towards the last years of the
Tempo era, Mizuno-Echizen-no-kami attempted a
drastic financial reform by strictly prohibiting extravagance, abolishing the guilds, lowering prices,
increasing taxes, enforcing contributions, and reclaiming and developing the Imba-numa Lake.
However, before he succeeded in his financial reform, he was forced to resign his post. When the
country's diplomatic relations with foreign powers
were marked by serious disturbances towards the
closing days of the Tokugawa period, the expenditure of the Shogunate was increased because of
the need of coastal defence which necessitated
the construction of fortresses and ship-building
yards as well as the purchase of war vessels. Its
financial difficulties increased at such a pace as to
make the final overturning of the Feudal Government inevitable.

3. THE SOURCES OF REVENUE

During the Tokugawa period, the size of feudal territories and the revenues of lords, *hatamoto* and ordinary *samurai* were expressed in terms of *koku* of rice; taxes were also paid in rice which, in fact, was the very basis of the finance and economy of the times. All this shows the important position of rice occupied in the revenues of the Shogunate. However, rice as the basic revenue of the Tokugawa Government was directly secured from its own lands in various parts of the country; and the Government had no claim over the crops of lands belonging to other feudal lords. There are some tax burdens besides the revenue from rice fields, but those are not so important. Thus, the main revenue of the Tokugawa Government was derived only from the lands directly under its own control; this system was radically different from the system that existed under the Muromachi Shogunate which collected military rice from all parts of the country as a tax. The difference between the two systems is worth noting. True, there was a system of forced contribution called *agemai* under the Tokugawa Shogunate and this was levied on the lands of feudal lords as an objective basis, still it was at best a temporary financial measure and not a permanent system. The following lands were exempted from this tax: the *shuinchi*, or lands such as the estates of shrines and temples or those which were exempted from all forms of public exactions by a Shogun's document; *jochi*, which comprised the compounds of temples and shrines and historic lands which were exempted from taxes by legal prescription; *munenguchi*, which comprised roads, marshes and sites of some public establishments; *misutechi*, which comprised grave-yards, crematories, slaughter houses, and execution grounds; *sonchi*, comprising lands desolated by landslides, inundation and other natural calamities. All other lands were regarded as being productive and therefore subject to taxation, although in some special cases exemption and allowance for tax deductions were permitted.

Besides land, there are some other sources of revenue, such as the business of commerce and industry — those taxes are called *unjō* or *myōga* — and the labour of mankind. But those are not of so much importance as the land.

Revenue from various privileges must be considered. When the Tokugawa Family rose to rule over the country, it confiscated the money saved by the Toyotomi Family, its predecessor and rival house, as well as by the fiefs of other lesser nobles. Revenue from all these sources undoubtedly added to the resources of the Tokugawa Government, which, however, had certain privileges that were used for securing further revenue. Its enterprises and the right of coinage need special mention.

The Shogunate had large pastures at Sakura and Kogane and managed mining enterprises in various parts of the country. We shall not dwell on the pastures because they were primarily necessary from the military standpoint. As to its mining enterprises, the most important ones were the gold and silver mines of Sado Island. This island originally belonged to the Lord of Uesugi, but as there were gold and silver mines on it, it was taken over by the Toyotomi Family and then by the Tokugawa Family. The Edo Government placed the Sado mines under the personal supervision of Ōkubo-Nagayasu and it was said that during the prosperous times, gold and silver on Sado produced " 1,000 *kan* during the day and 1,000 *kan* during the night." The silver mines in the provinces of Iwami and Izu were also actively worked, and provided an important addition to the Shogunate revenue.

The Shogunate also possessed the right of coining gold, silver and copper money which were circulated throughout the entire nation. The Government derived revenue by re-coining money in order to patch up its financial deficit; and thus its right of coinage was an important source of revenue.

The Shogunate also derived no small amount of revenue from contributions from feudal lords and other people, both in money and goods. Traders often were required to make loans called *goyōkin*, especially after the middle of the Tokugawa period, and this also was one of the principal sources of revenue. These *goyōkin* were rather forced from the *chōnin* class as well as from other wealthy people. We may then say that class property was one of the important revenue sources of the Edo Government.

Nor was this unnatural. Although the period being a feudal period whose economy was one of " rice economy," it was marked by the wide extension of money as the medium of exchange and by the rapid rise of the *chōnin* class. All these phenomena eventually determined the sources of the Government's revenue. Thus the land tax from the direct fiefs of the Shogunate, profits from re-coinage and *goyōkin* were important sources of public revenue.

4. THE SHOGUNATE'S RECEIPTS FOR THE THIRTEENTH YEAR OF TEMPO

Now that the sources of Government revenue have been explained, let us go deeper into this problem and consider it in detail. There is a very scanty historical source showing the facts concerning the administration of public finance during the feudal period. The following figures are given in the '*Suijinroku*,' edited by Katsu-Kaishū :

Receipts and Expenditure for the
thirteenth Year of Tempo

Ordina y revenue...........................925,099 *ryō*
Land tax .... 550,374 *ryō*

River navigation tax	3,203	*ryō*
Tax paid by the *hatamoto* in lieu of their labour service to the State	34,633	„
Contributions	16,633	„
Tax paid by traders at Nagasaki	22,792	„
Contributions raised for river administration	25,932	„
Debts paid back by *samurai*	76,686	„
Contributions made in goods valued at	146,846	„
Special revenue	587,049	*ryō*
Profit from re-coinage of gold and silver money	557,322	*ryō*
Annual quota of contribution from the lords in connection with the repair of the Nishimaru Palace	29,727	„
Government expenditure	1,453,209	*ryō*
Special expenditure	156,469	*ryō*
Deficit in ordinary accounts	528,110	*ryō*

The foregoing figures show that the total amount of the regular revenue of the Shogunate during the thirteenth year of Tempo (1842) was 920,000 *ryō* and that of the expenditure, 1,450,-000 *ryō*, the deficit being more than 528,000 *ryō*. The fact that the amount of special revenue constituted 40 per cent. of the total revenue and 63 per cent. of the ordinary revenue testifies to the financial stringency of the times and the financial instability of the Tokugawa Shogunate. The profit from re-coinage exceeds the revenue from the land tax and constitutes 38 per cent. of the total amount of revenue, thereby showing the important position it occupied in the finances of the Shogunate, and in relieving it from its financial difficulties.

We shall show in the following table how the tax burden was borne by the different classes so far as it is possible to specify them:

Burden on the *Samurai* Class

Contributions	16,633	*ryō*
Contributions raised for river administration	25,932	„
Tax paid in lieu of labour service	34,633	„
Percentage	12	%

Burden on the Farming Class

Land tax	550,374	*ryō*
Percentage	84	%

Burden on the *Chōnin* Class

River navigation tax	3,202	*ryō*
Tax paid by traders at Nagasaki	22,792	„
Percentage	4	%
Grand total	653,566	*ryō*
Percentage	100	%

The tax burden of the *chōnin* is not exactly represented in these figures inasmuch by the thirteenth year of Tempo, the system of *toiya* or guilds had been abolished by the Reform of Tempo and the tax paid by guilds was no longer enforced. However, it is undeniab'e that the overwhelming portion of the tax burden fell upon the farmers. On the other hand, if the loans or *goyōkin* made by the wealthy traders to the Shogunate are included — and in some cases they were never paid back — the tax burden of the commercial class would reach a considerable amount.

As the figures are not precise, it is impossible to go into detail, but, roughly speaking, the land tax borne by the farmers, the loans made by the *chōnin*, and the profit yielded by re-coinage make up the governmental income.

5. RELATIONS BETWEEN FINANCE AND RICE PRICE, RE-COINAGE AND *GOYŌKIN*

Relations between public finance and the price of rice. During the Tokugawa period, rice was not merely the principal staple product and food of the people; because of the peculiar economic conditions prevailing during that period, rice formed the foundation of the finances of the Shogunate and *daimyō*, and taxes were expressed and paid in terms of rice, and largely paid in the grain itself. On the other hand, money came to be used more and more extensively, and both the Shogunate and the feudal lords made payments in money as well as in rice, though the salaries of their retainers were usually paid in kind. Before payments in money could be made, one had to exchange his rice for money, and this necessity had dire effects upon the finance of the *samurai* class; for it was clear that fluctuations in the price of rice was inevitably accompanied by fluctuations in the amount of the revenue calculated in money.

One may think that the Shogunate derived an enormous revenue when the price of rice was exuberantly high, but this was not so, because the high price of rice was mostly caused by crop failures which meant a small amount of rice revenue ; moreover, the Government had to spend much money in the relief of poverty-stricken farmers and had to adopt various measures for the purpose of adjusting the price of rice. Thus, the prevalence of a high price of rice did not benefit the treasury of the Feudal Government. The fact that the Shogunate faced a financial predicament because of a bad crop is shown by a decree issued in May, in the seventh year of Kyōho (1722) which runs as follows : "In consequence of the failure of rice crops in recent years due to frequent storms and floods, a shortage has been reported in the official treasury, be it understood that there will be some delay in the distribution of rice to the *hatamoto* and in the payment to merchants."

Nor could it be said that a fall in the price of rice was necessarily followed by a reduction in the Shogunate treasury's revenue in money. As a fall in price is usually occasioned by a good harvest, the amount of rice turned in as tax was enormous. On the other hand, the amount of the proceeds from the sale of the revenue rice was not equally huge. When money economy was yet in its undeveloped stage, a good rice crop might

have made the finances of the Shogunate easy
and comfortable; as soon as money economy was
developed to such a point as to require the exchange of rice for money for the efficient administration of public finance, a depreciation in the
price of rice *ipso facto* was bound to affect the
public treasury unfavourably. A phenomenon like
this was bound to arise as a result of the para-
doxical economic organisation of the Tokugawa
period which was born of the co-existence of rice
economy and money economy. Although the effect
of the fluctuations in the price of rice on finance
is clear enough, such a fluctuation caused by a
good or a bad crop was liable to affect public
finance to a degree that is hardly imaginable at
a normal time when the price is maintained at
an appropriate rate.

Relations between finance and re-coinage. As
has been already pointed out, re-coinage was resorted to as a measure of relieving the Shogunate
of its financial difficulties. There is only one exception, that in the case of the re-coinage made
during the Kyōho era, the purpose of which was
to improve the debased currencies of the Genroku
era and revive the system of the Keichō era.
Almost all other cases of re-coinage had as their
aim to derive a profit therefrom and had the effect
of deteriorating the qualities of the currencies.

Arai-Hakuseki pointed out that the profit
called *deme* from the re-coinage of money during
the Genroku era amounted to about five million

ryō. Although it is impossible to find out the total amount of such profits during the entire period, the following are the figures for the eleven years between the third year and the thirteenth year of Tempo:

Year	Revenue	Expenditure	Deficit	Deme	Surplus or Deficit (marked Δ)
3	1,218,011	1,593,909	375,898	394,200	18,304
4	1,223,241	1,646,832	423,591	540,000	116,409
5	1,172,907	1,790,051	616,144	470,596	Δ 145,547
6	1,031,786	1,760,288	728,502	600,000	Δ 128,502
7	1,651,527	1,963,750	312,223	499,844	187,621
8	1,901,817	2,467,902	566,085	629,263	63,178
9	2,202,436	2,512,666	310,230	1,075,950	765,720
10	1,706,451	2,180,922	474,470	694,745	220,275
11	1,422,487	2,001,958	579,471	997,000	417,529
12	1,090,590	1,962,684	872,094	1,155,000	282,906
13	1,259,702	1,963,911	704,291	501,445	Δ 202,764

The foregoing table shows that not in a single year were the authorities of the Government able to make both ends meet; that they had to resort to re-coinage every year; and that thrice that method failed to adjust the balance between revenue and expenditure. The total amount of *deme* during the eleven years of the Tempo era was estimated at 7,558,043 *ryō.* What would have been the fate of the Shogunate, had no such financial scheme of relief been actually employed?

Now, it should be noted that the financial relief was the main reason for the adoption of this method by the Government; but the desire of officials in charge of the gold and silver mints to keep up their industrial activities was mainly responsible for the frequent re-coinings. These persons had an ample business while gold and silver were produced in great quantities; but, after the production of these metals had decreased, they were placed in a difficult position financially, and the only way to keep up their activities was re-coinage. The large-scale re-coinage during the Genroku era was planned out even as far back as thirty years before, or during the Kambun era, by the stoff of the gold and silver mints.

Relations between finance and *goyōkin*. These *goyōkin* were a financial burden placed on the merchants for the purpose of making up the deficit in the Government finance, and were supposed or held to be made voluntarily by them. Ostensibly they were to be redeemed, but in fact for the most part, they were not. They were rather to be regarded as forced or patriotic, so-called, loans.

Although the general purpose of such loans was to make up the deficit in the Government's finance, they were often spent on various individual instances. They might be spent for one of the following purposes: for the relief of the financial difficulties of some feudal lord or lords; on some gigantic public works; for the adjustment of the price of rice; and for military and coastal defense. The money, however, was to be used, in its fundamental aspect, in providing financial aid for the Shogunate, although the actual cases in which it was spent were diverse.

Wealthy *chōnin* in such cities as Edo, Kyōto, Hyōgo, Ōsaka, Nishinomiya, Sakai, etc. frequently received orders for loans from the Central Government; but those in Ōsaka most frequently received such orders. Those wealthy *chōnin* who received official " suggestions " for loans usually made petitions that the amount mentioned be reduced. Frequently, the differences between the amounts asked for and the amounts obtainable from such *chōnin* were considerable; nor did the Shogunate authorities always live up to the loan stipulations and pay either interest or principal.

One of the most frequent purposes of these loans was to raise the price of rice, for such a policy was beneficial to the ruling class which really supplied this staple product, for the high price of rice meant a relief for the poverty-stricken feudal lords and a financial surplus for the Shogunate itself. The policy of maintaining the price of rice at high levels, however, was aimed not only at the relief of the *daimyō* and the Shogunate, but that also of the *samurai* class in general as well as the farming population who were the tillers of the soil. On the other hand, the fact remains that the loans after the Tempo era were incurred almost exclusively for the benefit of the Central Government, for they played a signal rôle in making up its financial deficits.

6. EXPENSES OF THE SHOGUNATE

The expenses of the Tokugawa Government were divided into the following three groups: *jōshiki* (ordinary), *betsukuchi* (separate), and *rinji* (temporary). It is difficult to assign them to the prevailing classification of ordinary expenditure and extra-ordinary expenditure. Moreover, it is impossible to know the expenditure of the Tokugawa Government in detail, because of the extreme secrecy which was enforced. The following table shows the expenses of the Government for the thirteenth year of Tempo: [1]

Jōshiki Expenses	(*ryō*)
Kirimai and *yakuryō* payment	399,104
Expenses in the Shogun's palace	75,371
Expenses at the eight offices	277,077
Expenditures of the Shogunate's various offices	72,793
Expenditures outside Edo	27,213
Allowance to the *sanke*, and *sankyō* (six main branches of the Tokugawa Family) and others	32,162
Allowance to Sō-Tsushima-no-kami	8,655
Expenditures of the offices of *daikan*, (local government of the Shogunate)	21,803
Payments for timber	63,645
Expenditures for the transportion of rice	34,163
Expenditures for repair works, both in Edo	

---

[1] Takekoshi-Yosaburō, The Economic Aspects of the History of the Civilization of Japan, Vol. II, p. 338 etc.

and elsewhere and other miscellaneous   *(ryō)*
expenses 54,791
      Total 1,066,777

            Betsukuchi Expenses   *(ryō)*
Expenditures of river administration 33,329
Payments to be made out of the Shogun's
  loans 116,738
Payments to be made out of the interest on
  the Shogun's advances 8,163
Payments to be made out of the reserve fund 25,535
      Total... 183,766

            Rinji Expenses
Expenditures on repairs to the Nikkō Shrine
  and other shrines, on ceremonies, coinage,   *(ryō)*
  etc.. 172,713
      Grand total 1,423,256

Of the *jōshiki* expenses, the two chief items
are those on *kirimai* and *yakuryō*, and those for
the eight Government offices. *Kirimai* was a pension for *hatamoto* who had no domain land; it
was paid three times a year in both rice and
money. *Yakuryō* was a kind of salary for Government offices. These were in fact personnel expenditure. The *samurai* who received *kirimai* or
yakuryō lived on that revenue. This personnel
expenditure was the largest individual item in the
current expenditure of the Edo Government. By
the eight offices are meant the following: the
*onando, Nishimaru-onando, osakuji-kata, kobushin-
kata, on-makanai-kata, osaiku-kata, on-tatami-kata,
on-zaimoku-kata*. These and the next item, name-

ly, "expenditure of the Shogun's various offices," comprise the major portion of the Government expenditure of the Shogunate. Of the former, the expenditure for *onando, Nishimaru-onando* and *on-makanai-kata* is made up of the living expenses of the Shogun Family; and the second item, namely, expenses in the Shogun's palace must be the salaries of persons employed in the palace.

During the Tokugawa period, there was no budgetary system such as we have today. The maximum amount of revenue was made the basis of the expenditure. After the middle of the period, however, when the Shogun's Government was faced by serious financial difficulties, thrift began to be exercised, and it was after December in the third year of Kan'en (1750) that a sort of budgetary estimate was adopted. But this budget concerned only the living expenses of the Shogun Family and did not include the main items, such as the salaries of the *samurai* who received *kirimai* or *yakuryō*.

7. CONCLUSION

The chief principle of public finance during the Tokugawa period was to base expenditure upon revenue. Today, although we consider the ability of the people to bear tax burdens, we first decide on the amount of Government expenditure necessary for the administration of State affairs, and then the ways and means to derive

revenue necessary to cover that expenditure are
sought. Thus, expenditure precedes revenue. But
exactly an opposite principle was practised by the
authorities of the Tokugawa Shogunate. This
method was not limited to this period. It had, in
fact, been the established custom in all ages from
time immemorial, but the scholars of the Tokugawa period ardently upheld this principle both
in theory and in practice; and the statesmen of
the times also were fully conscious of it. Thus,
it must be noted that there was no difference in
principle between public finance and individual
household accounts; and in point of fact, it was
undeniable that in actual practice there was no
clear line of demarcation, naturally enough, between the finances of the Shogunate and the household accounts of the Tokugawa Family.

Except in its initial stages, the Tokugawa
Shogunate always suffered from financial difficulties due to various causes, such as crop failures
and other natural calamities, reduction in the output of gold and silver, outflow of currency, increase in Government expenditure, wide-spread
existence of luxury, personal corruption of officials
in charge of public finance, and a thousand and
one other causes. But the greatest and fundamental cause is to be found in the social economic
system of the time.

At first, the farm was almost the only means
of production and on the farm itself was the Feudal
Government founded. But with the advance of the

age, agriculture came to be faced by a deadlock, commerce and industry arose and currency came into use in greater degree ; the result being that the Shogunate became no longer able to exist on the revenue from the self-sufficient agricultural products of its own lands.   Accordingly, it had to welcome affably the moneyed *chōnin* newly coming into prominence, and treat with them for financial assistance and pretend to be grateful for the new economy that ushered them in.   In other words, the Shogun's Government was no longer able to depend upon the economic system on which it was based, and was compelled by circumstances to ask for the assistance of a class which it had previously disdained and disregarded.   It could no longer stand on its own bottom, and was obliged to trust in the development of a money economy which was inconsistent with its own economic foundation, for the improvement of its financial lot.   Therein lies the basic cause for the financial misery as well as the final collapse of the Tokugawa Government.

CHAPTER XI
THE NEW ECONOMIC POLICY IN THE CLOSING DAYS OF THE TOKUGAWA SHOGUNATE

1. INTRODUCTION

The period of about 260 years following the Keichō and Genna eras (1596–1623) is called either the Tokugawa period or the age of the feudal system based on the centralisation of power; but, needless to say, the situation in this period, as in other periods, was subject to a variety of changes. Especially in and after the middle part of the Tokugawa Shogunate, commerce and industry witnessed considerable development, currency was widely circulated and the *chōnin* class, or commercial interests, gained much influence in consequence of the growth of urban districts. This led to the development of the money economy in addition to the land economy already existing, a new economic power thus coming into being besides the agrarian economic power. Owing to this remarkable economic change, it became impossible for the *samurai* class to maintain their livelihood; and for the farming class to support the *samurai* class as under the old economic system, with the result that these classes had to bow to the new economic power and look to the *chōnin* for financial help. Some of those belonging to the former classes even turned *chōnin* themselves or became like *chōnin*. On the other hand, the *chōnin* class acquired the predominant social influence by virtue of their money power. They were able to prevail against even *samurai* authority and prestige, and to extend their authority over the farming interests also. In other words, economic changes gradually deprived all classes of their former characteristic status to give rise to a tendency for them to mix together. As it often occurred that people, for various reasons, forsook the class to which they belonged for another, class distinctions became blurred, with the natural result that the foundations of the feudal system were shaken.[1]

In the closing days of the Tokugawa Shogunate, disquieting rumours of possible invasion by a foreign power were in the air; while, on the other hand, there was the visit of the so-called "black ships" (the American squadron under the command of Commodore Perry) to these shores to demand the opening of the country for foreign commerce. In and after the Kaei and Ansei eras (1848–1859) especially, there took place particularly marked political, economic and social changes in consequence of the development of the relations with foreign countries. In those days, a new un-

---

[1] cf. Chap. VI.

precedented policy inconsistent with the traditional
policy of the Tokugawa Shogunate was adopted
with every prospect of another revolutionary
change coming over the social and economic conditions of the country. This chapter is intended
for a general survey of the circumstances prevalent at this momentous juncture.

2. INFLUENCES OF THE WESTERN CIVILISATION

The Tokugawa period was an age of national
exclusion, but the study of the conditions in
Western countries was not entirely neglected even
in these days of isolation. Western influence came
into this country through Nagasaki, where trade
with Holland was carried on. As early back
as the Genroku era (1688–1703), Nishikawa-Joken
wrote a book entitled the 'Kai Tsūshō Kō,' in which
he dealt with conditions abroad. In the Shōtoku
era (1711–1715), Arai-Hakuseki wrote the 'Sairan
Igen' and the 'Seiyō Kibun' on foreign affairs on
the strength of the information which he obtained
from Dutchmen about conditions in many countries. Particularly noteworthy is the fact that
Tokugawa-Yoshimune, the eighth Shogun, lifted
the embargo on the perusal of Dutch books,
allowing people to read all Western books except
those dealing with religious matters. Since then,
the study of Dutch made great progress. It was
at this time that Aoki-Kon'yō learned the Dutch
language from those Dutch officials who made

yearly visit to Edo to pay respects to the Shogun. Not only was Dutch studied as a language, but chemistry, medicine, the calendar, astronomy, military science, and other branches of scientific knowledge were introduced into this country through the medium of the Dutch language.

Towards the close of the Tokugawa Shogunate, further progress was made in the study of matters Western, and in the second year of Ansei (1855), the Yōgaku-sho (Foreign Language School) was established at the foot of Kudanzaka. This institution was renamed the Bansho Torishirabe-sho (Institute for the Study of Western Books) in the following year, and the Dutch language was taught there by Mitsukuri-Gempō, Sugita-Seikei and other scholars. Later, other languages such as English, French, German and Russian were added to the curriculum, and chemistry and mathematics were included among the subjects of study. At first, the students were limited to retainers of the Shogunate, but afterwards retainers of *daimyō* were also admitted. Foreign teachers were also engaged, and the practice of sending students abroad for study there was even then adopted. The pioneer institution again changed its name to the Yōsho Shirabe-sho, and then again to the Kaiseisho. It was the predecessor of the Tōkyo Imperial University. In short, the establishment of the Bansho Torishirabe-sho gave a fresh impetus to the study of Western knowledge, and it bears witness to the importance attached even in those days to the importation of Western civilisation.

In a memorial which Takashima-Kihei submitted to the Shogun in October of the sixth year of Kaei (1853) was mentioned: " Although the people in this country regard it as a shame to learn anything from foreign countries, foreigners praise those who learn things from other nations, because they think that these people are doing good patriotic service. Foreigners make voyages to various countries and if they find anything good in other countries, they are ready to adopt it so as to make up for what is lacking in their own countries. It is true that they are intent on trade and profits, but their motives are to enrich their fatherlands and add strength and activity to their fighting forces. As they are not in the habit of sticking to antiquated customs, they are by no means above learning from others. Nay, they look down upon those people who refuse to learn anything from other nations as bigoted." Thus, it will be seen that the idea of seeking knowledge in the outside world so that the shortcomings of the Japanese people might be made good and traditional evil customs might be discarded by adopting the good points of other nations, was held by some people as early as the closing days of the Tokugawa Shogunate.

3. FOREIGN INTERCOURSE AND TRADE

So far as the country's trade with foreign countries is concerned, Japan was trading with Holland and China at Nagasaki in those days, and besides, Tsushima maintained trade relations with Korea to a certain extent, while Satsuma carried on some amount of trade with China through Loochoo. The principal trade of the country was, however, that with China and Holland at Nagasaki. With the changes of the times, restrictions of various kinds were laid even on this tiny interchange of goods, and there was a decline in the volume of trade. Because the traffic in those days was passive and one-sided and also owing to the difference in the relative value of precious metals between Japan and the countries with which she traded, there was a remarkable outflow of Japanese gold and silver. Such being the case, many scholars in those days held the view that trade was absolutely uncalled for, and advocated the policy of seclusion. It is true that Honda-Toshiaki and some other thinkers held progressive ideas and urged the necessity of throwing the country open to foreign intercourse and trade, but they were rather exceptions.

The visit of American warships to Japan towards the close of the Tokugawa régime, however, changed the whole situation. The *rōjū* (a Minister of the Tokugawa Government) showed

the credentials submitted by the American Envoy
to the Shogunate to all the *daimyō* on July 1st
of the sixth year of Kaei (1853) calling for an
unreserved expression of views on the American
demands contained in them.   The replies made
by the *daimyō* were multigenerous.   Some *daimyō*
urged the rejection of America's demands at the
cost of opening hostilities with that country, and
other *daimyō* suggested that the Shogunate should
defer its reply to America, pending the completion of warlike preparations, while some others
held that America's demands should be partially
accepted with a view to a pacific settlement of
the situation.   Quite a number of *daimyō*, on the
other hand, maintained that it was no longer
possible for the Shogunate to adhere to the old
policy of seclusion, and the only feasible course
open to it was to throw the country open to
foreign trade.

Among the *daimyō* which advocated trade
with foreign countries were some which suggested
the acceptance of the American overtures simply
(as, for instance, the Gujo-Han in Mino province
and the Muramatsu-Han in Echigo province), but
many of them laid down various conditions for
acceptance.   There was quite a large body of
opinion in favour of trade being allowed for a
limited period, say, five or ten years.   During this
period of trade, some *daimyō* (the Lord of Iwa-
murata in Shinano province and the Tsuyama-
Han in Mimasaka province) insisted, the coastal

defence should be strengthened; some (the Sakura-Han in Shimōsa province) maintained that trade should be opened but that if it proved injurious to the national interests it should be suspended, and some others (the Uwajima-Han in Iyo province and the Oshi-Han in Musashi province) urged that on the completion of all preparations for war trade relations should be broken off. Besides the above, a *daimyō* (the Fukuoka-Han in Chikuzen province) took the line that trade should be opened with America and Russia but that it should be denied to England and France, while some (the Tsuyama-Han in Mimasaka province and the Obama-Han in Wakasa province) advocated trade through the intermediation of Dutchmen. Yet another *daimyō* (the Hikone-Han in Ōmi province) expressed the positive view of not only granting the American request for trade but reviving the *shuinsen* (vessels with the special permit of the Shogun for trading with foreign countries) for the development of foreign trade, declaring that it was the way of the world to exchange goods for reciprocal benefit. There were also some *daimyō* which urged that restrictions should be set both on the amount of trade and on the kinds of articles for trade. Memorials were also laid before the Shogun by Mukoyama-Gendayū and Katsu-Rintarō, both *kobushin* officials, as well as by other officials of the Shogunate, and certain scholars urging the necessity of opening trade with foreign countries. I will, however, refrain from describing them in detail here.   The facts enumerated above have been quoted from the 'Dainihon Komonjo, Bakumatsu Gaikoku Kankei Monjo' Volumes 1 to 3, and the incidents recorded all happened in the sixth year of Kaei (1853).   It is true that many of the views in favour of trade were evidently prompted chiefly by the underlying motive of gaining time for completing the armed defences, but seeing that the Hikone-Han advocated trade for trade's sake and that Mukoyama-Gendayū and Takashima-Kihei referred to trade as indispensable for making the country rich and strong, the country was not entirely free from people who were wide awake to the benefits accruing from commercial pursuits.   Granting that many people advocated trade as an expedient for meeting a serious situation claiming urgent attention at the time, it must be admitted that the very fact that such views found expression at all bears witness to the change of the times.

After much discussion, in which views such as those already stated were frankly set forth, foreign trade was eventually opened.   In the first year of Ansei (1854), the Shogunate opened Shimoda, Hakodate, Nagasaki and Kanagawa as trade ports.   The amount of trade at Yokohama (which was opened instead of Kanagawa) was as follows[2] :

---

[2] 'Yokohama Kaikō Gojūnen-shi'   Vol. II, p. 463.

Year	Exports	Imports	Total
Ansei 6 (1859)	¥ 578,907	¥ 543,005	¥ 1,121,912
Man'en 1 (1860)	3,194,688	2,996,568	6,191,256
Bunkyū 1 (1861)	2,343,755	2,198,406	4,542,161
,, 2 (1862)	4,113,092	3,858,016	7,971,108
,, 3 (1863)	3,704,484	3,474,749	7,179,233
Genji 1 (1864)	3,601,284	3,377,949	6,979,233
Keio 1 (1865)	5,318,767	4,988,921	10,307,688
,, 2 (1866)	6,794,439	6,373,079	13,167,518
,, 3 (1867)	6,764,749	6,345,229	13,109,978

The exports included coal and firewood for shipping use, and maritime products, in which Japan had been trading with China. The only new exports to Europe and America were tea, silkworm-egg cards, raw silk and yarns, but trade was no longer one-sided. The volume of exports was now equally as great and valuable as that of the imports. In this way, the traditional exclusionist policy of the Tokugawa Shogunate was discarded in the Ansei era, it being supplanted by the new policy of opening the country to foreign intercourse and trade.

4. INDUSTRIES

In the Tokugawa period, tranquillity prevailed in the country and the standard of living among the people advanced with the result that luxurious habits grew among the noble and the rich, and the demand for industrial goods increased. In consequence of the adoption by many *daimyō* of the policy for encouraging production, there was marked progress in industry. The popular forms of industry in those days were handicrafts and household industry. Factory industry was still unknown, nor was there much use of machinery. Towards the end of the Tokugawa Shogunate, however, these conditions underwent a change.

Some influence of European industrial arts on Japanese industry as early back as the closing days of the Muromachi period, and in the Tokugawa period articles were manufactured in imitation of imported goods. In the Kansei era (1789–1800), a plan was laid down to establish a woollen textile factory. Nabeshima-Kansō studied in Dutch books the method of manufacturing iron, and cast a gun with a reverberatory furnace in the third year of Kaei (1850). In the Kaei and Ansei eras (1848–1859) Shimazu-Nariakira also established a refinery in the garden of the castle of Kagoshima, where guns were cast and many things, including ceramics, glass, agricultural implements, shipbuilding machinery and oil-extracting machines were manufactured, mostly by Dutch methods. In the second year of Ansei (1855) an electric machine was constructed. In the third year of Keiō (1867) he established a factory of spinning mill in a new method. Tokugawa-Nariaki, Lord of Mito, not only made guns, rifles and ammunition, with reverberatories (in April of the first year of Ansei) but built a warship at a ship-building yard which he established at Ishikawa-jima (work began in the sixth year of Kaei and finished in the third year of Ansei). In the fourth year of Ansei, the Shogunate started work on an ironfoundry at Akunoura, Urakami-mura, Hizen province, and the work was completed in the first year of Bunkyū (1861) in charge of Dutchman. In the third year of Bunkyū (1863), the Government laid another plan to build a dockyard at Tategami, Urakami-mura (which was later abandon-ed) and in the first year of Genji (1864), it was decided to build a big dockyard at Yokosuka-mura, Sagami province. In connection with this plan, the Shogunate sent Shibata-Hyūga-no-Kami, *gaikoku-bugyō* (a high commissioner in charge of foreign affairs) to France and engaged a French expert and others, work being started in March of the second year of Keiō (1866). In November of the same year, the establishment of a branch of the Iron-works at Yokohama Hon-mura, Musa-shi province, was decided upon.

Thus, the Shogunate and the Saga, Kagoshima, Mito and other *han* took the lead in introducing Western industries. Although this importation was, of course, merely by way of experiment, it shows that the fact was then recognised by far-sighted men that the full development of industry was impossible under the handicraft industrial system, and that it was imperative that new in-dustries should be created by improving the industrial system through the utilisation of machines. They proceeded to translate their convictions into actual deeds. Here, also, a new policy widely different from the old one was being framed.

5. THE COMPANY AND MONOPOLY SYSTEMS

It may fairly be said that, generally speaking, commerce and industry in the Tokugawa period were under individual management. It is true that besides enterprises under private or individual management, there were works under the direct management of the Shogunate or Government works, and *han* works or undertakings under the management of the respective *han* and those monopolised by *han*, but all these were single enterprises in nature; they hardly deserved the name of joint enterprises. Again, although there existed bodies of merchants and industrialists known as *za* or *kabunakama*, they were supervising organisations, and their existence does not show that managements of the business were operated by organised bodies of men. In such circumstances, it must be admitted that enterprises were generally speaking, individual; yet were there some which was under the management of what may be called family organisations, a system which was somewhat different from individual management. For instance, the Mitsui-gumi, the Ono-gumi, and the Shimadagumi were organised by members and relatives of the same families for the transaction of various kinds of business in many places.

The following description[3] gives an idea of how these organisations were formed :

" Hachirōemon became so rich that he opened branches of his shop not only in the three big cities (Edo, Ōsaka and Kyōto) but in many prosperous castle-towns in the country, and at these shops many kinds of articles besides piece goods were sold. His brothers formed six branch families, but the property of both the head and the branch offices was made the common possession of all these families, which shared in losses as well as profits in equal proportions. Owing to this arrangement, they neither made excessive gains nor suffered heavy losses, so that there was no fear of any of these families going bankrupt. Nor did the clerks in their employ belong to any particular families. There were six head clerks in Edo, and these men were in charge of the shops at Suruga-chō and other places. Although they did not take part in the daily shop transactions, they had to attend the meetings which were held six times a month. At these meetings the leading clerks were called together and matters relating to the trade were discussed. Again, the principals of the six Mitsui families were made to serve in their shops with the clerks from their

---

[3] cf. 'The Origin of the Mitsui Family' in the 'Edo Kaishi.' Vol. I, no. 5.

childhood in order to learn the trade. To these six families were allowed certain fixed sums of money every year to meet the expenditure on clothing, food and daily necessaries, and they were strictly forbidden to waste money in excess of these sums. Such being the case, even the seniors of the six families were not in a position to have all things their own way. If any of them refused to observe the family regulations, he was immediately forced into retirement and his name was struck off the list of the families. Hachiroemon was the supreme head of these six families, and the others had their proper place assigned to them. If Hachiroemon either retired from active life or died, Hachirobei, who was next in order of seniority, succeeded to the name of Hachirōemon as the head of the Mitsui family, and Saburosuke who was next to Hachirobei in rank was promoted to the rank held by Hachirobei with his name changed also, and so forth. Regardless of the distance of blood-relationship, Hachiroemon of the time was always regarded as the supreme head of the six families, and the status of the heads of the other families was accordingly fixed. In this way, the same intimacy as exists among true brothers was kept up among them. It is said that it was due to these admirable family regulations that the six families have never showed signs of decline in their fortunes during the last century of their existence."

In the third year of Keiō (1867), a form of

joint enterprise developed. In that year, although the great sum of about eight or nine hundred thousand *ryō*, was required for completing the works of the foreign settlements in Kōbe and Ōsaka and for providing trading facilities, the Shogunate authorities found it difficult to put up the money by means of *goyōkin*, or compulsory levies collected from *chōnin*. Then the Shogunate caused the Ōsaka *chōnin* to establish a company on a joint-stock basis. In a memorial submitted by the *kanjō-bugyō* (a financial Minister of the Shogunate) and other officials of the Government in power at the time occurs the passage : " It is absolutely impossible to make the trade prosperous and advance the interests of the State, unless business is conducted in accordance with the company system." From this it is clear that the company formed by the Ōsaka *chōnin* by order of the Tokugawa régime was an attempt to copy the company system of the West. It is said that the plan to establish a company was mooted among the officials of the Shogunate about the first year of Keiō, and Oguri-Kōzuke-no-Suke, who, in the suite of the Japanese Envoy, visited the United States in the first year of Man'en and imported new financial and economic knowledge into this country, was a foremost advocate of the plan. Fukuzawa-Yukichi dealt with the company system in the ' *Seiyō Jijō*,' a book published in the second year of Keiō, and in the ' *Shōnan Ikō*,' a postmous work by Yokoi-Shōnan which was published in

the second year of Keiō and the ' *Keizei Shōgaku* '
by Kanda-Kōhei also, reference was made to this
system. Thus, the merits of the company system
and the need of its introduction into Japan were
recognised and urged by scholars. The wealthy
men in Ōsaka had, however, no experience of
foreign trade, nor had they any knowledge of the
company system. It was, therefore, only under
compulsion that they acquiesced, much against
their will, in the formation of the company. At
any rate, it is a fact worthy of special mention
that a company was actually organised in the
third year of Keiō (1867) on the basis of a joint-
stock partnership, a kind of association which had
never existed before. Although it was formed on
the model of Western organisations of the kind,
it was, of course, a very imperfect institution as
compared with companies such as we have today—joint-stock companies in particular. It was
nevertheless a very advanced idea on the part of
those who, not contented with the old system of
business management, introduced the company
system ruling in Western countries with a view
to a more effective execution of business in this
country, and it must be regarded as a very important new industrial policy.

Moreover at that time the Shogunate itself
attempted to adopt a system resembling monopoly
by establishing the *sambutsu-kaisho*. This was
planned in November of the second year of Ansei

(1855) and in November of the first year of Keiō
(1865), but each time the plan fell through.[4]

6. THE GOVERNMENT'S FINANCE AND PAPER
CURRENCIES

The Tokugawa Shogunate was in straitened
financial circumstances during the greater part of
its existence, being prosperous only in its earlier
period, and in its closing days its financial distress
became very acute. The occurrence of foreign
complications towards the end of the Shogunate
entailed on it new outlays in the way of coast
defences, the construction of forts and shipyards
and the purchase of warships, resulting in the increase of the annual expenditure.

Since the Hōreki era (1751–1763) the Shogunate often levied *goyōkin* (money requisitioned)
besides the regular taxes (which were paid in rice)
in an attempt to make good deficits in its treasury.
Before the Tempo era (1830–1843), the *goyōkin*
was levied chiefly for the purpose of forcing up
the price of rice and advancing money to various
daimyō, but after the Kaei era (1848–1853), it was
mainly for the purpose of meeting the expenses
involved in coast defences and in the settlement
of foreign problems and for providing the war
fund required for the campaign against the Chōshū-Han. This change of object throws a side-

4) cf. Chap. IV.

light on the changes of the times.

The Shogunate also had frequent recourse to recoinage to relieve the financial straits to which it was reduced. It is obvious that the profits accruing from recoinage went to help the Shogunate financially, and, indeed, all schemes of recoinage in those days, with the single exception of the one in the Shōtoku era (1711–1715), were prompted by the desire to realise these profits. The new gold coins minted in the first year of Man'en (1860) weighed about 8 *bu* and 8 *rin* a piece, of which only 5 *bu* was gold. As compared with one-*ryō* gold coins minted in the Keichō era (1596–1614), which contained 4 *momme* of gold, therefore, their actual value was reduced to one-eighth. Unlike many past cases, however, the object of issue in this case was to remove the difficulties arising out of the difference in relative value between Japanese and foreign gold and silver. This fact shows that the intercourse with foreign countries had created a new object in regard to coinage also.

The Shogunate patched up its finance by constant recourse to recoinage, as already noted, but it was thanks to this makeshift policy that it could for long refrain from the issue of paper money, to which device many *daimyō* had to resort. In this closing days, however, the Shogunate was obliged to depart from this traditional policy of avoiding the issue of paper money. The practice of raising money from *chōnin* by means of *goyō-kin* was followed in the closing days as well, but

frequent appeals to this practice in a short space
of time rendered it quite ineffective in raising the
requisite money. Moreover, as *goyōkin* levied in
the past had, in most cases, been treated as if
they had been donations, there was a natural
reluctance on the part of the *chōnin* concerned
to meet the Shogunate overtures. The fact that
goyōkin was levied in the first and second year
of Keiō in succession, coupled with the waning
influence of the Shogunate in consequence of
difficult problems confronting it at home and
abroad, made it all the more difficult for the
Shogunate to raise large sums by means of
goyōkin. Unable to gather the requisite money
by this means, it at last conceived the idea of
issuing paper money for the first time since its
establishment.

In the third year of Keiō (1867), the Shogunate
made the *ginza* in Edo issue notes of the seven
denominations of 100 *ryō*, 50 *ryō*, 25 *ryō*, 10 *ryō*,
5 *ryō* and one *ryō*, to be convertible within three
years after issue by Mitsui-Hachirōemon, purveyor
to the Shogunate, and these notes were put into
circulation in Edo, Yokohama, or the Kantō provinces. With regard to the opening of the port of
Hyōgo, it caused rich merchants in Ōsaka, Hyōgo
and other places to establish a company with their
joint contributions for the issue of convertible
notes of the six denominations of 100 *ryö*, 50 *ryō*,
10 *ryō*, one *ryō*, two *bu* and one *bu*, to the maximum amount of 1,000,000 *ryō*. These were put

into circulation in Ōsaka, Kyōto and near provinces on November 1st, and the payment of taxes in these notes were allowed. This device was adopted because it was difficult to raise large funds from rich merchants by traditional means. While making them put up the requisite money on the one hand, the Shogunate tried to obviate any loss through the circulation of this money in notes, on the other hand. Owing to a lack of confidence in the notes among the general public, however, many holders of notes applied for conversion with the result that the rich had to provide the funds doubly. Be the matter what it may, the issue of paper money by the Shogunate was a new departure from its traditional policy.

7. THE POLITICAL SYSTEM

I have so far described the new economic and financial policy of the Shogunate, and now I will make some reference to a big change that took place in political matters, that is, the reform of the *sankin-kōtai* system. The peculiar feudal system of the Tokugawa period and 250 years of tranquillity during this period are, of course, traceable to the various lines of policy pursued by the Shogunate, but they are most largely due to the *sankin-kōtai* system. This system was inseparably associated with the Shogunate. Tokugawa-Yoshimune, the eighth Shogun, effected some reform of this system and inaugurated the *agemai* system, but his underlying motive in carrying out this reform was rather to save the Shogunate from its financial difficulty. About nine years afterwards, the *agemai* system was abolished and the *sankin-kōtai* system was revived. Indeed, it was amply proved that in order to keep 300 feudal lords under effectual control it was very important for the Shogunate to maintain this system and that this traditional system always called for strict enforcement for the security of the Shogunate, and yet in the second year of Bunkyū (1862), the Shogunate was forced by the prevailing state of things to revise this system. The influence of the Shogunate declined towards its end, while many feudal lords had gradually become so impoverished that they attempted to shake off the yoke of the system which entailed heavy outlays on them. Not only was the strict enforcement of the system rendered impossible but the complicated foreign relations, which called for strong national defences and armaments and for a perfect unity of the nation to meet foreign aggression, made the *sankin-kōtai* system, which had for its sole object the control of the feudal lords by the Shogunate, inappropriate to the needs of the times. In such circumstances, the *sankin-kōtai* system, under which feudal lords were made to go up to Edo every other year to stay there in the Shogun's service, was abolished in favour of a new system, which enjoined on them visits to Edo once in three years to stay there in the

Shogun's service for one hundred days. It is self-evident that this change of the system played a very important part in accelerating the collapse of the Tokugawa Shogunate. The change of the *sankin-kōtai* system was as much against the traditional policy of the Tokugawa Shogunate as the opening of the country to foreign intercourse was against the traditional policy of seclusion, and it is hardly necessary to say that it was a remarkable departure from the beaten track.

Among the luminaries of the day were some who were convinced that the feudal system under which many *han* were formed in the country was no longer feasible and that it was necessary to introduce a new *gunken* (prefectural) system so that the whole country might be made one united body to deal effectually with other countries. This fact is evidenced by the following narrative in the '*Kaikoku Kigen*:'

"In October of the year before last (the first year of Genji) I (Katsu-Awa) got a reprimand and had since been living in retirement, when in May (of the second year of Keiō) I received unexpected orders from the Minister of the Shogunate to visit the castle. I was much puzzled, but as I could not very well disobey the order, I repaired to the castle. At the interview with the Minister, I was told that the Shogun, who was in Ōsaka at the time, had ordered my speedy visit to Ōsaka. I respectfully answered that I would willingly comply. Then, the Minister told me that the situation in the Kyōto-Ōsaka district was very serious and that I should therefore leave for the place of the Shogun's sojourn without delay. My summons to the castle amazed all the eminent officials who had an antipathy to me. Oguri-Kōzuke-no-Suke and two other officials took me to another room for secret conference. They said that on my arrival in Ōsaka I would surely be consulted by the Shogun on important State matters. The situation was very critical, and it was expected that on the arrival of a certain amount of gold and a few warships, which the Shogunate had ordered from France, a campaign against the Chōshū-Han would be launched. A punitive force might also be sent against the Satsuma-Han, if occasion demanded. After these *han* had been subjugated, there would be no powerful *han* left to interfere with the policy of the Shogunate. Following up the advantage thus gained, steps would be taken to reduce the fiefs of all feudal lords so as to faciliate the introduction of the prefectural system. This plan which was kept strictly secret, they said, was all but decided upon. They took it for granted that I would agree to this policy and asked me to urge on the Shogun and his high officials in Ōsaka the necessity of adopting this policy. I knew that it would be a waste of time and energy to argue the point with them, and so I refrained from any expression of my view, confining myself to listening to their views. On my arrival in Ōsaka, I waited on Itakura-Iga-no-Kami, when he asked my opinion on the views of the high officials in Edo.   In reply, I said that in view of the commencement of foreign intercourse, it was quite necessary for the prefectural system to be introduced, but that it was inadvisable for the Shogunate to try to reduce the fiefs of the feudal lords for the sake of its own security and to dictate to the country with supreme political power in its hands.   If this grand work was to be achieved for the advance of the true interests of the State, it was necessary for the Shogunate to be ready to curtail its own powers and put men of great wisdom and talent in high offices so that it might escape all charges of insincerity.   Such an attitude would certainly be approved not only by the gods but by the spirit of the founder of the Tokugawa Shogunate. The Shogunate must have faith in what it was doing, instead of hating and chastising the Satsuma-Han or the Chōshū-Han. If the Shogunate shaped its course in such a way, I would be ready to do all I could to promote the end in view. What the authorities were urging at present was very irrelevant, nor would their theory be practicable. If their policy were to be adopted, the Shogunate would provoke nation-wide resentment to the serious detriment of its own interests. I asked him to lay this view of mine before the Shogun."

Although the plan to introduce a new prefectural system was not adopted, it is a very momentous thing that the expression of such an opinion should have been made in that feudal period.

8. THE MEN OF THE DAY

The policy of opening the country to foreign intercourse, which was adopted in the Ansei era (1854-1859) was, to all appearances, rather forced upon the Shogunate than otherwise. The Shogunate knew that the rejection of the overtures of the United States for the opening of trade relations meant war, and that there was a very slender prospect of Japan's victory in war. In the circumstances prevailing at the time, the course pursued was probably the only alternative available. The opening of intercourse with foreign countries was a strong incentive to the Shogunate, which could no longer adhere to its old ways or indulge in fancied security. It had to pay much attention to the reform of politics and make special endeavours to introduce the new civilisation of the West so that Japan might keep abreast of the world. The appointment of men of talent to high Government offices, the grant of the liberty of petition, the establishment of iron-works, the casting of guns, the lifting of the embargo on the building of big ships, the purchase and construction of warships and the promotion of trade and commerce were carried out in such circumstances, and it was also due to the same incentive that the new economic policy to which I have already referred was framed.

In the first year of Man'en (1860), the Tokugawa Shogunate dispatched a mission to the United
States to exchange Notes on the Ansei Treaty.
Although this was the natural outcome of the
conclusion of the Treaty, it was nevertheless an
unprecedented course of action with the Shogunate
which had strictly prohibited the visit of Japanese
to foreign countries since the adoption of the
exclusion policy.   Shimmi-Buzen-no-Kami led the
mission as chief Envoy, with Muragaki-Awaji-no-
Kami as assistant Envoy and Oguri-Kōzuke-no-
Suke as *metsuke* (superviser).   The Envoy's suite
included Hirose-Hōan, a doctor hailing from Kai
province, and Fukuzawa-Yukichi, a young *samurai*
of the Nakatsu-Han.   They stayed in America for
several months, during which time they closely
inspected the civilised conditions there, and came
home with a good stock of new knowledge which
was not shared by others at home in those days.
Oguri-Kōzuke-no-Suke brought home as souvenirs
globes, new machines, etc., by way, it is said, of
arousing interest among the Japanese people in
the study of conditions abroad.

In the first year of Bunkyū (1861) and in the
third year of the same era also, Envoys were
dispatched to Europe.   In the first year of Keiō
(1865), Shibata-Hyūga-no-Kami and others were
sent to France and England in connection with
new schemes to establish shipyards and iron-works,
and in the following year a mission was sent to
Russia.   Again, in the third year of Keiō (1867), an

Envoy was dispatched to France on the occasion of the opening of an International Exhibition there. Besides these missions, the Chōshū Han and the Satsuma-Han as well as the Shogunate sent young men abroad for study. These students learned much through their personal observation of the Western civilisation and on their return home strove to impart new knowledge to the public. Some of them, who were subsequently appointed to high posts, endeavoured to administer financial and economic matters by the application of their new knowledge. It is conceivable that these men of new knowledge played an important part in the framing and execution of the new economic policy in the closing days of the Tokugawa Shogunate, to which reference has already been made.

9. AFTER THE RESTORATION

After the Restoration, Japan's economy underwent a very remarkable development. Contrary to the seclusion policy of the Tokugawa Shogunate, the country was thrown open to foreign intercourse and foreign trade prospered, though the first opening of the country to foreign trade and intercourse took place towards the end of the Tokugawa régime, as already noted.

The civilisation of the Meiji era was, in a sense, a mechanical civilisation. In the first ten years, the Meiji Government pursued a policy of direct interference in industry. It imported Western industry into Japan and established model factories of various kinds in order to set examples for the public to follow. Thus, by the importation of new machines and the dissemination of new technical art, the foundations of the new industry of Meiji were laid. As already mentioned, however, the need of mechanical industry was recognised by the Shogunate and some advanced *han* towards the end of that régime and attempts were then made to import new machines.

The Meiji era was also characterised by the vigorous growth of company enterprises. It is undeniable that the industrial development after the Restoration owed much to the company system. All important enterprises forming the arteries of national economy were operated according to this system. Nor can it be denied that it was largely through the encouragement of the Meiji Government that this system was widely adopted. At the beginning of the Meiji era, the *Tsūshō Kaisha* (Trading Companies) and the *Kawase Kaisha* (Exchange Companies) were established, and the *Kokuritsu Ginko* (National Bank) was organised in the fifth year of Meiji (1872), after which the growth of the company system was rapid. The need of company enterprise was, however, already recognised in the closing days of the Shogunate, when a company, though a very imperfect one, was established. Such being the case, it may fairly be said that the company system in Japan germinated before the Meiji era.

The Meiji Government also resorted to the practice of levying *goyōkin* at the time of the Restoration in order to make up a deficit in the war and administrative funds, as it could not otherwise find the requisite money. This device of raising funds was soon found unworkable, and the Government next took to the issue of paper money to meet the urgent needs of the time. Indeed, the issue of inconvertible notes, which took place at frequent intervals, and their adjustment occupied a large share of the attention of the authorities in the first half of the Meiji era. The issue of paper money, as I have already mentioned, was resorted to by many *han* under the Tokugawa Shogunate, and the Shogunate itself had recourse to it in the third year of Keiō (1867).

As regards the political organisation, whereas the feudal system operated in the Tokugawa period, the prefectural system was adopted in the Meiji era. Even in the Tokugawa period, however, it became so difficult to maintain the feudal system towards its end that the *sankin-kōtai* system had to be revised, and the introduction of the prefectural system was seriously considered by men of advanced ideas, as already noted. Had the policy advocated by Oguri-Kozuke-no-Suke and other Shogunate officials been adopted at the time, the prefectural system might have been introduced under the Tokugawa Government, just as the Satsuma-Chōshū Government was formed in the new Meiji régime.

It is noteworthy that various lines of economic policy pursued after the Restoration — in the first ten years of Meiji in particular — were in contemplation or actually carried out to some extent in the closing days of the Shogunate.

*   *   *
*   *

As I have already explained, the political power actually remained with the *samurai* class, in spite of the change of régime from the Tokugawa Shogunate to the Meiji Government. What occurred was merely the transfer of power from the upper class *samurai* to the lower class *samurai*. The economic development after the Restoration also embodies nothing but the gradual growth of the seed sown in the closing days of the Shogunate, as will be clear from my explanation of the economic changes in those days. In other words, it is a mistake to think that all the important economic policies adopted after the Restoration were unknown before that time. The facts which I have so far enumerated will be helpful in the study of the true nature of the Meiji Restoration.

CHAPTER XII

THE IMPORTANCE OF *GOYŌKIN* OR FORCED LOANS IN THE MEIJI RESTORATION

1. FINANCIAL DISTRESS OF THE MEIJI GOVERNMENT

"The Imperial régime has been at last restored; the fundamental policy of the State has been duly established; the Emperor will hereafter administer State affairs in person; and all things pertaining to the State are about to be provided. But there is one thing lacking — State revenue. This is due to the fact that Tokugawa-Keiki has not yet transferred to the new Government the State revenue which he should have transferred at the time he gave up the political power in favour of the new Government. Although the Imperial Court has to defray various expenses for the disposition of State affairs, it has no source of revenue at its command."

The above is a quotation from a public declaration issued by the *Dajōkan* or Council of State on May 8, the first year of Meiji (1868). It clearly indicates the extreme financial distress to which the Meiji Government was subjected at the beginning of its existence.

Reviewing the series of momentous events that took place at that time, one will find that it was on October 14, the third year of Keiō (1867) that Tokugawa-Keiki addressed a memorial to the Throne requesting Imperial permission to transfer the political power to the Imperial Court. The permission asked was granted on the very following day, namely, October 15, and a public declaration of the Restoration of the Imperial régime was made on December 14, the same year. But even at that time Keiki was still occupying the official position of *Naidaijin* or Prime Minister, and still held his domain; while the *daimyō*, shrines and temples likewise held their respective fiefs. The newly formed Meiji Government enjoyed a very feeble existence, as its only source of revenue was a domain which annually yielded 30,000 *koku* of rice and which the Imperial Court had held in possession during the feudal period. It was obvious that such a negligible amount of revenue was utterly insufficient for the administration of the new Government. Truly, "there was one thing lacking — State revenue."

The financial distress of the Meiji Government at that stage of its existence can never be adequately imagined. Iwakura-Tomomi urged the priests of temples such as the Higashi-Honganji and the Nishi-Honganji to make monetary contributions to the Government. He also instructed the leading merchants of Kyōto such as Mitsui-Saburōsuke, Ono-Zensuke and Shimada-Hachiro-

zaemon to do likewise. He also ordered Kumagai-
Kyūemon to urge wealthy merchants and landowners of Kyōto and its vicinity to lend their
financial assistance to the Imperial Government.
On December 26, the Kinkoku-Suitōsho or Revenue Office gave out the following instruction to
the Mitsui-gumi:

"Now that the Shogunate Government has
returned the political power to the Imperial Court
and the Shogun himself has withdrawn to Ōsaka
Castle, all government orders shall hereafter be
issued by the Imperial Court. However, as the
transfer of revenue affairs has not yet been made
by the Shogunate Government, the Imperial Court
is confronted by financial want. Accordingly, the
Revenue Office has been established for the purpose of securing the necessary State revenue.
Indications at present are that hostilities may be
commenced at any moment between the Imperial
Court and the Shogunate, and we are constrained
to secure revenue for the general administration
of State affairs and conducting military campaigns
in order to maintain peace in the realm. Now,
as your firm has been in the financial service to
the Imperial Court from the olden time, you are
ordered to be in service of the Revenue Office
hereafter. Consider the gravity of the present
condition of the Imperial Court and serve it with
all your fidelity."

The Mitsui-gumi responded to this order with
promptitude and made a donation of 1,000 *ryō*.

The same firm also presented 1,000 *ryō* to the
army of the Satsuma-Han quartered at the Shōko-
kuji, Kyōto, and which was faced by a serious
financial want with its resulting blow to the
morale of the soldiers. This forced loan or contribution was made on the eve of the Fushimi-
Toba Battle that really heralded the open hostilities of the Imperial Court and the crumbling
Shogunate. In January, next year, the Mitsui-
gumi together with the two families of Ono and
Shimada made a loan of 2,000 *ryō* to the new
Government.

There were other instances of such loans.
The transfer of the political power by the Shogunate placed a heavy financial burden on the
new Government and the burden was further
increased in weight by the Battle of Fushimi-
Toba. As the Government had no permanent
source of revenue, it inevitably depended on the
donations and loans by wealthy *chōnin* in the
disposition of its immediate problems.

2. *GOYŌKIN* DURING THE EARLY
YEARS OF MEIJI

The Revenue Office was established on December 23, the third year of Keiō (1867) and Hayashi-
Samon and Mitsuoka-Hachirō (Kimmasa-Yuri) were
appointed as its directors, and charged with the
duty of securing revenue for the Government.
The Mitsui-gumi was represented by several of

its own men at the Revenue Office. These men carried out the financial work. They often found it impossible to make both ends meet, and the Mitsui-gumi had to make up the deficit by accommodating loans. According to an official statement made under date of January 15, the first year of Meiji (1868), Mitsui, together with Ono and Shimada, filled the financial requirements of the Government by accommodating loans out of the bills of exchange which people had drawn with these three financial houses on their credit. There was a persistent danger of an over-imposition of *Goyōkin* or forced loans resulting in a stoppage of the payment of the bills and thus in a loss of confidence in the credit power of these houses — which loss would have prevented them from further serving the Revenue Office. Accordingly, on January 17, the same year, the Revenue Office issued a statement saying that funds given to the Government were to be regarded as loans and would not be therefore confiscated (as was often done under the old régime) and that the payment of bills of exchange in big sums might be suspended at the convenience of the Government. On January 19, a loan of 10,000 *ryō* was made jointly by Mitsui, Ono and Shimada.

Thus, the forced loans extended by these three financial houses enabled the new Government to defray its immediate expenses. But it was faced by the need of raising funds for sending a punitive expedition to Edo, which step became necessary after the Battle of Fushimi-Toba. The Council of State met on January 7 in order to discuss the problem. The meeting was presided over by Iwakura-Tomomi and attended by the following officials: Mitsuoka-Hachirō, Ōkubō-Ichizō, Hirozawa-Hyōsuke, Gotō-Shōjirō, etc. Hirozawa expressed his opinion that a fund of 200,000 *ryō* was required for undertaking the proposed military expedition to the seat of the old government, but Mitsuoka argued that at least 3,000,000 *ryō* was absolutely required. The meeting accepted Mitsuoka's opinion and decided to raise it at once.

On January 21 the Revenue Office assembled the representatives of Mitsui and other houses which were in its service and asked them to present a list of the names of leading business firms and wealthy citizens in Kyōto, Ōsaka and near by districts. This instruction was followed by the presentation by these firms of three lists of such names. The first list included such names in Kyōto and its vicinity; the second list contained those of Ōsaka and of its neighbourhood; and the third list contained those of Ōmi province. The new Government accordingly invited more than 100 merchants of Ōsaka and Kyōto to the Imperial Palace of Nijō on January 29, and asked them for their cooperation for raising a fund of 3,000,000 *ryō*.

The Mitsui-gumi wrote a letter to the Revenue Office under date of February 2 regarding the right method of rising this fund. It urged that the only way to overcome the difficulty involved was to despatch an official of the Revenue Office to Ōsaka for the purpose of securing the agreement of the wealthy citizens of that city as a preliminary step for raising the needed fund.

This suggestion was accepted and on February 12 Mitsuoka-Hachirō was despatched to Ōsaka. On the following day he summoned 15 leading merchants of Ōsaka headed by Kōnoike-Zen'emon. These men were instructed to assist the Revenue Office in raising the proposed fund and put under the employment of the Revenue Court. On February 19 and 20, 650 wealthy citizens of Ōsaka were summoned (322 on the first day and 328 on the second day) and were instructed to assist the new Government in its attempt to raise the fund.

This fund (*goyōkin*) the Revenue Office tried to raise was really a domestic loan redeemable through the tax on land. When the Emperor Meiji's visit to Ōsaka as a preliminary step for sending a punitive expedition to Edo was decided on February 3, a fund of 50,000 *ryō* each was raised at both Kyōto and Ōsaka to be used as the travelling expense of the Imperial visit. The stupendous difficulty the officials of the new Government faced in raising the needed fund of 3,000,000 *ryō* is described by the ' *Kōjō-oboegaki* ' which gives an account of the efforts made by the Mitsui-gumi in conjunction with the two houses of Ono and Shimada at the command of the Government under date of November, the second year of Meiji (1869). It says in part: "When the Revenue Office tried to raise the funds, many expressed their misgivings (as to the possibility of redemption) and we had to act as guarantors. We have collected the money from the persons whose names are given in the list attached. The total amount now collected at Kyōto and other places is about 1,300,000 *ryō*." In a report to the Government by Iwakura-Tomomi in May of the same year, he says: "Recently we tried to raise only 3,000,000 *ryō* and we fail to understand why we have not succeeded in raising even half of that amount." It appears, however, that even Mitsuoka had not really believed that he could raise the amount he proposed; he wanted to impress the wealthy merchants with the statement of the amount in his wish to raise as much as possible under the circumstances.

Prior to all this, just before Iwakura set out on his journey to Tōsandō following the decision to send an expedition against Edo, the Mitsui-gumi was ordered to join his suite and two representatives of the firm joined it (January of the first year of Meiji; 1868). They were given the full privilege of *samurai* and proved instrumental in raising funds on many occasions on the way. At Ōtsu, they donated a fund of 3,000 *ryō* (January 24), another 10,000 *ryō* at Ōgaki (February 21); they purchased 1,000 bales of polished rice after the party had arrived at

Warabi in Musashi province (March 13) and stored them in the Mitsui warehouse at Fukagawa, Edo (the value being 1,712 *ryō*); on April 16 a donation of 25,000 *ryō* and at later date another donation of 10,000 *ryō* were made to the headquarters of the Iwakura expedition. Still another donation of 30,000 *ryō* was made after H.I.H. Prince Taruhito (Arisugawanomiya), commander-in-chief of the Expeditionary Army arrived at the Zōjōji Temple, Shiba, Edo.

In leap-month April of the same year, the Government levied a loan of 500,000 *ryō* among the wealthy merchants and trade guilds of Ōsaka and its vicinity, as the expense of sending a superintendent-general to Edo. Prior to this the Imperial Army took over Edo Castle. Although discontented *samurai* betook themselves to Ueno for the purpose of resistance, no move was made by the Imperial Army because it was under financial privation. It was because of this that Sanjō-Sanetomi was ordered to go to Edo in the capacity of superintendent-general. But there was another reason for raising this fund; the Government had to purchase a warship. The fund was apportioned as follows: 100,000 *ryō* among 15 merchants headed by Kōnoike who were in the service of the Revenue Office; 50,000 *ryō* among Mitsui, Ono and Shimada who were engaged in the exchange business; 344,000 *ryō* among some 87 guilds of various trades such as *sake*-brewing, pawning, exchange, etc. The merchants in the service of the Revenue Office actually turned in 80,000 *ryō* and Mitsui and two others paid 40,000 *ryō*; but the amount paid by the various commercial guilds is unknown.

The Government on May 15 issued the so-called *Dajōkan* notes (Notes of Council of State), but it was unable to defray all expenses with these notes. It had to use cash in the payment of salaries to the soldiers of the Imperial Army in the Ōu district where people were not accustomed to the use of such paper money, and also in the purchase of military weapons from foreign countries. The Government, accordingly, had to depend on the Mitsui-gumi in securing the needed cash. On May 22, the firm furnished the Government with a fund of 50,000 Mexican dollars. Again, on August 25, the Government summoned the representatives of Mitsui and other firms in Tōkyō to the Imperial Palace at Tōkyō in order to raise a fund of 860,000 *ryō*. On this occasion, Mitsui, Ono, and Shimada supplied a total of 60,000 *ryō*. This loan was redeemed entirely by gold paper notes when they were issued in December, the second year of Meiji (1869).

3. THE SIGNIFICANCE OF *GOYŌKIN*

The foregoing account will be enough to show the financial distress under which the Meiji Government laboured in the early years of the new régime. The following table indicates the receipts and disbursements of the Government in four different periods:

	1st Period *(Dec. 1867– Dec. 1868)	2nd Period (Jan. Sept. 1869)	3rd Period (Oct. 1869– Sept. 1870)	4th Period (Oct. 1870– Sept. 1871)
	(yen)	(yen)	(yen)	(yen)
Ordinary Revenue	3,664,780	4,666,055	10,043,627	15,340,922
Extraordinary Revenue	29,424,533	29,772,348	10,915,871	6,803,675
Sub-division :				
Dajōkan Notes	24,037,389	23,962,610		
Funds and Domestic Loans	3,838,107	811,000		
Foreign Loans	894,375	100,500		
Total Revenue	33,089,313	34,438,404	20,959,499	22,144,597
Ordinary Expenditure	5,506,253	9,360,230	9,750,003	12,226,382
Extraordinary Expenditure	24,998,832	11,425,609	10,357,669	7,008,775
Total Expenditure	30,505,085	20,785,839	20,107,672	19,235,158

As the above figures show, the extraordinary revenue constitutes the greater portion of the total revenue of the first period. The same is true to some extent of the second period, but just the reverse is the case for the third period. The extraordinary revenue during the first period was derived from three sources, namely, *Dajōkan* notes, money contributed or loaned by citizens, and foreign loans. Because of the difficulty of accounting, the Government raised or loaned money first

---

* The first year of Meiji falls on 1868.

from among the citizens of Tōkyō, Kyōto, Ōsaka,
Hyōgo and Ōtsu and then further from those in
other parts of the country. The Government also
commandeered rice stored in the municipal warehouses of Tōkyō and Yokohama with a promise
to pay for it at later dates. As to foreign loans,
the Government borrowed 500,000 dollars from
the Oriental Bank, a British financial house in
Yokohama and 400,000 dollars from a British
firm. *Dajōkan* notes also constitute a greater
portion of the extraordinary revenue during the
second period and domestic as well as foreign
loans are also included.

The foregoing statistics in the first and second
periods in the government finance of the early
Meiji years evince the fact that Government found
it impossible to cope with its financial distress
only by depending on financial accommodations
by the wealthy merchants in Kyōto, Ōsaka, etc.—
a policy which had been handed down from the
Shogunate days. Thus, the Government felt the
necessity of issuing notes and borrowing from
foreign sources. In other words, the three financial policies of raising funds and domestic loans,
of seeking the aid of paper money and of borrowing foreign capital, were employed in order to
patch-up the financial problem of the time. I
have above dwelt chiefly on one of these three
policies, namely, the policy of raising *goyōkin* or
forced loans the Government raised from wealthy
citizens. Now, it is to be noted that *goyōkin*

during the feudal days was not the same with that in the period under our consideration. During the Tokugawa period, *goyōkin* and *kenkin* or monetary contribution was differentiated only in name, and although the redemption of *goyōkin* was presupposed, it was not actually practised. In some cases, *goyōkin* was arbitrarily changed into *kenkin* afterwards. Let us now consider the nature of *goyōkin* as it was raised by the Meiji Government. As we have already pointed out, the Government declaration issued on January 17, the first year of Meiji (1868) made it clear that the *goyōkin* raised by the Government was to be regarded as loans and would not be confiscated. We regret that very little is known now of the methods of raising this money and of the conditions of it subscription, etc., each time it was raised by the Meiji Government.

When 3,000,000 *ryō* was raised as the basic fund of the Revenue Office, the tax on land was made security. And we know that the land tax was the only source of revenue for the Government at that time. Later, when the Government announced its intention to raise money as the expense for the Imperial expedition, the assurance was given that no subscribers would be placed in a condition of distress, thereby hinting that the money would be paid back at some future date. When another fund was raised as the expense of sending a superintendent-general to Edo, the rate of interest was specified as 1.5 per cent. a month, and the Government assured lenders that the money would be paid back within October. Thus, the Government promised as to the rate of interest as well as the time of redemption. The Government fulfilled its promises. It paid a monthly interest of one per cent. for the Revenue Office fund and 1.5 per cent. for the money which was raised on the occasion of the sending of the superintendent-general to Edo.

Both the principal and interest of the *goyō-kin* raised by the Meiji Government were paid, as the following table of figures indicates:

	1st Period (yen)	2nd Period (yen)	3rd Period (yen)	4th Period (yen)	Total (yen)
Funds Raised	3,838,107	811,000	—	—	4,649,107
Funds Redeemed	263,293	1,465,301	1,449,318	1,471,193	4,649,105
Interest Paid	197,636	202,724	195,963	84,089	680,412

The interest paid includes that which was paid on foreign loans. The very fact that both principal and interest were paid back shows that the *goyōkin* raised by the Meiji Government during the first few years of its existence was radically different from that which was raised under the Tokugawa régime.

It is clear that the funds raised by the Meiji Government were used mostly for political and military affairs during the turbulent period immediately following the Meiji Restoration. But even the wealthy citizens of that time had no magic box from which they could produce as much money as they wished. Many of them were unable to raise the amount specified by the Government. Take the Mitsui case, for instance. That firm was commanded to turn in 50,000 *ryō* in cash and in a lump sum on August 25, of the first year of Meiji (1868), at Tōkyō. The firm paid 20,000 *ryō* immediately and promised to pay 10,000 *ryō* more in the following month, but the Government allowed no delay and demanded the immediate payment of the remainder. There was no other way than to submit to the order, and Mitsui had to sell gold and silver wares it had kept in its safe in order to raise the necessary amount of money. Merchants in Ōsaka also faced similar distress. Mitsui's report to the Revenue Office stated that some of the well-known merchants in Ōsaka had closed their doors and discontinued business. A statement issued by a drug dealers' guild pointed out the dire effects of the Government's attempt to raise money on its members who were forced to financial embarrassment thereby. Thus, it was impossible for wealthy merchants to comply with the Government's demand to the latter's complete satisfaction. The Government felt the obvious necessity of altering its financial policy. Thus, there appeared the policy of issuing the so-called *Dajōkan* notes, promulgated on leap-month April 19.

As these notes were inconvertible, they failed to circulate smoothly, and the Government had to

issue decrees several times urging their circulation. (For instance, on July 18 and 23 of the
first year of Meiji; 1868.) Various other methods
were employed in order to facilitate the circulation
of the notes.   Later, the Government established
the Commercial Office (*Shōhōshi*) which loaned out
Dajōkan notes to *daimyō* and merchants in Kyōto,
Ōsaka, etc., as industrial funds.   In Ōsaka, the
notes were given to those who possessed the
certificates of subscription to *goyōkin*.   As the
goyōkin collected under the Tokugawa régime was
not paid back, merchants of Ōsaka thought it much
safer to take the notes and they eagerly accepted
them.   Thus, they received these notes with the
certificates of the funds they had paid on various
occasions as securities.   As the rate of interest
on the Revenue Office funds was one per cent.
per month and the merchants had to pay an
interest of 0.6 per cent. per month, what the Government did amounted to the issuance of bearer
certificates at the interest rate of 0.4 per cent.
per month.   But the rate of interest on the notes
was not uniform.   In the case of the fund raised
for the purpose of sending a superintendent-general
to Edo, the rate was one per cent. per month
instead of 0.6 per cent. in other cases.   This is
because of the fact that the interest rate on that
particular fund was 1.5 per cent. per month.   In
consequence, in this case the Government's action
amounted to the transfer to the merchants of
bearer certificates at the interest rate of 0.5 per

cent. per month.

Let us next consider how the funds were paid back. The Ōsaka Prefectural Government issued the following notification on October 20, the second year of Meiji (1869):

"The Government since last spring has on several occasions raised funds to be used for military campaigns. The money so raised will be eventually repaid in due course of time. The Government is ready to repay in cash the loans it raised when it purchased the steel warship on which Lord Sanjō was despatched to Tōkyō in leap-month April. Creditors are hereby asked to present themselves at the Finance Department on the 24th instant to get repayment. Those having received notes for the loan certificates shall return them to the Finance Department to receive the cash payment."

Again, on November 28, the following notification was issued by the same Prefectural Government:

"Both the principal and interest of the loans raised in the three cities shall be repaid to the creditors after the end of November. The creditors shall present themselves to the Finance Department to get repayment. As cash and notes have equal value, the payment will be paid in either of them. Those wishing to receive cash shall return the notes they received from the Government in exchange for loan certificates."

We may assume then that the loans were

repaid by the Government. As the creditors had received the notes in exchange for their loan certificates as a rule, they must have received cash by presenting the notes to the Finance Department. In case the presentation of a great sum of notes was impracticable, the amount representing the difference between the loans (*goyō-kin*) and the notes was repaid, we presume, by the Government. In other words, the loans were redeemed in notes issued by the Government. There is an historical record showing that the loan of 50,000 dollars and the loan of 60,000 *ryō* accommodated by Mitsui and others, were all redeemed in notes. We may summarise the policy of loan redemption by the Government as follows: the Government insisted on the delivery of notes the same as bond certificates. Then, taking advantage of the great difficulty of their delivery, the Government settled the debts by paying the difference between the loans and notes. The Government adopted the rate of 120 *ryō* in notes for every 100 *ryō* of gold in the settlement of the loans incurred in the second year of Meiji (1869).

4. ADDENDUM

We have seen that the Government was able to secure revenue in the early part of the Meiji era through Mitsui and other wealthy families of the time. Under the old régime, the *daimyō* entertained before wealthy merchants, offered them social positions and treated them the same as *samurai*, in return for the financial assistance then rendered. The Meiji Government also made similar recompenses to Mitsui, Kōnoike and other wealthy merchants for the financial help they had given. There is no doubt, of course, that loyalty was the motive of their act; they could not stand seeing the financial distress of the struggling Government and offered their helping hands in coping with the financial exigencies of the time. However, the fact remains that the new Government succeeded in securing the financial help of these merchants and in carrying out its work of overthrowing the feudal régime, because it could attract these merchants by the slogan of loyalty to the Imperial Court.

Ōsaka was the financial centre of Japan during the feudal period and the Shogunate Government often levied *goyōkin* on the wealthy merchants of the city. There were such instances of requisitioning funds during the closing years of the period. When the critical stage of the Shogunate régime was reached, both the authorities of the Edo Government as well those of the new Government cast coquettish glances towards Ōsaka. When the new Government summoned the wealthy merchants of Ōsaka on December 29, the third year of Keiō (1867) to present themselves at Kyōto, they failed to present themselves under one pretext or another. But on January 7 Shogun Keiki returned to Edo on board the Kaiyō-

Maru and on January 10th, H.I.H. Prince Yoshiakira (Ninnajinomiya) went to Ōsaka in the capacity of the commander-in-chief of the Imperial Expeditionary Force. This was followed by the Imperial visit of the Emperor Meiji to Ōsaka and the city was placed under the control of the Imperial Court. The firm establishment of the new Government was greatly aided by the financial aid thus rendered by the wealthy merchants of Ōsaka and other cities. This financial cooperation was made by few wealthy citizens at times, but it was rather necessary to secure money from many citizens. We have already stated that the Government summoned 650 *chōnin* of Ōsaka when it tried to raise three million *ryō* as the fund of the Revenue Office. There is no way of knowing the exact number of the merchants who made contributions, but the following figures taken from the Ōsaka Section of the Government Revenue Ledger will indicate the general outline of the loans:

Loans (*ryō*)	Number of Creditors	Amount (*ryō*)
10,000 and above	1	50,000
Between 5,000 and 10,000	5	32,593
Between 1,000 and 5,000	76	149,800
Between 500 and 1,000	84	55,102
Between 450 and 500	17	7,294
Between 400 and 450	26	10,865
Between 350 and 400	38	13,316
Between 300 and 350	67	20,986

Between 250 and 300	48	12,803
Between 200 and 250	95	19,969
Between 150 and 200	176	28,452
Between 100 and 150	354	41,232
Between 50 and 100	552	35,073
Below 50	185	5,629
Total	1,724	483,114

The loans accommodated by various guilds:

10,000 and above	2	40,000
Between 1,000 and 10,000	29	53,234
Between 500 and 1,000	30	19,146
Between 100 and 500	72	17,884
Below 100	36	1,294
Total	169	131,558

The foregoing figures regarding the individuals' burden of loans indicate that the number of the persons who contributed 500 *ryō* or more each, constitute 60 per cent. of the total amount; but the number of persons who contributed less than 150 *ryō* each constitute 73 per cent. of the total number of persons. This shows how comparatively small amounts were raised from among a large number of *chōnin*.

It was on occasion of despatching the superintendent-general to Edo in leap-month April that an enormous burden was imposed on the various guilds; but the foregoing figures show that the guilds also shared the burden of raising the Revenue Office funds.

The same is true of the raising of the Revenue Office funds in the city of Sakai, as the following figures indicate :

Loans (ryō)	Number of Creditors	Amount (ryō)
1,000 and above	2	2,300
Between 500 and 1,000	2	1,450
Between 400 and 500	2	960
Between 300 and 400	2	740
Between 200 and 300	6	1,265
Between 100 and 200	34	4,510
Between 50 and 100	48	3,060
Between 30 and 50	57	1,948
Between 20 and 30	53	1,175
Between 10 and 20	372	4,115
Total	578	21,523
Sake brewers' guild in Sakai		1,400
Sake brewers' guild in Kishiwada		125

The number of those contributed less than 100 *ryō*, especially those whose amounts were 10 or 20 *ryō*, is very large. This is additional evidence of the fact that the money was raised from many people in small amounts.

When the Emperor Meiji's expedition to Ōsaka was decided, a sum of 50,000 *ryō* was raised from Kyōto and Ōsaka each. Although a few wealthy persons played a prominent rôle in the raising of this money, many others in Ōsaka, Sakai, Nishinomiya, Itami and other points in the old province of Settsu made contributions in various amounts. The money is subdivided as follows :

Individuals' burden (*ryō*)	Number of persons
1.500	2
1,000	6
700	1
600	3
500	8
400	9
Between 300 and 400	38
200	1
100	2
70	1
50	1
Total	72

There are also many cases in which a number of persons jointly contributed, their number sometimes being several scores. A group of persons numbering 893 made a contribution of 84,035 *ryō*, the average amount per person being little over 94 *ryō*.

As the above table shows the number of individuals who contributed less than 100 *ryō* and only four and the total amount is comparatively large. But if we think of adding the case of contributions made by groups of individuals, the total number of persons is 965 and they raised a total sum of 167,000 *ryō*. This is another proof to the undeniable fact that the raising of the funds was participated in by many instead of few.

We have already seen that the Government no longer could raise funds through forced loans and had to resort to the policy of issuing *Dajōkan* notes which was regarded as similar to bond certificates. In a debate held among an official council in March, the second year of Meiji (1869), arguments pro and con were advanced regarding the proposed abolition of the system of *goyōkin*. The council decided in favour of its abolition in April of the same year and addressed a memorial to the Throne in favour of the replacement of *goyōkin* by a system of government loans. The memorial was accompanied by the following recommendations :

" As we have decided to abolish *goyōkin* and establish a system of government loans, we recommended that all indispensable government expenditure be met by floating loans, that all *goyōkin* which have been levied on landlords and merchants since the Restoration be turned into government loans without delay ; and that the interest on the loans be paid at the request of the bondholders."

However, as the grant of *Dajōkan* notes was made in order to carry out the same function as government loans, one may say that the idea contained in the above memorial to the Throne had been carried out before the presentation of the memorial.

It was the *samurai* of the lower ranks who actually carried out the political reformation of the Meiji Restoration, and there is no denying that the activities of *chōnin* participated in the same movement were characterised by passivity. But would the establishment of the Meiji Government have been possible without the financial assistance of *chōnin*? We gravely doubt such a possibility. The accomplishment of the Restoration was possible because the Meiji Government could raise *goyōkin* from wealthy merchants and then issue paper money. For this reason, the efforts made by the *chōnin* in the Restoration movement cannot be lightly regarded, although they appear to have been passive. Moreover, although few *chōnin* played the rôle of leadership, a large number of *chōnin* also participated in the movement and its final success was due to their cooperation and assistance. We may then say that the power of the many rather than of the few brought about the Restoration and gave it their support.

SUPPLEMENT

THE DEVELOPMENT OF THE STUDY
OF ECONOMIC HISTORY
IN JAPAN

1. INTRODUCTION

The histories which we have hitherto had are histories of politics, of diplomacy, of wars, or histories in which the lives of great men are predominant. Not much importance was formerly attached to the historical study of economic facts. Not that there was no historical study of economic aspects in days of yore. We come upon narratives of economic activities in many histories compiled in ancient and medieval times. Not a few histories were compiled in the Tokugawa period treating of currencies and economic activities. It was, however, in and after the nineteenth century even in the West that the study of economic facts was made a specialised and independent branch of scientific research. In Japan, such a study is of quite recent growth. For economic matters attracted little public attention in ancient times, and people were prone to hold them in contempt. They were rather asham-

ed of talking of economy or money-making. Social conditions underwent remarkable changes in
modern times, however. Business acquired much
importance, so much so that economic activity has
become an indispensable factor in politics and
in armaments. Because economic problems have
come to attract the anxious attention of the
public and also because, in consequence of the
marked progress of political economy as one
branch of science, the inquiry into the history
of economic facts has become very necessary, the
study of economic history has gradually acquired
increasing importance of late.

2. THE STUDY OF THE ECONOMIC HISTORY OF
JAPAN IN THIS COUNTRY

Many histories compiled in ancient and medieval times in this country contain many references to economic facts. For instance, the six
national histories (the ' Nihon Shoki,' the ' Shoku
Nihon-gi,' the ' Nihon Kōki,' the ' Shoku Nihon
Kōki,' the ' Montoku Jitsuroku,' and the ' Sandai
Jitsuroku '), which were compiled by Imperial command, give some facts relating to economic activities. The ' Ruishū Kokushi,' a history compiled
by Sugawara-Michizane, by gleaning the same
affairs dealt with in these six histories, also records facts relating to the prices of commodities,
monetary circulation, the land system, etc. The
' Ryō no Shūge,' commentaries on the Taihoryo,

clearly shows that the history of the systems relating to land, Government granaries and taxes
was studied by the jurists of the day. If this does
not necessarily mean that the economic history of
the country was specifically studied, it testifies to
the fact that the history of the economic system
engaged some attention of the scholars of those
days, as did that of other systems and things. In
the Kamakura and Muromachi periods, literature
was on the decline, and it was then largely the
concern of Buddhist priests. Nothing worthy of
special mention was, therefore, published in those
days in the matter of economic history, though
in the way of religious history, fairly good books,
such as the ' *Genkyō Shakusho*,' were produced.
In the Tokugawa period, however, things were
considerably different from those obtaining in
the previous periods, none-the-less because it was
equally an age of military ascendency, and matters bearing on finance and economy were held
in greater regard than before. Some scholars in
that period paid considerable attention to these
aspects of activity. Prompted by references to
economic activities in Chinese books, some attempts were made by scholars of Chinese classics
in those days to look into the study of history
from the standpoint of economics. Traces of this
are discernible in the books written by distinguished scholars of the period, such as Arai-
Hakuseki, Muro-Kyūso, Ogyū-Sorai, Itō-Tōgai and
Dazai-Shundai.   Many books on economy includ-

ed in the '*Nihon Keizai Sōsho*' and in the '*Kinsei Shakai Keizai Sōsho*' treat of the history of economic facts in this country. As the more notable of such books may be mentioned the '*Dainihonshi Shokkashi*,' Kondō-Morishige's works, the '*Senroku*' and the '*Kingin Zuroku*,' and the '*Sanka Zui*' by Kusama-Naokata. In this way, the study of economic history made much progress in the Tokugawa period. It was nevertheless still very imperfect, for no scientific methods of research such as are now employed then were used.

In the reforms effected at the time of the Meiji Restoration, the old ideas were almost completely discarded in favour of imported Western ideas. This provoked some reactionary ideas. In politics, the theory of the rights and liberty of the people found vigorous expression. In the field of historiology, however, these reforms seem to have produced no marked effects. Influenced by the loyalism which witnessed a considerable growth in the closing days of the Tokugawa Shogunate, the '*Dainihonshi*' and the '*Nihon Gaishi*' were still widely read. The time was still unripe for a new historical study to appear. After the establishment of the Bureau of History in the Government in January, the second year of Meiji (1869), a search was made for any missing volumes in the historical records of the country, and historical materials were collected. In the tenth year of Meiji (1877), the Historiographical Bureau was provided in the *Dajōkan* (Government), but this

Bureau did nothing beyond compiling the '*Meiji Shiyō.*' At that time, the late Dr. Taguchi-Ukichi produced the '*Nihon Kaika Shōshi,*' which was published in the tenth-fifteenth years of Meiji (1877–1882). This book dealt with the progress of Japanese civilisation with a glance at European affairs and from the economic point of view, and as such it put a new meaning on the study of history in this country. Since then, the study of history in various fields has become active, and many historical works have been published, old history books reproduced and historical writings generally have become more frequent.

With regard to economic history also, nothing worthy of note was written during the first ten years of Meiji. In the ninth year (1876), the '*Dainihon Kaheishi*' (compiled by the Finance Department); in the tenth year (1877), the '*Kyūten Ruisan Denseihen*' (compiled by the Genrōin) and the '*Nōsei Suitōki*' (compiled by the Industrial Board); in the eleventh year (1878), the '*Kōgei Shiryō,*' (compiled by the Imperial Museum); in the fifteenth year (1882), the '*Dainihon Sozeishi*' (compiled by the Finance Department) and '*Dainihon Teikoku Ekiteishikō oyobi Dainihon Teikoku Ekiteishikō Kōshō* (compiled by the Department of Communication); in the sixteenth year (1883), the '*Kyū Bakufu Rizai Kaiyō*' (compiled by the Finance Department), in the eighteenth year (1885), the '*Kasei Kōyō Hōreihen*' (compiled by the Finance Department), and in the twentieth year (1887), the 'Meiji Kasei Kōyō' (compiled by the Finance Department) were published, but there were no private publications of the kind which deserve mention during the interval. Just as the Government pursued a policy of direct interference in industry in that period so as to awaken the nation from its long slumbers and to promote industrial development, so was literary work in respect of industrial history chiefly undertaken by the Government in the first half of Meiji. It was, so to speak, the age of official publications. This was, no doubt, partly due to the fact that the services of scholars were largely requisitioned for the Government's historiographical work, but it is at the same time conceivable that it was, in no small measure, owing to the fact that, as the time happened to be immediately after the Restoration, business had not yet fully developed and few persons had any mind for the study of economic history, a history which is somewhat different from ordinary history. At any rate, the first half of Meiji was the age of official publications. The methods of study then adopted were mostly antiquated. The chronological and unscientific methods were followed in many instances.

In the nineteenth year of Meiji (1886), the 'Kaiun Shiryō' by Kozasa-Kiyone,' and in the twenty-first year (1888), the 'Nihon Kodai Tsūkakō' by Hamada-Kenjirō, the 'Dainihon Fudōsanhō Enkakushi' by Yokoi-Tokifuyu, the 'Shōenkō' by Kurita-Hiroshi, and the 'Tokugawashi Kaheishi' by Saitō-Tanzō were published. The 'Dainihonshi Shokkashi' by the Mito-Han was also published in the same year. In the twenty-second year (1889), the 'Nihon Seidotsū' by Hagino-Yoshiyuki and Konakamura-Yoshikata and the 'Nihonbashi Uoichiba Enkaku Kiyō' by Sakamoto-Jisaburō were issued. In the following year, the 'Suijinroku' and the 'Suijin Yoroku' by Count Katsu, and the 'Nihon Zaiseishi' by Hagino-Yoshiyuki were published. Again, in the twenty-fourth year (1891), Endō-Yoshiki published the 'Nihon Shōgyōshi' and Ōbayashi-Yūya wrote the 'Dainihon Sangyō Jiseki,' while the twenty-fifth year (1892), witnessed the publication by Suganuma-Teifū of his book entitled the 'Dainihon Shōgyōshi.' In this way, private publications on economic history became more numerous every year, and some of them were of great value too. Regarding the books officially compiled, there were published in the twenty-third and twenty-fourth years (1890 and 1891) the 'Dainihon Nōshi' by the Department of Agriculture and Commerce, and the 'Kokusai Enkaku Ryaku' by the Finance Department, in the twenty-fifth year (1892), the 'Teikoku Denshin Enkakushi' by the Department of Communications, and in the thirtieth year (1897), the Dainihon Nōsei Ruihen' by the Department of Agriculture and Commerce. As compared with the first half of Meiji, however, the number of official publications was very small. In short, the age of official publications was being superseded by that of private publications. In many quarters, either by individuals or by compilation societies, researches of various kinds were undertaken. With the importation of Western science, methods of study gradually improved. In the methods of description also, the old chronological and unscientific modes of description were discarded by degrees in favour of a scientific method of making clear the cause and effect of events. Thus, a marked change was noticeable between the former and the latter half of Meiji in the study of the economic history of Japan.

The study of the economic history of Japan made unprecedented progress in the Taishō and Shōwa eras. Scholars made extraordinary efforts in quest of basic historical materials, by means of which they endeavoured to achieve an elaborate and accurate scientific study so as to put the economic development of this country in its true perspective. Many reports made and many books written as the results of these researches were consequently of great value. I will here desist from a detailed reference to these admirable books and articles. Suffice it to say that the great progress made in this line of study since the closing days of Meiji is really astounding. At present, in all aspects of economic history, results of study, either general or specific, are made public almost daily in book form or in magazine articles.

The study of the economic history of Japan has thus made great strides of late in this coun-

try, and it is admitted on all hands that the
late Dr. Yokoi-Tokifuyu, former professor of the
Tōkyō Higher Commercial School, and the late
Dr. Uchida-Ginzō, former professor of the Kyōto
Imperial University, both scholars of profound
learning, were the leading pioneers in this field
of study. The former scholar wrote the ' *Nihon
Kōgyōshi*,' which was published in the thirtieth
year (1897), and the ' *Nihon Shōgyōshi*,' published
in the next year, while the latter scholar's complete works were issued in the tenth year of
Taishō (1921), Volumes first and second of which
are devoted to the study of economic history.
The late Dr. Miura-Hiroyuki, former professor
of the Kyōto Imperial University wrote many
respectable essays referred the Japanese economic
history which are find in his ' *Hōseishi no Kenkyu* '
and other works. The late Dr. Fukuda-Tokuzō,
former professor of the Tōkyō Commercial Col-
lege wrote a book entitled the ' *Nihon Keizaishiron*,' which was originally published in German with the title : " Die gesellschaftliche und
wirtschaftliche Entwicklung in Japan " (Stuttgart,
1900). He was one of the Japanese scholars who
took special interest in the study of the economic
history of Japan. Dr. Takimoto-Seiichi, professor
of the Keiō University, who died in the seventh
year of Shōwa (1932), wrote the ' *Nihon Keizaishi* '
and also published a collection of books on economics in the Tokugawa period. It is widely
known that under his editorship, the ' *Nihon*

Keizai Sōsho' and the '*Nihon Keizai Taiten*' were published.   These scholars combined to lay the foundations of the present growth of the study of the economic history of Japan.   They were all men of first-class learning in their special line.   Mr. Takekoshi-Yosaburō also produced a voluminous book entitled the '*Nihon Keizaishi*,' the English translation of which entitled 'The Economic Aspects of the History of the Civilization of Japan' (3 vols. London) was recently issued. The English title of the book faithfully describes its contents.

3. THE STUDY OF FOREIGN ECONOMIC HISTORY IN JAPAN

In the Tokugawa period already, there was some study in this country of the economic history of the Orient — the economic history of China in particular.   As the late Dr. Uchida pointed out some times ago, it is on record that Itō-Jinsai, Itō-Tōgai, Komiyama-Fūken, Asaka-Konsai, Kameda-Hōsai and Yamada-Shōsai stud ed the history of the land system and agricuture of ancient China.   Many books dealing with economics were published in China and imported into this country.   The study of scholars in the Tokugawa period was based on materials supplied by these books.   In the Meiji and Taishō eras, such study made further progress and the results of these researches into the economic history of the Orient were made public in book form and in magazine articles. But in compared with the study of the economic history of Japan, such studies were quite infrequent.

So far as the study of the economic history of the West in this country is concerned, it is on record that Western political economy was imported into Japan in the closing days of the Tokugawa Shogunate, through, for instance, books written by Adam Smith[1]. After the Restoration, books treating of the economic history of the West were translated into Japanese. For example, Taguchi-Ukichi translated 'The History of British Commerce' by Leone Levi in the twelfth year of Meiji (1879), and in the eighteenth year (1885) 'The Technical History of Commerce' by John Yeats was translated by Ōshima-Sadamasu and published by the Department of Education. Subsequently many books on the economic history of the West were translated into Japanese. The practice of translating Western economic books, whether of old editions or of new, is still briskly going on. Since the latter days of Meiji, however, works have been published in this country in which the authors, instead of contenting themselves with mere translation of Western books on economics have made a deep study of them with reference

---

[1] For this fact I am indebted to Professor Mutō-Chōzō, of the Nagasaki Higher Commercial School.

to certain facts and put these facts in a new light according to their own points of view, or restated them according to a system of their own. It seems that this kind of study has made very marked progress of late. For instance, books have been published in which European economic history is systematically summarised in a general way, or the development of capitalism, industrial revolution and other individual subjects are re-examined and studied in the light of Western literary records. As it is, of course, very difficult to obtain in Japan basic historical materials relating to Western economic history, it is quite natural that the study of Western economic history in this country should take such a course.

4. THE LATEST STATE OF THE STUDY OF ECO-NOMIC HISTORY IN JAPAN

There is no comparison between the latter years of Meiji and the present day as to the state of study and the teaching of economic history in Japanese universities, especially in universities with departments of politics and economics. In the closing days of Meiji, economic history rather meant Western economic history, and there were practically no scholars who made a special study of this branch of science. Lectures on Western economic history were then given by those, whose speciality was something else, merely to fill in the regular curricula[2]. There was no independent Chair of Economic History, as a rule. Since the Taishō era, however, Japan has had scholars who have made a special study of either Japanese or Western economic history. An independent Chair of Economic History was created in the Kyōto Imperial University in the eleventh year of Taishō (1922), and one in the Tōkyō Imperial University in the fifth year of Shōwa (1930). In other Imperial, Government and Private Universities also, lectures were established on Western and Japanese economic histories. Moreover, economic history or commercial history is being taught at the various Higher Commercial Schools.

As already stated, the study of economic history in this country has made remarkable progress, but no technical encyclopedia of economic history has yet been produced, though the 'Nihon Shakai Jii,' the third edition of which was published in the fortieth year of Meiji (1907), and the 'Keizai Daijisho,' published by the Dōbunkan from the forty-third year of Meiji to the fifth year of Taishō (1910–1916), give many items bearing on economic history. The 'Keizaigaku Jiten,' recently compiled by the Institute for Economic Research in the Ōsaka Commercial University, contains particularly numerous items of this kind.

---

[2] In some Colleges of Literature, on the other hand, there were professors who lectured on and made a speciality of the history of Japanese legislation and of the economic history of Japan.

With regard to scientific societies and magazines pertaining to economic history, professors,
researchers and students of economic history at
the Kyōto Imperial University organised in the
fourth year of Shōwa (1929) a society called the
Keizaishi Kenkyūkai, which has been issuing a
monthly magazine called the '*Keizaishi Kenkyū*'
since November of the same year.   Besides, it has
already published in book form two memoirs con-
taining the results of research conducted by its
members in collaboration.   These are the '*Nihon
Kōtsūshi no Kenkyū*' and the '*Meiji Ishin Keizaishi
Kenkyū.*'   In the sixth year of Shōwa (1931), the
Shakai Keizaishi Gakkai was established in Tōkyō.
From May of the year of its establishment, the
Society issued its quarterly magazine, the '*Shakai
Keizaishigaku.*'   This was converted into a month-
ly magazine in April of the seventh year (1932).
A general meeting of the Society is held once a
year and lecture meetings are organised under its
auspices.

5.   THE ESTABLISHMENT OF THE NIHON KEIZAISHI
KENKYŪSHO (INSTITUTE FOR RESEARCH IN
ECONOMIC HISTORY OF JAPAN)

The Nihon Keizaishi Kenkyūsho (Institute
for Research in Economic History of Japan) has
its origin in the Seminar of Economic History
of Japan, which started in the fifteenth year of
Taishō (1926) in the Department of Economics of

the Kyōto Imperial University under the charge
of Professor Honjō-Eijirō. In July, the fourth
year of Shōwa (1929), the Keizaishi Kenkyūkai
(Society for the Study of Economic History) was
organised, and in November of the same year was
issued the first number of its monthly journal
entitled '*Keizaishi Kenkyū*.' Drs. Honjō-Eijirō and
Kokushō-Iwao, both professors of the Kyōto Imperial University, were the chief promoters of this
Society. In December, the seventh year (1932),
Dr. Kokushō planned the establishment of the
Institute for Research in Economic History of
Japan; and a two-storied wooden building, with
a four-storied ferro-concrete library, was erected
in the neighbourhood of the Kyōto Imperial University. The Institute was opened for research
and other business on May 15, the eighth year
(1933). It has four directors and a regular staff of
five investigators, together with other investigators
who have their main duties elsewhere. The four
directors are Professor Honjō-Eijirō (Department of
Economics), Professor Kokushō-Iwao (Department
of Agriculture), Assistant Professor Nakamura-
Naokatsu (Department of Literature), and Professor Kanno-Watarō (Ōsaka Commercial University). There is, besides, an advisory council.

The work of the Institute comprises (1)
researches by individual members, (2) joint inquiries, (3) publication of books and journals, (4)
collection of books and materials for study, and
their utilisation, (5) holding of research and

lecture meetings, special courses of study, and exhibitions, etc. It has already published the ' *Nihon Keizaishi Bunken* ' compiled by Dr. Honjo, the ' *Wagakuni Kinsei no Sembai Seido* ' edited by Mr. Horie-Yasuzō, the ' *Matsuehan Keizaishi no Kenkyū* ' by late Mr. Hara-Tsutae, the *'Shizoku Jyusan no Kenkyū'* by Kikkawa-Hidezō and the '*Keizaishi Gairon*' by Honjō-Eijirō. The journal ' *Keizaishi Kenkyū* ' became to be issued by the Institute as its organ. For the publication of the results of researches made by the members of the Institute monthly meetings are held. The work of compiling the ' Dictionary of the Economic History of Japan' is now making good headway.

*   *   *   *

Such is the development which the Japanese scientific world concerned with the study of economic history has witnessed in recent years. Historians in general have come to evince more interest in economic history, so that the results of the study of economic history are constantly made public in ordinary historical magazines. Owing to the fact that most articles on economic history are published in Japanese in this country, few are made known to the Western world of science. The ' Kyōto University Economic Review,' is, however, printed in European languages, and consequently the articles appearing in it are read by Western scholars and the articles are often quoted and reviewed by them, a fact which marks one phase of progress in the study of political economy in Japan — the study of economic history in particular.

APPENDICES

I. CHRONOLOGICAL TABLE

Nengō (name of Era)	After the accession of the Emperor Jimmu (Jimmu Era)	Christian Era
The Nara (奈良) Period*		
Taika (大化)	1305–1309	645–649
Taihō (大寶)	1361–1363	701–703
Yōrō (養老)	1377–1383	717–723
Tempyō (天平)	1389–1408	729–748
Tempyō-Shōhō (天平勝寶)	1409–1416	749–756
The Heian (平安) Period*		
Engi (延喜)	1561–1582	901–922
The Kamakura (鎌倉) Period*		
Bun'ei (文永)	1924–1934	1264–1274
Einin (永仁)	1953–1958	1293–1298
The Yoshino (吉野) Period (The Nambokuchō 南北朝 Period)		
The Muromachi (室町) Period* (The Ashikaga 足利 Period)		
Eikyō (永享)	2089–2100	1429–1440
Bummei (文明)	2129–2146	1469–1486

* The eras indicated in this period are only those referred in the text.

The Sengoku (戰國) *Period*

The Azuchi-Momoyama (安土桃山) *Period*
(*The Shokuhō* 織豐 *Period*)

The Tokugawa (德川) *Period*

Keichō	(慶長)	2256-2274	1596-1614
Genna	(元和)	2275-2283	1615-1623
Kan'ei	(寛永)	2284-2303	1624-1643
Shōho	(正保)	2304-2307	1644-1647
Keian	(慶安)	2308-2311	1648-1651
Jōō	(承應)	2312-2314	1652-1654
Meireki	(明曆)	2315-2317	1655-1657
Manji	(萬治)	2318-2320	1658-1660
Kambun	(寛文)	2321-2332	1661-1672
Empō	(延寶)	2333-2340	1673-1680
Tenna	(天和)	2341-2343	1681-1683
Jōkyō	(貞享)	2344-2347	1684-1687
Genroku	(元祿)	2348-2363	1688-1703
Hōei	(寶永)	2364-2370	1704-1710
Shōtoku	(正德)	2371-2375	1711-1715
Kyōho	(享保)	2376-2395	1716-1735
Gembun	(元文)	2396-2400	1736-1740
Kampo	(寛保)	2401-2403	1741-1743
Enkyō	(延享)	2404-2407	1744-1747
Kan'en	(寛延)	2408-2410	1748-1750
Hōreki	(寶曆)	2411-2423	1751-1763
Meiwa	(明和)	2424-2431	1764-1771
An'ei	(安永)	2432-2440	1772-1780
Temmei	(天明)	2441-2448	1781-1788
Kansei	(寛政)	2449-2460	1789-1800
Kyōwa	(享和)	2461-2463	1801-1803
Bunka	(文化)	2464-2477	1804-1817
Bunsei	(文政)	2478-2489	1818-1829
Tempo	(天保)	2490-2503	1830-1843
Kōka	(弘化)	2504-2507	1844-1847
Kaei	(嘉永)	2508-2513	1848-1853

Ansei	（安政）	2514–2519	1854–1859
Man'en	（萬延）	2520	1860
Bunkyū	（文久）	2521–2523	1861–1863
Genji	（元治）	2524	1864
Keiō	（慶應）	2525–2527	1865–1867

After The Restoration

Meiji	（明治）	2528–2571	1868–1911
Taishō	（大正）	2572–2585	1912–1925
Shōwa	（昭和）	2586–	1926–

II. WEIGHTS, MEASURES AND MONEYS

MEASURES OF LENGTH

1 *ri* (里)=36 *chō* (町)=2,160 *ken* (間)=2.44030 miles=3.92727 $^{\text{Kilo-}}_{\text{metres}}$
1 *ken* (間)=6 *shaku* (尺)=60 *sun* (寸)=5.965163 feet=1.81818 metre
1 *shaku* (尺)=10 *sun*(寸)=100 *bu* (分)=0.994194 foot=0.30303 metre
1 *shaku* (尺) (cloth measure)=1.25 *shaku* (尺)

Metric system:

$$1 \text{ kilometre} = \left\{ \begin{array}{l} 0.62137 \text{ mile} \\ 3{,}280 \text{ feet } 10 \text{ inches} \end{array} \right\} = 9.16667 \; chō \text{ (町)}$$

1 metre $\qquad\qquad\qquad$ =3.3 *shaku* (尺)

MEASURES OF WEIGHTS

1 *kan* or *kwan* (貫)=1,000 *momme* (匁)

$$= \left\{ \begin{array}{l} 8.26733 \text{ lb. (Avoir.)} \\ 10.04711 \text{ lb. (Troy)} \end{array} \right\} = 3.75000 \text{ kilogrammes}$$

1 *momme* (匁)=10 *fun* (分)

$$= \left\{ \begin{array}{l} 0.13228 \text{ oz. (Avoir.)} \\ 0.12057 \text{ oz. (Troy)} \end{array} \right\} = 3.75000 \text{ grammes}$$

1 *kin* (斤)=160 *momme* (匁)

$$= \left\{ \begin{array}{l} 1.32277 \text{ lb. (Avoir.)} \\ 1.60754 \text{ lb. (Troy)} \end{array} \right\} = 0.60000 \text{ kilogramme}$$

Metric system:

1 kilogramme=2.20459 pounds (Avoir.)=0.26667 *kan* (貫)
1 gramme $\qquad\qquad\qquad\qquad$ =0.2666667 *momme* (匁)

MEASURES OF CAPACITY

1 *koku* (石)=10 *to* (斗)=100 *shō* (升)

$$= \left\{ \begin{array}{ll} 4.96006 \text{ bushels (Dry)} & \text{England} \\ 39.6804 \text{ gallons (Liquid)} & \text{,,} \\ 5.11902 \text{ bushels (Dry)} & \text{U. S. A.} \\ 47.95389 \text{ gallons (Liquid)} & \text{,,} \end{array} \right\} = 1.80391 \text{ hectolitre}$$

1 *shō* (升)=10 *gō* (合)

Metric system :

1 hectolitre = $\begin{Bmatrix} 2 \text{ bush., } 3.35 \text{ pecks (Dry)} \\ 26.42 \text{ gal. (Liquid)} \end{Bmatrix}$ = 5.54352 *shō* (升)

MEASURES OF SURFACE

1 square *ri* (里)=1,296 *chō* (町)=5.95505 sq. miles=15.42347
1 *chō* (町)=10 *tan* (段)=3,000 *tsubo* (坪)   sq. kilometres
                                    =2.45064 acres=99.17355 ares
1 *tsubo* (坪) or *bu* (歩)=3.95369 sq. yards=3.30579 centiares

Metric system :

1 are   = $\begin{Bmatrix} 100 \text{ sq. metres} \\ 119.6 \text{ sq. yards} \end{Bmatrix}$ = 30.25000 *bu* (歩)

1 sq. kilometre = $\begin{Bmatrix} 0.386 \text{ sq. mile} \\ 247.10 \text{ acres} \end{Bmatrix}$ = 0.06484 sq. *ri* (里)

MONETARY UNITS

1 *ryō* (兩)=4 *bu* (歩)=16 *shu* (朱). . . . . *old units*
1 *ryō* (兩) in gold = 60 *momme* (匁) in silver = 4,000 mon (文) in
copper . . . . *old units*
1 *ryō* (兩)=1 *yen* (圓). . . . . *at the Meiji Restoration*
1 *yen* (圓, ¥)=100 *sen* (錢)=1000 *rin* (厘) . . . . . *current units*

III. JAPANESE BIBLIOGRAPHY

Bakumatsushi (幕末史　小林正次郎著)
History of the closing days of the Tokugawa régime, by Kobayashi-Shōjirō.

Chirizuka-dan (塵塚談　小川顕道著)
Miscellaneous topics on the manners and customs, by Ogawa-Kendō.

Chōnin Bukuro (町人囊　西川如見著)
Merchant's bag, namely sundry notes for the information and instruction of merchants, by Nishikawa-Joken.

Chōnin Kōkenroku (町人考見録　三井高房著)
How the wealthy citizens of Kyōto fell into ruin, mainly on account of the loans to *daimyō*, by Mitsui-Takafusa (Hachiroemon).

Dainihon Fudōsanhō Enkakushi (大日本不動産法沿革史　横井時冬著)
History of Japanese real estate law, by Yokoi-Tokifuyu.

Dainihon Kaheishi (大日本貨幣史　吉田賢輔等編)
History of currency in Japan, compiled by Yoshida-Kensuke and others, edited by the Finance Department.

Dainihon Komonjo, Bakumatsu Gaikoku Kankei Monjo (大日本古文書幕末外國關係文書)
A collection of documents dealing with the foreign intercourse in the closing days of the Tokugawa shogunate.

Dainihon Nōsei Ruihen (大日本農政類編　農商務省編)
Materials for a history of Japanese agriculture, by the Department of Agriculture and Commerce.

Dainihon Nōshi (大日本農史　農商務省編)
History of Japanese agriculture, by the Department of Agriculture and Commerce.

Dainihon Sangyō Jiseki (大日本産業事蹟　大林雄也著)
Japanese industrial events, by Ōbayashi-Yūya.

Dainihonshi (大日本史　徳川光圀編)
History of Great Japan, compiled by Tokugawa-Mitsukuni.

Dainihonshi Shokkashi (大日本史食貨志)
Treatise on political economy in the "Dainihonshi."

Dainihon Shōgyōshi (大日本商業史　菅沼貞風著)
History of Japanese commerce, by Suganuma-Teifū.

Dainihon Sozeishi (大日本租税志　野中準等編)
History of taxation in Japan, compiled by Nonaka-Jun and others, edited by the Finance Department.

Dainihon Teikoku Ekiteishikō oyobi Dainihon Teikoku Ekiteishikō Kōshō (大日本帝國驛遞志稿及大日本帝國驛遞志稿考證　青江秀等編)
History of communications in Japan, compiled by Aoe-Shū and others, edited by the Department of Communication.

Edo Machikata Kakiage (江戸町方書上)
Family records of the prominent *chōnin* in Edo, compiled during the Bunsei era (1818–1829).

Genkō Shakusho (元亨釋書　僧師錬著)
History of Buddhism in Japan from Emperor Suiko to the Genkō era, by Priest Shiren.

Genshōkanki (元正間記)
Record of the Genroku and Shōtoku eras, by an anonymous.

Ginroku (鈐錄　荻生徂徠著)
Memoirs on armaments, by Ogyū-Sorai.

Goningumi-chō (五人組帳)
Record of the *gonin-gumi* (autonomic cooperation organised by every five families for mutual aid and solidarity on police, litigant, tax-paying, moral and other social matters.)

Hōseishi no Kenkyu (法制史の研究　三浦周行著)
Essays on Japanese legal institutions, by Miura-Hiroyuki.

Hyakushō Bukuro (百姓蠹　西川如見著)
Farmer's bag, namely sundry notes for the information and instruction of farmers, by Nishikawa-Joken.

Jikata Ochiboshū (地方落穂集)
A collection of scattered rice-ears from the country, i.e. a compendium of agronomical and agrimensorial informations, by an anonymous.

Kaijō Kōtsū Shiron (海上交通史論　辻善之助著)
History of overseas communication, by Tsuji-Zennosuke.

Kaikoku Kigen (開國起源　勝海舟著)
How the Country was opened, by Katsu-Kaishū.

Kai Tsūshō Kō (華夷通商考　西川如見著)
Polyhistorical description of the commerce of China and barbarous countries, by Nishikawa-Joken.

Kaiun Shiryō (海運史料　小笹清根著)
Historical materials of shipping, by Kozasa-Kiyone.

Kaseikōyō Hōreihen (貨政考要法令篇)
Statutes regarding currency, compiled by the Finance Department.

Kashoku Yodo (家職要道　正司考祺著)
Essential principles of private economy, by Shōji-Kōki.

Keiseidan (經世談　櫻田虎門著)
A treatise on statesmanship, by Sakurada-Komon.

Keizai Daijisho (經濟大辭書　同文館版)
Dictionary of economics, published by the Dōbunkan.

Keizaigaku Jiten (經濟學辭典　大阪商科大學經濟研究所編)
Dictionary of economics, compiled by the Institute for Economic Research in the Ōsaka Commercial University.

Keizai Ikkagen (經濟一家言　瀧本誠一著)
Essays in economic studies, by Takimoto-Seiichi.

Keizai Mondō Hiroku (經濟問答祕錄　正司考祺著)
Secret memoirs of dialogues on political economy, by Shōji-Kōki.

Keizairoku (經濟錄　太宰春臺著)
Politico-economical investigations, by Dazai-Shundai.

Keizairoku Shūi (經濟錄拾遺　太宰春臺著)
Supplement to politico-economical investigations, by Dazai-Shundai.

Keizaishi Kenkyū (經濟史研究)
The study of economic history, a monthly journal published by the Nihon Keizaishi Kenkyūsho.

Keizai Shōgaku (經濟小學　神田孝平著)
Elementary economics, by Kanda-Kōhei.

Kingin Zuroku (金銀圖錄　近藤守重著)
Graphical record of gold and silver coins, by Kondō-Morishige.

Kinsei Shakai Keizai Sōsho (近世社會經濟叢書　本庄榮治郎，土屋喬雄，中村直勝，黑正巖編)
Library of social economy of Tokugawa period compiled by Honjō-Eijirō, Tsuchiya-Takao, Nakamura-Naokatsu and Kokushō-Iwao.

Kōgei Shiryō (工藝志料　黑川眞賴著)
Historical materials of technology, compiled by Kurokawa-Mayori, edited by the Natural History Board.

Kōjō Oboegaki (口上覺書　陶山鈍翁著)
Notes from colloquium on agricultural subjects, by Suyama-Don'ō.

Kokusai Enkakuryaku (國債沿革略　大藏省編)
Brief history of National Loans, edited by the Finance Department.

Kokushi Sōron oyobi Nihon Kinseishi (國史總論及日本近世史　內田銀藏著)
General history of Japan and the history of Tokugawa period, by Uchida-Ginzō.

Kyūten Ruisan Denseihen (舊典類纂田制篇　橫山由淸等編)
History of land system in Japan, in the "Kyūtenruisan" (old book series), compiled by Yokoyama-Yoshikiyo and others, edited by the Genrōin.

Meiji Ishin Keizaishi Kenkyū (明治維新經濟史研究　本庄榮治郎編)
Study of the economic history of the Meiji restoration period, compiled by Honjō-Eijirō.

Meiji Kasei Kōyō (明治貨政考要　大藏省編)
History of currencies in the Meiji era, compiled by the Finance Department.

Meiji Shiyō (明治史要　修史局編)
Survey of the Meiji era, edited by the Historiographical Bureau.

Minkan Seiyō (民間省要　田中丘隅著)
Essentials of civic life, chiefly discourses on taxes, water regulation and communication, by the Tanaka Kyūgū.

Montoku Jitsuroku (文德實錄　藤原基經撰)
Authentic record of the reign of Emperor Montoku, official chronicle compiled by Fujiwara-Mototsune by the Imperial Order.

Nihonbashi Uoichiba Enkaku Kiyō (日本橋魚市場沿革紀要　坂本二三郎著)
Historical survey of the Nihonbashi Fish Market, by Sakamoto-Jisaburo.

Nihon Gaishi (日本外史　賴山陽著)
Private record of Japanese history, by Rai-Sanyō.

Nihon Kaika Shōshi (日本開化小史　田口卯吉著)
Historical sketch of Japanese civilisation, by Taguchi-Ukichi.

Nihon Keizaishi (日本經濟史　竹越與三郎著)
The economic history of Japan, by Takekoshi-Yosaburō. English translation: "The Economic Aspects of the History of the Civilization of Japan."

Nihon Keizaishi (日本經濟史　瀧本誠一著)
Economic history of Japan, by Takimoto-Seiichi.

Nihon Keizaishi Bunken (日本經濟史文献　本庄榮治郎編)
Bibliography on the economic history of Japan, compiled by Honjō-Eijirō.

Nihon Keizaishiron (日本經濟史論　福田德三著)
Treatise on economic history of Japan, by Fukuda-Tokuzō. German original edition: "Die gesellschaftliche und wirtschaftliche Entwickelung in Japan."

Nihon Keizai Sōsho (日本經濟叢書　瀧本誠一編)
Bibliotheca œconomiæ politicæ japonicæ, compiled by Takimoto-Seiichi.

Nihon Keizai Taiten (日本經濟大典　瀧本誠一編)
Magna bibliotheca œconomiæ politicæ japonicæ, compiled by Takimoto-Seiichi.

Nihon Kodai Tsūkako (日本古代通貨考　濱田健次郎著)
Inquiry into the currencies of ancient Japan, by Hamada-Kenjirō.

Nihon Kōgyōshi (日本工業史　横井時冬著)
History of Japanese industry, by Yokoi-Tokifuyu.

Nihon Kōki (日本後記)
Historia postera japonica, namely official chronicle from Emperor Kammu to Emperor Junna, compiled by the Imperial Order.

Nihon Kōtsūshi no Kenkyū (日本交通史の研究　本庄榮治郎編)
A study of the history of communications in the Tokugawa period, compiled by Honjō-Eijirō.

Nihon no Keizai (日本の經濟　戸田海市著)
Japan's economy, by Toda-Kaichi.

Nihon no Keizai to Bukkyō (日本の經濟と佛教　河田嗣郎，岡本一郎共著)
Japan's economy and buddhism, by Kawada-Shirō and Okamoto-Ichirō.

Nihon Seidotsū (日本制度通　萩野由之，小中村義象共著)
Political and social institutions of Japan, by Hagino-Yoshiyuki and Konakamura-Yoshikata.

Nihon Shakai Jii (日本社會事彙　經濟雜誌社編)
Japanese social encyclopedia, edited by the Keizai Zasshisha.

Nihon Shōgyōshi (日本商業史　遠藤芳樹著)
History of Japanese commerce, by Endō-Yoshiki.

Nihon Shōgyōshi (日本商業史　横井時冬著)
History of Japanese commerce, by Yokoi-Tokifuyu.

Nihon Shoki (日本書記)
Historia japonica, namely official chronicle since the Mythical
Age to Empress Jitō, compiled by the Imperial Order.

Nihon Zaiseishi (日本財政史　萩野由之著)
History of Japan's public finance, by Hagino-Yoshiyuki.

Ninzu Zōgen Kakiagechō (人數增減書上帳)
Population record.

Nōsei Suitōki (農政垂統記　織田完之, 高畠千畝共著)
History of agriculture in Japan, compiled by Oda-Kanshi and
Takahata-Sempo, edited by the Industrial Board.

Rōjin Zatsuwa (老人雑話　江村宗具著)
An old man's tales, namely miscellaneous notes on worldly
affairs, by Emura-Munetomo.

Ruijū Kokushi (類聚國史　菅原道眞撰)
Official record methodically classified after the nature of
events, compiled by Sugawara-Michizane and others by the
Imperial Order.

Ryō no Shūge (令集解)
Commentaries on the Taihōryō.

Sairan Igen (采覧異言　新井白石著)
Foreign topography, by Arai-Hakuseki.

Sandai Jitsuroku (三代實錄)
Authentic record of the three Emperors' (Seiwa, Yōzei and
Kōkō) reigns, namely official chronicle compiled by the
Imperial Order.

Sanka Zui (三貨圖彙　草間直方著)
A graphical cyclopædia of the three (gold, silver and copper)
coins, by Kusama-Naokata.

Seidan (政談　荻生徂徠著)
Political discourses, by Ogyū-Sorai.

Seiyō Jijō (西洋事情　福澤諭吉著)
Things Western, by Fukuzawa-Yukichi.

Seji Kemmon Roku (世事見聞錄)
Observations on worldly affairs, by an anonymous.

Seiyō Kibun (西洋紀聞　新井白石著)
Notes on Western things, by Arai-Hakuseki.

Senroku (錢錄　近藤守重著)
Record of currencies by Kondō-Morishige.

Shakai Keizaishigaku (社會經濟史學)
Social and economic history, a monthly magazine published by the Shakai Keizaishi Gakkai.

Shōenkō (莊園考　栗田寛著)
Study of manors in Japan, by Kurita-Hiroshi.

Shōhei Yawa (昇平夜話)
Night tales on political abuses existing in the Tokugawa era, by an anonymous.

Shoku Nihongi (續日本紀)
Historia japonica secunda, namely official chronicle from Emperor Mommu to Emperor Kammu, compiled by the Imperial Order.

Shoku Nihon Kōki (續日本後記)
Historia japonica postera secunda, namely official chronicle from Emperor Junna to Emperor Nimmei, compiled by the Imperial Order.

Shōnan Ikō (小楠遺稿　横井小楠著)
A posthumous work of Yokoi-Shōnan.

Shōzei-chō (正税帳)
Treasury-book, i.e. the book showing the settlement of accounts of the Ōchō period, namely the amount of the cereals paid by people in taxation and the defrayals made in the previous year.

Shūmaiken Josho (收米權上書)
A memorial presented to the authorities on abolishing the evils perpetrated by rice-merchants, through establishing the government monopoly of rice trade, by an anonymous.

Sōbō Kigen (草茅危言　中井竹山著)
Bold words of a burgher, by Nakai-Chikuzan.

Suijinroku, Suijin Yoroku (吹塵錄, 吹塵餘錄　勝海舟著)
Collections of materials of political and economic activities in the Tokugawa period, by Katsu-Kaishū.

Taiheisaku (太平策　荻生徂徠著)
Policy to maintain peace at home, by Ogyū-Sorai.

Tamakushige Beppon (玉くしげ別本　本居宣長著)
Essays on political, moral and worldly affairs, by Motoori-Norinaga.

Teikoku Denshin Enkakushi (帝國電信沿革史)
History of the telegraphic service in the Empire, by the Department of Communication.

Tokugawashi Kaheishi (德川氏貨幣志　齋藤坦藏著)
Record of the currencies in the Takugawa régime, by Saitō-Tanzō.

Yokohama Kaikō Gojūnenshi (橫濱開港五十年史)
History of fifty years of the opening of the port of Yokohama.

Yume no Shiro (夢の代　山片蟠桃著)
Sundry treatises of polyhistorical contents, including among others, institutional, political and politico-economical inquiries and essays, on the lines of Nakai-Chikuzan and Nakai-Riken, by Yamakata-Bantō.

Wagakuni Kinsei no Sembai Seido (我國近世の專賣制度　堀江保藏著)
Monopoly system in the Tokugawa period, by Horie-Yasuzō.

IV. JAPANESE VOCABULARY

Agemai (上ゲ米) The extraordinary taxation levied upon *daimyō* by the Eighth Shogun Tokugawa-Yoshimune for the amendment of the *sankin-kōtai* system. One hundred *koku* of rice in every ten thousand *koku* of fief was paid.

Ashigaru (足輕) The lowest of the feudal retainers; a footman.

Be (部) [Also called *tomo* 伴] A body of subjects belonged to *uji* in Ancient Times, whose service was hereditarily confined within a certain branch of industry and other activities as the governed class.

Betsukosaku (別小作) A kind of *shichiji-kosaku* (質地小作), namely the tenancy of farm in pledge by persons other than its owners.

Bonge (凡下) Commoner; non-*gokenin*.

Bugyō (奉行) Officials of various degrees and duties under the feudal government. They were such as *Jisha Bugyō* (寺社奉行 Minister of Temples and Shrines), *Kanjō Bugyō* (勘定奉行 Minister of Finance) etc. The *Machi Bugyō* (町奉行), of which there were two in the city of Edo, correspond to the present day Governor with the difference that the former possessed not only administrative but military and judicial functions.

Buke-hatto (武家法度) *Samurai*'s Law enacted by the Tokugawa Government stipulating *samurai*'s duties, manners, etc.

Bukeyaku (武家役) Tax on *samurai*.

Bushidō (武士道) The *samurai* cult; Japanese chivalry.

Buyaku (賦役) Labour exacted from the lower people by a government or statute labour in Ancient times; a corvée.

Chinso (賃租) The farm tenancy system in the *gunken* régime. *Chin* means the rent collected in advance at the time of sowing seeds in spring, while *so* means the payment of the rent at the time of harvesting crops in autumn.

Chishi (地子) A kind of land tax.

Chō (調) A kind of tribute in cloth and other things customarily paid to the Government in the Ōchō period.

Chōja (長者) A wealthy man; a millionaire.

Chōnin (町人) Merchants and artisans.

Chōsan (逃散) Farmers' desertion from their lord's fief, due to the tax burden in the Tokugawa period.

Chōyōsen (調庸錢) *Chō* and *yō* paid in coins. See *chō* and *yō*.

Chūgen (仲間) A *samurai*'s attendant; a lackey.

Daikan (代官) Governors of small domains under the direct control of the Tokugawa Government.

Daimyō (大名) A feudal lord; a feudal chief having an estate worth more than 10,000 *koku* of rice.

Dajōkan (太政官) Council of State in the Meiji Government abolished in 1885.

Deme (出目) The profit by a recoinage under the Tokugawa Government.

Dosō (土倉) An earthy storehouse of a pawnbroker in the Muromachi period, in which the pawned goods were kept; a money-lender or a pawnbroker.

Eikosaku (永小作) Tenancy of farm for a term of over twenty years.

Emishi (蝦夷) [also called *ezo* 蝦夷]. Barbarian, often indicates the Ainu.

Eta (エタ) A class of people who has continued to occupy the lowest social position until the Meiji Restoration, their chief occupations having been those of leather dressers, cobblers, or buriers of dead animals.

Fudai-daimyō (譜第大名) A *daimyō* in hereditary vassalage to the Tokugawa family.

Fudasashi (札差) A person specially licensed to exchange rice into money for *samurai*; a money-lender to *samurai*.

Gaikoku-bugyō (外國奉行) The Minister of Foreign Affairs of the Tokugawa Government.

Ginza (銀座) Government's mint in the Tokugawa period where silver coins were made. Ginza were established at Edo, Kyōto, Ōsaka and Nagasaki.

Gokamon (御家門) The branch families of the Tokugawa Shogunate except the *Gosanke.*

Gokenin (御家人) Low grade vassals of the feudal government.

Gosanke (御三家) The most important branch families of the Tokugawa Shogunate: Owari, Kii and Mito.

Gōshi (郷士) A kind of *samurai* who lived away from the castle-town of their liege *daimyō,* and cultivated land.

Goshuinchi (御朱印地) Domains of shrines and temples certificated by the Government's charter in the Tokugawa period.

Gōso (強訴) An urgent complaint or petition to the Government made by mob.

Goyōkin (御用金) Compulsory levies collected chiefly from *chōnin,* sometimes from farmers.

Gun (郡) Subdivision of *ken* (after 1871); Subdivision of a *kuni* (國—province) (before 1870); a county.

Gundai (郡代) The chief magistrate of *gun* in the Tokugawa régime.

Gunken-Seido, or—system (郡縣制度) A term designating a monarchical form of government in distinction to the *hōken-seido* (封建制度—feudal system); prefectural system.

Gunnai-ori (郡內織) A stuff woven at Gunnai.

Gunshi (郡司) Superintendent of *gun* in the *gunken* régime.

Habutae (羽二重) A kind of glossy silk.

Han (藩) A feudal clan.

Hanchi (半知) The reduction of the stipends of *samurai.*

Handen (班田) Fields granted by the Government in the Ōchō period.

Hatamoto (旗本) The immediate vassals or the household troops of the Shogun in the Tokugawa period.

Hinin (非人) A begger; a pariah.

Hitokai (人買)　A kid-napper; a slave-dealer.

Hōken-seido, or — system (封建制度)　Feudal system.

Honsho (本所)　A lord of a land in the *Shōen* system.

Hyakushō (百姓)　A farmer; a husbandman; a peasant.

Hyakushō-dai (百姓代)　Village officials appointed from among farmers in the Tokugawa period.

Hyakushōyaku (百姓役)　Tax on farmers in the Tokugawa period.

Ikkō-shū, or — sect (一向宗)　A subsect of the *Jōdo* denomination of Buddhism, originated by a priest named Shinran; old name of *Shinshū* (眞宗).

Imikura (齋藏)　The Imperial warehouse in which the offerings to the Gods were stored in Ancient Times.

Ine (稻)　Rice; rice-plant; seed-rice.

Jiki-kosaku (直小作)　A kind of *shichiji-kosaku* (質地小作) namely the tenancy of farm in pledge by its owners.

Jitō (地頭)　A local administrative official of the Kamakura Government who had charge of taxation and administration of the fiefs.

Jochi (除地)　Lands of temples or shrines, or a historic land which was exempted from taxes by legal prescription.

Jōshu (城主)　A *daimyō* who possessed his own castle.

Jun-kokushu (準國主)　A *daimyō* who possessed a territory next in size to those of the *kokushu* (國主).

Kabane (姓)　The name indicating the status and standing of a family in Ancient Times.

Kabunakama (株仲間)　A guild authorized by the Tokugawa Shogunate.

Kachi (徒士)　A *samurai* who attends on foot when a *daimyō* goes out; a foot-soldier.

Kakeya (掛屋)　A financial agent for *daimyō* and *samurai* in the Tokugawa period.

Kampaku (關白)　The highest official who formerly acted as the prime minister.

Kami (神) God; a deity; a supernatural being.

Kamigata (上方) Kyōto, Ōsaka and its districts.

Kanjō-bugyō (勘定奉行) Minister of Finance in the Tokugawa Government.

Kanjō-gimmiyaku (勘定吟味役) Inspectors of Finance of the Tokugawa Government.

Kanzei (關税) A custom duty.

Karō (家老) The principal retainer of a *daimyō*.

Kashikin-kaisho (貸金會所) A sort of credit organ which was created under the reign of the Shogun Tokugawa-Ieharu.

Kawase-kaisha (爲替會社) The exchange companies established soon after the Meiji Restoration.

Ken (縣) A prefecture.

Kenkin (献金) Presenting or contributing money (as for some public purposes).

Kien (棄捐) The act of letting off or cancelling debts as was done by the Tokugawa Government for the *samurai*.

Kirimai (切米) A part of salary paid by rice to the *hatamoto* in the Tokugawa period.

Kimono (着物) Clothing; cloths; a dress.

Ko (戸) A house or a family.

Kobushinkata (小普請方) *Hatamoto* and *gokenin* who earned below 3,000 *koku* of rice.

Kokubunji (國分寺) National temples which were erected in every province by the Imperial command of Emperor Shōmu.

Kokuritsu-Ginkō (國立銀行) The national bank which was established in the early years of the Meiji period after the American banking system.

Kokushi (國司) The governor of a province in Ancient Times.

Kōri (郡) Another designation of *gun*; a county.

Koseki (戸籍) An official register book of family.

Kubunden (口分田)   The land granted to each person in the *handen* system.

Kuge (公家)   The name of the nobility attached to the Emperor and residing in Kyōto in former times; a court noble.

Kugadachi (探湯)   A sort of ordeal by means of boiling water.

Kumigashira (組頭)   A village official appointed from among farmers in the Tokugawa period.

Kuni-ikki (國一揆)   A political riot for the purpose of over-throwing the local magistrate or the *samurai* class.

Kuni-no-miyatsuko (國造)   A local official in Acient Times.

Kura (藏)   A warehouse.

Kuramoto (藏元)   A keeper of the warehouse in a *kurayashiki* (藏屋敷) under a *kurayakunin*, i.e., one who was in charge of the receiving and delivery of warehouse goods of a *kurayashiki* in the Tokugawa period.

Kurayaku (倉役)   Pawnbroking tax in the Muromachi period.

Kurayakunin (藏役人)   A warehousing official who was in charge of each *kurayashiki*.

Kurayashiki (藏屋敷)   In the Tokugawa period, many *daimyō* had warehouses in Ōsaka, Edo and other cities for the purpose of selling rice and other products of their respective provinces. These warehouses called *kurayashiki*.

Mabiki (間引)   Infanticide prevailed in the Tokugawa period.

Metsuke (目付)   Officers of different ranks in the feudal governments, whose duty was to keep an eye (whence their name) on other officials and report on their conduct, as public censors; a superviser.

Miso (味噌)   Bean-cheese.

Misutechi (見捨地)   A land exempted from the tax, in which comprised grave-yards, crematories, slaughter houses and execution grounds.

Mitsugi (貢)   A tribute or tax in Ancient Times.

Monzenmachi (門前町)   Towns in front of temples and shrines.

Mujin (無盡), **or Mujinkō** (無盡講) A mutual financing association, in which many persons agree to invest each a certain sum of money, and use it in turn by drawing lots.

Mujinsen (無盡錢) Money lent by *dosō* with a security of pawned goods in the Kamakura period; also indicates this financial system itself.

Munebetsusen (棟別錢) House tax in the Kamakura and Muromachi periods.

Munenguchi (無年貢地) A land exempted from taxation, namely, roads, marshes and sites of some public establishments.

Muraji (連) A kind of *kabane*.

Myōga (冥加) A sort of monetary contribution or tax in the Tokugawa period.

Myōden-kosaku (名田小作) Tenancy of farm belonging to a landowner.

Na (名) Personal name as distinguished from family name.

Naidaijin (内大臣) (1) Anciently a high official ranking next to *Dajōdaijin* (太政大臣—prime minister); (2) later the official below *Udaijin* (右大臣—Minister of the Right); (3) at present the Lord Keeper of the Privy Seal.

Nichiren-shū, or—sect (日蓮宗) A sect of Buddhism popularly called *Hokkeshū* (法華宗), originated by the priest Nichiren.

Nimbetsu-chō (人別帳) A register book of populationi in the Tokugawa period.

Nishijin-ori (西陣織) A textile produced at Nishijin, Kyoto.

Ōchō (王朝) Dynasty. By the " Ōchō period " means the period of Imperial Rule, namely, the period before the Kamakura period since the Accession of the Emperor Jimmu.

Okakae (御抱) Temporary retainers.

Ōkura (大藏) The Imperial warehouse in which the goods belonging to the State were stored in Ancient Times.

Omemie (御目見得)   Audience of the Shogun ; a rank in the direct retainers of the Tokugawa Government, *samurai* in this rank being granted the audience to the Shogun.

Ōmetsuke (大目付)   An official in the Tokugawa Government whose duty was to inspect, and report upon, the conduct of *daimyō* and other officials.

Omi (臣)   A kind of *Kabane*.

Ōmuraji (大連)   The head of the *muraji*.

Onando (御納戸)   An official of the Tokugawa Government who had charge of the Shogunate's treasury.

On-makanai-kata (御賄方)   An official of the Tokugawa Government who had charge of the purveyance.

On-tatami-kata (御疊方)   An official of the Tokugawa Government in charge of the *tatami* (疊―mat) in the Shogunate Palace.

On-zaimoku-kata (御材木方)   An official of the Tokugawa Government in charge of the building materials.

Ōomi (大臣)   The head of the *omi*.

Osaiku-kata (御細工方)   An official of the Tokugawa Government who had charge of providing weapons, saddleries, *shōji* (障子―paper-screens), etc.

Osakuji-kata (御作事方)   An official of the Tokugawa Government who had charge of building.

Oyakata (親方)   Master.

Ramma (闌間)   The open ornamental work over the sliding doors or paper-screens between the lintel and the ceiling ; Transom window.

Rōjū (老中)   Minister of State in the Tokugawa Government.

Rōnin (浪人)   (1) In the Ōchō period, a vagrant; (2) in the Tokugawa period, a *samurai* dismissed from the service of his lord.

Ryōke (領家)   A landowner in the *Shōen* system.

Ryōmin (良民)   Good people ; law-abiding citizens.

Sakaya (酒屋) A *sake*-dealer.

Sake (酒) A fermented liquor brewed from steamed rice mixed with yeast and water.

Sambutsu-kaisho (產物會所) Also called *Bussan-kaisho* (物產會所) or *Kokusan-kaisho* (國產會所). An official organ for monopoly and industrialisation in the Tokugawa period.

Samurai (侍) Also called *bushi* (武士). A general name for the persons who wore two swords in former times, from the Shogun down to the lowest retainers of *daimyo*'s vassals; a warrior.

Sankin-kōtai (參覲交代) Alternative sojourns of *daimyo* in Edo by turns where the Shogun reside.

Sekisho (關所) A place where guards are stationed to examine the passenger; where the custom duty was levied in the Middle Ages.

Shichiji-kosaku (質地小作) Tenancy of mortgaged farm.

Shingaku (心學) Philosophy of *chōnin* in the Tokugawa period.

Shindō (神道) Shintoism.

Shiro (代) An unit of the measure of farm in Ancient Times.

Shizoku (氏族) Family, or all persons bearing the same family name; clan.

Shōen (莊園) The territory of a noble in the Ōchō period; a manor.

Shōgun (將軍) [Cont. form of *Seii-taishōgun* 征夷大將軍]. The barbarian-subjugating generalissimo; head of the shogunate.

Shōhōshi (商法司) Commercial Office in the early days of the Meiji Government.

Shōji (障子) A paper sliding-door; a paper-screen.

Shōji (莊司) The directer of a *shōen*.

Shōke (莊家) The residence of the Lord or his representative in a *shōen*.

Shokunin (職人) A handicraftsman; a journeyman.

Shōya (庄屋) The head of a village in former times; A village-master.

Shugo (守護) An official (warden) sent by Minamoto-Yoritomo to the respective provinces to keep an eye over the conduct of the governors and at the same time to assist the latter in putting down rebels.

Shuinchi (朱印地) Also called *Goshuinchi*. See *Goshuinchi*.

Shuinsen (朱印船) Vessels with the *shuinjo* (朱印狀—Shogunate's Charter) for trading with foreign countries.

So (租) Land tax.

Sonchi (損地) The lands desolated by landslides, inundation and other natural calamities which were exempted from the land tax in the Tokugawa régime.

Suiko (出擧) A sort of loans for consumption in Ancient Times, namely, the system under which the seed-rice, of the official or the private possession was lent to farmers in spring and they had to pay it back with interest after the harvest in autumn.

Taihō-ryō (大寶令) Ordinance of the Taihō era.

Tanomoshi (賴母子), **or Tanomoshikō** (賴母子講) Same as *mujin*; An association of mutual financial aid.

Tansen (段錢) A tax in currency (*sen*) levied on farm land according to the *tan* (段) acreage in the Middle Ages.

Tashidaka (足高) A system of supplying the shortage when the sum of the fief were less than that of the official situation.

Tenryō (天領) The territories of the Tokugawa Shogunate, namely, the lands under the direct possession of the Shogunate.

Terakoya (寺小屋) A private school-house where children were taught to write, read and cipher.

Tokusei (德政) Practice of repudiating all rights and obligations concerning contracts of loan, sale and mortgage signed within a certain stipulated period, in the Kamakura and Muromachi periods.

Tomitsuki (富突) A sort of lottery.

Tomo (伴) See *be*.

Tomo-no-miyatsuko (伴造) Another name of *miyatsuko* which is a kind of *kabane*.

Totei (徒弟) Apprentice.

Totō (徒黨) Confederacy; faction; conspiracy.

Tozama-daimyō (外樣大名) A *daimyō* who was not hereditary vassal of the Tokugawa Shogunate.

Tsuchi-ikki (土一揆) A riot caused by the populace in the Muromachi period.

Tsūshō-kaisha (通商會社) The trading company in the early days of the Meiji era.

Uchikowashi (打毀) Wrecking of rice shops or rich man's house by rioters in the Tokugawa period; then also means a rice riot.

Uchikura (内藏) The Imperial warehouse in which the goods belonging to the Imperial Family were stored in Ancient Times.

Uji (氏) Lineage; pedigree; clan.

Ujigami (氏神) A god of a family, or of a birth-place.

Uji-no-kami (氏上) The patriach or the head of a *uji*.

Utokusen (有德錢) Contributions collected from rich families in the Ashikaga period.

Yakko (奴) A slave.

Yakuryō (役料) The salary of a government official in the Tokugawa period.

Yamato-minzoku (大和民族) The Japanese race.

Yō (庸) Tax in kind which was paid in compensation for the statute labour in the Ōchō period; a corvée.

Yonezawa-ori (米澤織) A textile produced at Yonezawa.

Yōnin (用人) A chamberlain in a *daimyō*'s court.

Yoriki (與力) A constable in former times, higher in grade than *dōshin* (同心), the low-grade officials under the Tokugawa Government.

Yōsen (徭錢) Tax payment in coins in compensation for a corvée.

Yūshu (邑主) A *daimyō* who possessed only his own military camps.

Za (座) A guild of merchants or craftsmen in the Middle Ages; A guild under the direct control of the Shogunate in the Tokugawa period.

Zayaku (座役) Tax on *za* in the Middle Ages.

INDICES

I. NAMES OF PERSONS

II. GEOGRAPHICAL NAMES

III. SUBJECTS

NH